ISMS
&
OLOGIES

ISMS & OLOGIES

453 Difficult Doctrines You've Always Pretended to Understand

by ARTHUR GOLDWAG

Quercus

First published in Great Britain in 2007 by

Quercus
21 Bloomsbury Square
London
WC1A 2NS

Originally published in the United States of America by Madison Park Press,
a trademark of Bookspan, in 2007

A CIP catalogue record for this book is available from the British Library

ISBN 1 84724 176 X
ISBN-13 978 1 84724 176 4

Printed and bound in Great Britain by Clays Ltd, St Ives plc.

10 9 8 7 6 5 4 3 2 1

CONTENTS

ALPHABETICAL LIST OF TERMS

Introductionism
by Michael Lewis

n. An obscure cult inside American publishing devoted to finding people willing to praise new books, typically written by their friends. In the ideal case the author of the book is a complete unknown, whereas the writer of the introduction is slightly less obscure, and deeply in debt not only to the author but also to the publishing house. The cult's single sacred belief is that any new book, no matter how ineptly written, can be sold with the right sales pitch.

If that is a fair definition of *introductionism*, this introduction counts as heresy. I'd never heard of the author, Arthur Goldwag, and his book was sent to me by a publisher to whom I owe nothing at all. This manuscript, with its odd title, just arrived in the mail, and I started to read it. Reaching the passage in the author's note in which Goldwag describes his love of *henotheism*—"the belief that while there is more than one God, only one of them is worth worshipping"—I was put in mind of Ambrose Bierce, who wrote *The Devil's Dictionary,* a rare reference book that succeeds without even pretending to be useful. But I read on and found that Goldwag's purpose wasn't merely to amuse. There was indeed such a thing as *henotheism,* and while the author's prose might be witty, *ISMS & OLOGIES* is intended to be a learned and useful work of reference, a thing a person might keep around as a reminder of the origin and meaning of all sorts of fancy terms that tend to be hurled around indiscriminately. For instance, *surrealism* wasn't invented so that American teenagers would have a word to describe every unusual thing that ever happened to them. *Chiliasm* is not a Mexican food. A *Spenglerism* has nothing in common with a *spoonerism*. *Quietism*, on the other hand, is fairly quiet. And *idiotism* is (interestingly) idiotic.

This strange encyclopedia turned out to be more than a reference book, however. For it did not merely answer my questions; it answered questions I had never thought to ask, but wished I had. (See *auteurism* to understand, for instance, why Hollywood directors are able to grow rich and famous expropriating other people's creations without anyone thinking twice about it—how, say, Francis Ford Coppola can take a book written by Mario Puzo, make it into a film, and call it "Francis Ford Coppola's *The Godfather*.") Goldwag also introduced me to concepts I could hardly believe anyone ever bothered to think up. I knew about *necrophilia*, for example, but never imagined there could be such a thing as *eproctophilia*—"sexual excitement from flatulence." And I'm betting that even the most ardent sports fans will be surprised to learn of *plushophilia*—"the sexual attraction to people in costumes, such as team mascots or theme park characters . . ." (Goldwag strays, in places, from his stated mission to demystify only words that end in *ism,* and demystifies a few other words too. He strays well.)

Almost inadvertently the author has written a pithy history of intellectual perversion. "The formulation of isms is something that people do," Goldwag writes, "and something that they overdo as well; it's also something they resist and resent. The more isms, the more schisms." By compressing all major and most minor religious, political, and artistic movements into a single volume, he has distilled the madness of mankind: its tendency to create sects and cults and private clubs of the mind. Outside the club, employed as the bouncers, stand a phalanx of bewildering words and concepts and beliefs, and these have much to fear from Arthur Goldwag. I've never met the man, but I can introduce his book freely and honestly, without fear of being labeled an introductionist. He's achieved something few authors achieve, and created in the same package a path to understanding and a highway to pleasure. He's led his readers under the red velvet ropes, past the bouncers, and into the club.

Author's Note

ISMS AND OLOGIES CAN serve as invaluable intellectual and social shorthand. When a philosopher declares himself to be a logical positivist, or a Christian identifies herself as a premillennial dispensationalist, at least their peers understand what they're talking about. But as anyone who's struggled through a humanities quarterly well knows, isms too often substitute for ideas or analysis; they are as likely to obfuscate as illuminate. A single paragraph picked virtually at random from one reputable journal yielded "nomadism," "post-feminist," "racism," "masculinism," "patriarchy," and the tongue-twisting phrase "possible homologation in an allegedly gender-bending post-modern flux of identities." And academics aren't the only ones with a penchant for jargon. In the fall of 2005, an otherwise thoughtful article in Melbourne, Australia's the *Age* compared Iraq's chaotic present to Bosnia's ten years after the ratification of the Dayton Accords.

> Bosnia remains heavily scarred by intense nationalism, cultural chauvinism and irredentism. There is also an undercurrent of Wahhabism, the austere Islamic creed, imported to the Balkans by mujahideen from Afghanistan, Chechnya and the Middle East.
>
> The multiculturalism that defined pre-war Sarajevo in the minds of many is long gone.

Never mind your feelings about the Serbs and the Croats, or about nation building in general, that's a lot of isms to swallow all at once. Even the most educated of readers might have forgotten what "irredentism" means or what precisely "Wahhabism" is.

And there are plenty of isms that we might have forgotten—or never really known at all—closer to home. We've all been offered free copies of the *Watchtower* by evangelizing Jehovah's Witnesses, but do we know how the tenets of their faith differ from those of Baptists? How many of us would take it upon ourselves to explain to a room full of our contemporaries just what it means to be existential?

For that matter, what is dialectical materialism? What is the difference between a Jacobite and a Jacobean, an Augustinian and an Augustan, a Platonist and a NeoPlatonist? Rastafarianism is firmly linked in the popular mind to Bob Marley and dreadlocks and ganja, but is it a religion or a political ideology or something else? Do Buddhists pray to Buddha? How modern can modernism be if all the famous modernists are dead? The political pundit George Will styles himself a Whig; the late Senator Barry Goldwater called himself a paleoconservative; I. Lewis "Scooter" Libby, the indicted former chief of staff to Vice President Dick Cheney, was known to be one of the most powerful neoconservatives in the Bush administration. What distinguishes all these flavors of conservatism? What are their basic tenets?

In the following pages I provide answers to all these questions and more. But as I immersed myself in the world of isms and ologies, I became increasingly aware of their limitations. What makes a religion a religion, a political movement a movement, or for that matter, a sexual perversion perverse goes well beyond their formal definitions. Take capitalism. No one would deny that Donald Trump or Bill Gates is a consummate capitalist, but what drives them—what makes these extraordinary people who they are—is a combination of acquisitiveness, self-aggrandizement, will to power, creativity, ruthlessness, and their own unique forms of entrepreneurial genius. However ardent its defenders might be, capitalism is neither a philosophical system nor a faith; it's an after-the-fact description of the particulars and consequences of certain kinds of human behavior that developed within the contexts of particular social arrangements and historical contingencies, combined with educated observations about the ways that money and goods and other signifiers of value tend to behave when they are traded. Or let's go back to Wahhabism. If you want to understand what inspires young Islamist terrorists to strap bombs to their bodies and blow themselves and busloads of innocents to kingdom come, the teachings of radical sheiks will only tell you so much. Human character and culture are complex and often irrational and contradictory; isms are just one of the many tools that we use when we try to get a handle on ourselves.

It occurs to me that isms might bear some of the blame for how unlistenable so much contemporary art music is and why the Whitney Biennial show inspires such predictable outrage among middlebrow art critics. Ever since music and art historians began to organize their textbooks according to a chronological succession of isms—impressionism following realism, serialism following post-Romanticism—creative artists have felt pressured to do more than merely create; they feel an obligation to advance their idiom as well, lest critics characterize their work as revanchist. But outside of academia and the art world, most of us find Neolithic cave paintings of mammoths to be far more memorable than the generic abstract sculptures that grace the lobbies of so many office buildings; few of us are immune to the charm of a songbird's warbling. Aristotle, who gave his name to one of the longest-lasting and most influential isms of all, believed that the artistic impulse arose out of the desire to imitate nature. To call attention to primitive art's undiminished appeal isn't to disparage avant-gardism per se—it's simply to suggest that the critical impulse is not always in synch with our instinctive sensibilities, that a song that we can whistle or a pretty picture of a flower needn't be shallow or sentimental. And never mind what isms have done to the arts. Almost every war in recorded history was fought over one ism or another.

But if isms and ologies are confusing and dangerous and often reductive, they're undoubtedly fascinating as well. The big ones define whole eras; the more obscure ones lead us down some of the less-traveled highways and byways of human culture. A friend of mine telephoned not too long ago to tell me about a word that Chicano Lowriders in Los Angeles use to describe their values: *amigoism.* When another friend challenged me to name an ism he'd never heard of, I told him about *henotheism,* the belief that while there is more than one God, only one of them is worth worshipping. One morning when I sat down to work on this book, I noticed a Post-it note stuck to my computer monitor. Written on it in my younger son's unmistakable scrawl was one enigmatic word: *tractor-trailerism.* I have no idea what he was getting at, but I'm sure he'll be delighted to see his contribution in print.

Not too long ago, I saw a still photograph from the original Broadway production of *Strike Up the Band* in which a chorus line of raffish protesters brandished crude, handmade placards. One of them read "Down with Ismism!" I wondered if "ismism" was a real word.

It wasn't in my *Oxford English Dictionary,* but I got lots of hits when I Googled it. Among other things, I learned that an American writer named Rupert Hughes (1872–1956) had used the word in a novel called *We Can't Have Everything,* which was made into a silent movie in 1918.

> There were tomboys and hoydens and solemn students; hardworking sculptresses and dreamy poetesses; girls who wanted to be boys, and girls who wanted to be nuns; girls who were frantic to vote, and girls who loathed the thought of independence; girls who ached to shock people, and girls of the prunes-and-prismatic type, patricians and precisians, anarchists and Bohemians.
>
> She encountered girls who talked appallingly about breeding dogs and babies, about Freudian erotics, and new schools of art, Futurism, Vorticism. Their main interest was Ismism.

I'd never heard of Hughes, but upon further investigation I was astonished to learn that he was not only an uncle of the reclusive billionaire Howard Hughes, but was formerly renowned in his own right as a vastly prolific novelist, short story writer, playwright, Hollywood scenarist, movie director, and biographer (his three-volume life of George Washington was his proudest achievement)—that he was, in short, as the *Los Angeles Examiner* eulogized him in his obituary, "for more than 50 years, a towering figure in the literary life of our nation." Who knew? Sic transit gloria mundi.

My search for Ismism might have turned out to be something of a wild-goose chase, but the scenery along the way was full of surprises. I hope that readers will enjoy similar serendipities as they browse through *ISMS & OLOGIES*; if you use it as a reference, I hope you'll find what you need. But treat my definitions with due caution—many of the topics I cover are worthy of an entire library in their own right. To paraphrase Shakespeare, there are more isms on heaven and earth than you could possibly dream of; *ISMS & OLOGIES* is merely the tip of the iceberg. While I have strived to maintain an unbiased tone, I am not without prejudices and opinions, and I'm sure that some of them are apparent. I apologize in advance to whomever I might offend.

In *The Language Instinct* (1994), the neuroscientist Steven Pinker suggested that certain human attributes and proclivities are encoded in the very structure of the brain. Among them, he speculates, is an intuitive sense of physics and biology that derives from an instinctive propensity to classify and taxonomize. Our desire to organize vast tracts of undifferentiated emotional, spiritual, intellectual, and scientific terrain into neatly labeled counties, townships, boroughs, municipalities, villages, and lots, is as innately human as our capacity for open-ended wonder; our taste for order goes hand in hand with our attraction to mystery. The formulation of isms is something that people do—and something that they overdo as well; it's also something they resist and resent. The more isms, the more schisms. Perhaps that's the ultimate dialectic of human progress.

ISMS
&
OLOGIES

Politics
& History

ABOLITIONISM

The eighteenth- and nineteenth-century movement to ban the institution of slavery. Sentiment against slavery had become widespread in England by the 1780s; led by Quakers, and with the support of Methodists and Baptists, the movement scored its first significant victory in 1807 with the passage of the Abolition of the Slave Trade Act. On August 1, 1834, all slaves in the English empire were emancipated.

The first abolitionist society in America, the Society for the Relief of Free Negroes Unlawfully Held in Bondage, was founded in Philadelphia in 1775. Benjamin Franklin, an ambivalent slave owner (he arranged to have his slave freed upon his death but outlived him), was a member. Other prominent founding fathers, such as John Jay and Alexander Hamilton, advocated the elimination of slavery. George Washington, though sympathetic to their position, avoided committing himself to it publicly—he, too, made arrangements to free his slaves in his will. But it wasn't until the 1820s and 1830s that, inspired by the preaching of Charles Grandison Finney (1792–1875) and other charismatic evangelical preachers and the journalism of William Lloyd Garrison (1805–79), the abolitionist movement reached critical mass. The American Anti-Slavery Society was organized in Philadelphia in 1833; James G. Birney (1792–1857) ran for president in 1840 and 1844 as the candidate of the abolitionist Liberty Party. In the mid-1840s both the Methodists and the Baptists split into Northern and Southern denominations over the issue; in 1852 Harriet Beecher Stowe (1811–96) published *Uncle Tom's Cabin*. When Abraham Lincoln met her, he is reported to have said, "So you're the little woman who wrote the book that made this great war."

AFROCENTRISM

A contemporary outgrowth of Pan-Africanism. Formulated in the early twentieth century, Pan-Africanism is the idea that black-skinned people around the world—the African diaspora—form a distinct nationality. This idea was promoted by black nationalists, such as Marcus Garvey (1887–1940), Malcolm X (1925–65), and adherents of the Nation of Islam, as well as more mainstream figures like W. E. B. DuBois (1868–1963).

Temple University scholar Molefi Kete Asante coined the term *Afrocentrism* in 1980, which is the belief that African history and culture must be reexamined on their own terms, because they are necessarily distorted, suppressed, and marginalized when they are viewed through a Eurocentric, colonialist lens. Afrocentrists promote a positive view of African heritage, emphasizing the achievements of its civilizations, its unique spirituality, and its communal values. Though the holiday of Kwanzaa was created by the African American scholar Maulana Karenga in 1966, it is obviously a product of the same zeitgeist; the Howard University scholar Carter G. Woodson (1875–1950) created Negro History Week as early as 1926.

Martin Bernal, a white professor emeritus at Cornell University who was a sinologist for most of his career (and who is the grandson of Sir Alan Gardiner, a towering Egyptologist of the last century), is one of the most visible and controversial advocates of Afrocentrist history today. In his multivolume work *Black Athena* (1987), he argues that the roots of classical Greek civilization are in the Semitic and black African cultures of the Middle East, among the latter of which he includes Egypt. Classical scholars have favored an Aryan view of Greek origins, he says, because of their unacknowledged racism and anti-Semitism.

ANARCHISM

From the Greek *an* (the absence of) and *archos* (authority; or a ruler), anarchy is a principled opposition to all but the most rudimental and noncoercive governments.

Anarchism was first propounded as a philosophical stance by Zeno of Citium (333–261 BCE), the founder of the philosophical school of Stoicism, who declared that governments and other hierarchical institutions are not only unnecessary, but responsible for most of society's ills. Since people are inherently rational, anarchists believe, the most equable form of government is one in which citizens freely agree to live together, sharing their property and abiding by voluntary rules.

The leading theorists of anarchism in the nineteenth century were the Englishman William Godwin (1756–1836); the Frenchman P. J. Proudhon (1809–65), who coined the phrase "Property is theft"; the Russians Peter Alexeevich Kropotkin (1842–1921), also known as the Anarchist Prince, and Mikhail Bakunin (1814–76), who broke with Marx over the question of whether government should be banned immediately after the revolution or allowed to gradually wither away after communism had taken root. The 1886 Haymarket riot in Chicago was blamed on anarchists; anarchists were forbidden to enter the United States in 1901 after Leon Czolgosz, a mentally disturbed anarchist sympathizer (and a former Republican), assassinated President McKinley. Emma Goldman (1869–1940) was arrested and briefly imprisoned as a suspected conspirator. When, after many more arrests, Goldman was finally deported in 1919, J. Edgar Hoover, then the twenty-four-year-old head of the General Intelligence Division of the Justice Department, called her "one of the most dangerous anarchists in America." The trial of the anarchists Sacco and Vanzetti would rivet the nation in 1921 (they were finally executed in 1927). Noam Chomsky, the renowned linguist and political gadfly, remarked in a 1995 interview that

> I was attracted to anarchism as a young teenager . . . and haven't seen much reason to revise those early attitudes since.

I think it only makes sense to seek out and identify structures of authority, hierarchy, and domination in every aspect of life, and to challenge them; unless a justification for them can be given, they are illegitimate, and should be dismantled, to increase the scope of human freedom.

Many of the groups involved in the antiglobalization movement today are deeply influenced by anarchist principles.

Antarchy, a word that has largely fallen out of use, literally means "against government" and is sometimes used to distinguish between the philosophy of conservative libertarians, who oppose big government but not private property, and the radical egalitarianism of anarchists, anarcho-syndicalists, and the like.

ANARCHO-SYNDICALISM

Also called syndicalism, *anarcho-syndicalism* is a version of anarchism in which labor unions join together to overthrow capitalism via general strikes and other nonpolitical means. ("One Big Union" was the slogan of the Industrial Workers of the World, better known as the Wobblies.) Once a classless society is achieved, the syndicalists believe, a voluntary confederation of unions could fill the role formerly played by governments. Anarcho-syndicalists were at the vanguard of the revolution in Spain in 1936.

One of the many humorous anachronisms in the film *Monty Python and the Holy Grail* (1975) occurs when Arthur hails himself to a peasant as the king of the Britons. Nonplussed, the peasant replies, "I didn't know we had a king. I thought we were an autonomous collective." When Arthur demands to know who his lord is, the peasant angrily replies, "I *told* you, we're an anarcho-syndicalist commune."

ANTIDISESTABLISHMENTARIANISM

Antidisestablishmentarianism was coined to describe the movement that arose in opposition to Prime Minister W. E. Gladstone's (1809–98) ultimately successful efforts to disestablish the Church of Ireland (i.e., revoke its status as the official, state-sanctioned religion). The act passed parliament in 1869, freeing Ireland's Roman Catholics from the onerous obligation of tithing to the Anglican Church as well as their own. The word lived on as a novelty; it is seldom heard nowadays except at spelling bees.

Antidisestablishmentarianism is frequently cited as the longest nonmedical, nonscientific, or nontechnical word in the English language. It's not—a facetious coinage dating from the eighteenth century, *floccinaucinihilipilification*, beats it by one letter. A portmanteau of three Latin words (*flocci, nauci,* and *pili*), which all mean "having little or no value," plus *nihil,* which means "nothing," and the suffix *fication,* which means "the making of," *floccinaucinihilipilification* is thus the act of deciding that something has no value. North Carolina's former senator Jesse Helms briefly put the word on the map in 1999 when he used it in reference to his evolving thoughts about the Comprehensive Test Ban Treaty, which he had come to oppose. He said he learned it from Senator Pat Moynihan.

Sesquipedalianism, another playful coinage that frequently finds its way into trivia contests and spelling bees, is of a much older vintage than either of the words defined above; it comes from "Proicit ampullas et sesquipedalia verba," a line in Horace's (65–8 BCE) *The Art of Poetry,* which can be translated as "He throws aside his paint pots and his words that are a foot and a half long." *Sesquipedalianism* (or "foot-and-a-half-longism") is used today, almost always ironically, to mean the propensity for using very long words.

ANTIGLOBALISM   *See* Globalism.

ANTI-SEMITISM

Hatred of Jews as a matter of moral and political principle. The word implies more than mere prejudice; it embraces political and social policies designed to purge Jews from positions of status, authority, or economic independence. In its most extreme manifestations, anti-Semitism seeks the outright extermination of the Jews.

The word was coined in 1879 by Wilhelm Marr (1819–1904),

a journalist, racial theorist, and the founder of the League of Anti-Semites, an organization dedicated to expelling Jews from Germany. Marr believed that the Jews, who had only been officially emancipated eight years earlier, had already managed to seize control of German finance and industry and were threatening to destroy the German people. By 1882 an anti-Semitic party controlled some seats in the Reichstag; in the 1890s Karl Lueger (1844–1910) won the mayoralty of Vienna with an explicitly anti-Semitic platform, deeply impressing the young Adolf Hitler (1889–1945).

Marr, of course, was not the first to see the Jews as an imminent threat to civilization. The word he coined was a euphemism for the harsher German word Judenhass, or Jew hatred, a sentiment that dates back at least to the beginnings of the Christian era. Indeed, some of the Gospels, such as John 19:6–7, in which Jewish priests and officials howl for Jesus' crucifixion, portray the Jews as his chief adversary. Christian grace was understood to have succeeded Mosaic law; Judaism was not just superannuated but discredited.

As the renowned Holocaust historian Raul Hilberg wrote in his landmark volume *The Destruction of the European Jews* (1961), in the Christian era,

> there have been three anti-Jewish policies: conversion, expulsion and annihilation. The second appeared as an alternative to the first, and the third as an alternative to the second . . . The missionaries of Christianity had said in effect: You have no right to live amongst us as Jews. The secular rulers who followed had proclaimed: You have no right to live among us. The German Nazis at last decreed: You have no right to live.

European Jews had been slaughtered by the thousands during the time of the Crusades; they were expelled from England in 1290 and from the Iberian peninsula in 1492. Throughout the Middle Ages and the time of the Reformation and on into the twenty-first century in Russia, they have been accused of preparing their Passover matzos with the blood of Christian children, of practicing witchcraft, and of spreading the plague. Forbidden to own land or join craft guilds, they were forced into trade and money lending, for which they were excoriated as usurers and accused of seeking to control the world's economic systems. In rural Eastern Europe they were the victims of periodic pogroms; until relatively recent times, most European cities confined them to ghettos. Martin Luther, in his *On the Jews and Their Lies* (1543), counseled Europe's rulers to treat their Jewish subjects as a physician treats a gangrenous limb:

> Cut, saw, and burn flesh, veins, bone, and marrow. Such a procedure must also be followed in this instance. Burn down their synagogues . . . force them to work, and deal harshly with them, as Moses did in the wilderness, slaying three thousand lest the whole people perish . . . If this does not help we must drive them out like mad dogs, so that we do not become partakers of their abominable blasphemy and all their other vices and thus merit God's wrath and be damned with them.

In 1903 a czarist official named Serge Nilus published *The Protocols of the Learned Elders of Zion,* which purported to be a document produced at the First Zionist Congress in Basel, Switzerland, in 1897, where Jews and Freemasons had supposedly plotted to take over the world. Though it has long been exposed as a hoax—it was adapted from a French anti-Masonic tract called *Dialogues in Hell,* whose protagonists are Montesquieu and Machiavelli—it continues to be widely circulated, especially in the Arab world.

Adolf Hitler's *Mein Kampf,* published in two volumes in 1925 and 1926, vividly described the monstrousness of the Jews:

> With satanic joy in his face, the black-haired Jewish youth lurks in wait for the unsuspecting girl whom he defiles with his blood, thus stealing her from her people. With every means he tries to destroy the racial foundations of the people he has set out to subjugate. Just as he himself systematically ruins women and girls, he does not shrink back from pulling down the blood barriers for others, even on a large scale. It was and it is Jews who bring the

Negroes into the Rhineland, always with the same secret thought and clear aim of ruining the hated white race by the necessarily resulting bastardization, throwing it down from its cultural and political height, and himself rising to be its master.

In 1933, when Hitler became Germany's chancellor, he was finally in a position to put his theories into practice. Twelve years later, between five and six million European Jews had been systematically murdered.

Today the most virulent anti-Semitic rhetoric can be heard in the Islamic world, which, though far from homogenous in its beliefs or politics, is seemingly unanimous in its detestation of Zionism and Israel. In 2003, Mahathir Mohamad, the prime minister of Malaysia, received a standing ovation at the Tenth Islamic Summit Conference of Islamic nations when he declared, "Jews rule this world by proxy. They get others to fight and die for them."

AUTHORITARIANISM   *See* **Totalitarianism.**

BALKANISM
The state of being balkanized is when a stable country, empire, or confederation is carved up into smaller, frequently hostile units; the term evokes the bloody history of the Balkans in the twentieth century. After the collapse of the Ottoman and the Austro-Hungarian empires, two world wars, the rise and fall of the Soviet Union, at least three Balkan wars, and the breakup of Yugoslavia, whatever overarching sense of identity that might have once bound together the countries and territories of the Balkan peninsula (Albania, Bosnia, Herzegovina, Bulgaria, Croatia, Greece, Macedonia, Serbia, Montenegro, Moldova, Romania, Slovenia, and Kosovo) has long since departed; the region is now definitively fractured along ethnic and religious lines.

"Shared moral principles enable people with a variety of backgrounds and interests to interact with one another within a commonly understood framework," wrote the conservative thinker Thomas Sowell in the July 2001 issue of *Capitalism Magazine.*

But busybodies who Balkanize our morality, our language and our political life are destroying that framework. Patriotism is more than a sentiment. It is a necessity. To keep what history has presented to us, Americans must either love it or lose it. Balkanize America and you risk becoming the Balkans.

BILATERALISM   *See* Unilateralism.

BOLSHEVISM

The most radical of the Marxist groups active in Russia in the early twentieth century, *Bolshevik* literally means "one of the majority." At the second party congress of the Russian Social-Democratic Labour Party (RSDLP) in 1903, Vladimir Lenin (1870–1924) debated Julius Martov (1873–1920) on the question of whether party membership should be restricted to a small cadre of professional revolutionaries. Although the majority of the rank and file advocated Martov's view, that the party should be broadly inclusive, Lenin's thinking prevailed with the leadership. Martov's faction thus became known as the Mensheviks, literally "members of the minority."

The party didn't formally split until 1912, but the differences between the factions were significant. Though both sides agreed that Russia's bourgeoisie was too weak to overthrow the feudalistic czar (a bourgeois revolution is a prerequisite, in classic Marxism, for the subsequent proletarian revolution), Lenin believed that Russia's economy could be developed under a dictatorship of the proletariat. The Mensheviks took a more gradualistic approach; rather than an immediate revolution, which they feared would replace one authoritarian regime with another, they sought to work with liberal elements of the middle class to develop capitalism to a point where socialism would become economically and socially feasible.

Leon Trotsky (who allied himself with both factions at different times) recalls in his memoirs that George Plekhanov (1857–1918), one of the founders of the RSDLP and a leader of the Mensheviks, initially supported Lenin at the 1903 party congress. Even so, Trotsky relates, after listening to one of Lenin's speeches, Plekhanov presciently remarked, "Of such stuff Robespierres are made."

CHARTISM
Radical political reform movement in Great Britain that began in 1838. It took its name from the People's Charter, drafted by the London Working Men's Association and presented to Parliament, which demanded universal male suffrage, voting by ballot, and annual parliaments whose MPs would not have to meet property requirements, would receive salaries, and represent equal-sized districts. Divisions within the ranks crippled the movement, as did the arrest of many of its leaders after riots broke out. Chartism faded as trade unions gained strength; though the economic crisis of 1847 sparked a brief revival, the movement fizzled soon thereafter.

COLONIALISM   *See* Imperialism.

COMMUNALISM
A social system that is organized around small, self-sufficient, idealogically or religiously homogenous communities or communes, as in the phalanxes of Fourierism and the Shaker farms in the eighteenth and nineteenth centuries. The word is also used as a pejorative for placing the interests of one's immediate religious group or ethnicity above that of the larger collective (as in ethnocentrism); in India the word is used in the sense of sectarianism, when religious/ethnic communities—the Sikhs, Hindus, Muslims—are in violent conflict with each other.

COMMUNITARIANISM
A contemporary nonpartisan movement, spearheaded by the sociologist Amitai Etzioni, that believes, as the Web site of the Institute for Communitarian Policy Studies puts it, "that the pendulum of contemporary society has swung too far in the direction of individual autonomy at the expense of individual and social responsibility."

Communitarianism springs from the recognition that the human being is by nature a social animal as well as an individual with a desire for autonomy. Communitarians recognize that a healthy society must have a correct balance between individual autonomy and social cohesion. Much recent thinking has focused on an assumed conflict between the rights of the individual and the responsibilities of the government. When you put "community" back into the equation, you find that the apparent conflict between the individual and the government can be resolved by public policies that are consistent with core American values and work to the benefit of all members of our society.

COMMUNISM   *See* Marxism.

CONSERVATISM

Abraham Lincoln famously defined conservatism as "adherence to the old and tried, against the new and untried"; the political writer William Safire defined a conservative as "a defender of the status quo who, when change becomes necessary in tested institutions or practices, prefers that it come slowly and in moderation."

The classic expression of political conservatism can be found in *Reflections on the Revolution in France,* by the English statesman Edmund Burke (1729–97), who wrote, "Good order is the foundation of all things." Burke regarded the American Revolution as a justifiable response to the intransigence, greed, and overreaching of Parliament and George III; confident that the former colonies would adopt a limited government in the best English tradition, he urged his countrymen to reconcile with them as quickly as possible. However, Burke deplored the French Revolution for its unremitting hostility to religion and monarchy, and especially for its militant egalitarianism, which he regarded as an assault on the very basis of civil society.

Traditionally, conservatives are capitalists; they are skeptical of utopian panaceas for poverty, prejudice, and other stubborn social ills because they know that people are inherently unequal. They believe that the invisible hand of the market is more honest and efficient in allocating services and income than any bureaucratically concocted set of regulations and procedures could ever be. No matter how noble their aims, conservatives say, government programs inevitably waste revenue and encourage corruption; worse, they cause unintended consequences that inevitably exacerbate the very problems they try to deal with.

It is ironic that conservatives so often invoke America's revolutionary founders, most of whom were classic liberals, as their supposed role models, but conservatism, like any other ideology, tends to accrue contradictions as its leaders gain real power. The alliance of the religious Right with the Republican Party has produced notable strains within American conservatism in recent years. Libertarian conservatives find it difficult to reconcile the ideal of limited government with the intrusions into the bedrooms, classrooms, and sickrooms of American citizens that are part and parcel of the culture wars that many fundamentalist Christians are engaged in. The interventionist foreign policy and nation building advocated by the neoconservatives in the administration of George W. Bush have not sat well with old-line paleoconservatives. The oxymoronic appellation "radical conservative" has attached itself to many of George W. Bush's key supporters as well as to Bush himself.

Senator Barry Goldwater (1909–98), the author of the book *The Conscience of a Conservative* (1960), a failed presidential candidate in 1964, and "the father of modern conservatism," once said:

> I have little interest in streamlining government or in making it more efficient, for I mean to reduce its size. I do not undertake to promote welfare, for I propose to extend freedom. My aim is not to pass laws, but to repeal them. It is not to inaugurate new programs, but to cancel old ones that do violence to the Constitution or that have failed their purpose, or that impose on the people an unwarranted financial burden.

But in the last years of his life, Goldwater also said, "You don't have to be straight to be in the military; you just have to be able to shoot straight"; and "A lot of so-called conservatives don't know what the word means. They think I've turned liberal because I believe a woman has a right to an abortion. That's a decision that's up to the pregnant woman, not up to the pope or some do-gooders or the Religious Right."

COSMOPOLITANISM   *See* Globalism.

DIXIECRATISM
In general use, a catch-all name for the beliefs of southern, conservative, segregationist Democrats. Specifically, the popular name for the States' Rights Democratic Party, formed in 1948 when thirty-five southern delegates withdrew in protest from the Democratic Party's national convention after civil rights planks championed by Hubert Humphrey (1911–78) were incorporated into its platform. These latter-day secessionists held their own convention in Birmingham, Alabama, where they nominated South Carolina's governor Strom Thurmond (1902–2003) for president. Thurmond would receive more than a million popular votes in the general election that fall.

At Strom Thurmond's one-hundredth birthday celebration in 2002, Senate majority leader Trent Lott, who represented Mississippi, infamously declared, "I want to say this about my state: When Strom Thurmond ran for president, we voted for him. We're proud of it. And if the rest of the country had followed our lead, we wouldn't have had all these problems over all these years." The ensuing controversy cost Lott his leadership position.

DYSTOPIANISM   *See* Utopianism.

EDWARDIANISM
Anything related to the politically complacent reign of Edward VII of Britain (1841–1910), who was crowned in 1901 after the death of his long-lived mother, Queen Victoria. In Europe this same era is known as the Belle Epoque. The dominant style in clothing, ad-

vertising, graphic and decorative arts was art nouveau, with its stylized, serpentine figures and curlicues; cubism also arose during this decade. H. G. Wells (1866–1946), George Bernard Shaw (1856–1950), and E. M. Forster (1879–1970) all rose to prominence; Henry James (1843–1916) wrote his great late novels, and Edith Wharton (1862–1937) wrote her early ones. Cinema began during the Edwardian era, as did powered flight, and motor cars began to vie with horses as a means of transportation. In fashion, the tiny-waisted Gibson Girl dominated in America; in Europe the S-bend corset emphasized the bosom and the hips.

The sinking of the *Titanic* in 1912 was a harbinger of more bad things to come; World War I and the Russian Revolution would deal a devastating blow to most comfortable Edwardian assumptions.

ETHNOCENTRISM   *See* Nationalism.

EXPANSIONISM   *See* Imperialism.

FALANGISM
From the Spanish version of the Greek word *phalanx,* which means a body of infantry troops gathered into a close formation. The Falangist Party was founded in Spain in 1933 and hewed closely to Fascist ideology. After the Civil War of 1936, it became the official party of Generalísimo Francisco Franco's (1892–1975) Spain.

FASCISM
From the Latin word *fascis,* a cylindrical bundle of sticks with an ax head sticking out of its side, a symbol of authority and power that was borne by lictors (bodyguards) before Roman imperial officials such as consuls, proconsuls, praetors, propraetors, and dictators on ceremonial occasions.

Benito Mussolini (1883–1945) was appointed prime minister of Italy in 1922 and became its dictator in 1925. Writing in the *Italian Encyclopedia* in 1932, he defined Fascism as a militaristic, quintessentially imperialistic philosophy: "Fascism . . . repudiates the doctrine of Pacifism . . . War alone brings up to its highest tension all human energy and puts the stamp of nobility upon the peoples who have courage to meet it." The opposite of Marxist socialism, Fascism repudiates democratic liberalism and egalitarianism equally emphatically. In Mussolini's words,

> The foundation of Fascism is the conception of the State, its character, its duty, and its aim. Fascism conceives of the State as an absolute, in comparison with which all individuals or groups are relative, only to be conceived of in their relation to the State.

Borne out of middle- and upper-class fear of a coming class war, frustration with the economic and political uncertainties of post–World War I Europe, nostalgia for past national glories, the romantic frisson of surrendering to a supreme leader with an indomitable will, and seemingly justified by the tenets of social Darwinism, fascistic regimes took hold of power in Spain and Germany a decade after Mussolini had secured his grip on Italy. Though Hitler and Mussolini did not survive the war they started, Spain's Generalísimo Francisco Franco (1892–1975), who once declared, "Our regime is based on bayonets and blood, not on hypocritical elections," was still ensconced in power when he died of old age in 1975.

FEDERALISM
A constitutional form of government in which power is divided between a group of smaller, semiautonomous entities and a central authority. The United States began its independent existence as a loose confederation of sovereign states. Though the national government had nominal oversight of war, the postal service, foreign and Indian affairs, weights and measures, and coinage, the Articles of Confederation, drafted in 1777 and ratified in 1781, didn't grant it the teeth it needed to raise troops or money from the states.

The Constitution that was submitted to the states for ratification in 1787 divided power between the states and a much more substantial national government, which was divided in turn into three equally powerful branches: the executive, the legislative, and the judiciary. The Anti-Federalists—prominent among them were Patrick Henry (1736–99), George Clinton (1739–1812), and George Mason (1725–92)—opposed the Constitution for various reasons, including its failure to guarantee basic liberties (freedom of speech and worship, the right to bear arms, freedom from cruel and unusual punishment, unreasonable search and seizure, etc.); hence the rapid passage of the Bill of Rights after the Constitution's ratification. Thomas Jefferson initially opposed the Constitution for its lack of a bill of rights; as vice president and president he clashed bitterly with the Federalist Party led by Hamilton and John Adams. Jeffersonianism is sometimes considered the antithesis to Federalism's thesis.

The Federalist Papers were a series of eighty-five articles written by Alexander Hamilton (ca. 1755–1804), John Jay (1745–1829), and James Madison (1751–1836) that appeared over the signature "Publius" in New York newspapers in 1777 and 1778. Though the specific purpose of the articles was to defend the Federalist system enshrined in the Constitution as a guarantor of liberty, a hedge against tyranny, and with its separation of powers, the most stable (if not the most efficient) form of representative government possible, they compose one of the more eloquent treatises on the strengths and weaknesses implicit in republicanism. "If men were angels," the fifty-first Federalist Paper eloquently declares, "No government would be necessary."

> In framing a government which is to be administered by men over men, the great difficulty lies in this: you must first enable the government to control the governed; and in the next place oblige it to control itself . . . This policy of supplying, by opposite and rival interests, the defect of better motives, might be traced through the whole system of human affairs, private as well as public.

FEMINISM

"I myself have never been able to find out precisely what feminism is," wrote Rebecca West. "I only know that people call me a feminist whenever I express sentiments that differentiate me from a doormat or a prostitute." Essentially, feminism is the elevation of so-called women's issues—equal pay for equal work, political equality, legal access to contraceptives and abortion, protection from rape, liberation from gender stereotypes, etc.—into a full-blown ideology or worldview. Mary Wollstonecraft's (1759–97) *A Vindication of the Rights of Women* is one of the great feminist manifestos: "Let woman share the rights and she will emulate the virtues of man; for she must grow more perfect when emancipated."

The Seneca Falls Declaration of 1848, an adaptation of the Declaration of Independence, marked the beginning of the woman suffrage movement in the United States. The Nineteenth Amendment of the Constitution, which grants women the vote, was not adopted until 1920. The Equal Rights Amendment, drafted in 1921, states that "Equality of rights under the law shall not be denied or abridged by the United States or by any state on account of sex." It has yet to be ratified.

FENIANISM

Taking their name from the legendary Fianna, the hunters, bandits, and mercenaries who served the High King as soldiers in Irish myth, the Fenian Brotherhood, a revolutionary group dedicated to expelling the British from Ireland, was organized in the United States in 1858 by the exiled John O'Mahony (1816–77). James Stephens (1825–1901), the founder of the newspaper the *Irish People,* led the movement in Ireland, where it was known as the Irish Republican Brotherhood.

In 1866, General John O'Neill (1834–78), a veteran of the Union Army, launched an abortive invasion of Canada with an army of eight hundred Fenians; several other attempted attacks on Canada were also thwarted. O'Neill later founded the Irish settlement of O'Neill, Nebraska. Shortly before his death he declared, "I have always believed in striking at England wherever we could reach her." In 1867 a ship called *Jacmel Packet,* rechristened *Erin's Hope* at sea, sailed from New York to Sligo, manned by fifty fighting men and carrying seven thousand rifles. Most of the crew were arrested upon its arrival, and the ship returned to New York with its cargo undelivered. Arthur Griffith (1872–1922), the founder of Sinn Fein, was a former Fenian.

FEUDALISM

A pyramidal system of obligations between members of the upper classes that arose in Europe between the ninth and fifteenth centuries. Though there were national and local variations, the broad outlines of feudalism are as follows: The king granted pieces of land (fiefs) to the most powerful aristocrats, who became his vassals, or loyal servants, and promised to bear arms in his defense; those senior aristocrats then subdivided their holdings among the next layer of aristocracy, who became *their* vassals, and so on. At the bottom of the pyramid were the serfs, or villeins. Their rights and obligations are spelled out in the system of manorialism (also known as seigneurialism), and are defined in their own entry.

The word *feudalism* is much newer than the system it describes; it was coined by lawyers in the seventeenth century to describe the traditional obligations of the military aristocracy. Eighteenth-century French radicals used it as a shorthand for the abuses of the ancien régime; Marxists would adopt the term in the next century to describe the privations of the peasantry in a rigid, class-based society. In recent years, a number of historians have argued that feudalism was nowhere near as universal—or as straightforwardly hierarchical—as it was once believed to be.

GARVEYISM

After Marcus Garvey (1887–1940), the founder of the Universal Negro Improvement Association. An early proponent of black nationalism and a forerunner of black separatists like Elijah Mohammed and Louis Farrakhan, Garvey came of age in Jamaica and Central America, where he was a union leader and journalist;

he moved to Harlem in 1916. Known as the Black Moses, he rhapsodized about the glories of bygone African civilizations in his speeches and his newspaper, *Negro World*. His "back to Africa" movement envisioned an Africa that was free from white imperialism, where a strong, black-ruled country would begin the process of unifying "all the Negro peoples of the world into one great body." Believing that integration was a futile goal (he supported the Ku Klux Klan for this reason), he established the Negro Factories Corporation to aid in the creation of a separate black economy. His own extensive business interests included restaurants, laundries, and groceries. His efforts to found a steamship line led to his conviction for fraud in 1925. After serving two years in prison, he was deported to Jamaica.

GAULLISM

The political philosophy, the personal charisma, and the abiding sense of France's grandeur epitomized by General Charles de Gaulle (1890–1970). De Gaulle was wounded three times in World War I and made five escape attempts after the Germans captured him at Verdun. A maverick military theorist during the interwar years, he was the only French commander who was able to drive back the invading Germans, albeit temporarily, in 1940. On June 18, 1940, a few days before France capitulated, he spoke on the BBC:

> I, General de Gaulle, now in London, call on all French officers and men who are at present on British soil, or may be in the future, with or without their arms; I call on all engineers and skilled workmen from the armaments factories who are at present on British soil, or may be in the future, to get in touch with me. Whatever happens, the flame of the French resistance must not and shall not die.

Winston Churchill recognized him as the leader of Free France; the Vichy regime sentenced him to death in absentia.

Though his relationship with Churchill and Roosevelt was anything but smooth, he entered Paris with the U.S. Army in

1944 and would be one of the four signatories of the German Act of Unconditional Surrender on May 8, 1945.

He retired from politics to write his memoirs in 1953, but was elected president again in 1958 at the height of the Algerian crisis. Determined to return France to superpower status, he developed an independent nuclear capability, blocked Britain, which he regarded as a U.S. satellite, from joining the European Economic Community, and sought an independent détente with the Soviet bloc. In 1966, his relations with the United States strained over Vietnam, de Gaulle withdrew France from the integrated command structure of NATO, evicting all foreign troops from French soil.

"France cannot be France without greatness," de Gaulle characteristically declared in his memoirs. "More than just a form of nationalism," John J. Miller wrote in the *New York Times,* "Gaullism insists that France must exert an outsized influence on the course of human events."

GLOBALISM

"The new electronic interdependence," Marshall McLuhan wrote back in 1962, "recreates the world in the image of a global village." Almost half a century later, the world is even smaller. Jet travel is much faster and more affordable (if less comfortable); cell phones, satellite phones, and the Internet allow for instantaneous communication; corporate brands like McDonald's are ubiquitous in locations as far-flung as Russia, China, the United Arab Republics, Paraguay, and Azerbaijan; Bollywood and Hollywood set the standards for big-screen entertainment; and CNN and *Baywatch* flicker across the screens of battery-powered TVs in Outer Mongolian yurts. Cosmopolitanism, literally "world citizenship," begins to seem like less of a utopian notion, though in practice, the more economically and culturally potent members of the world community still subsume the smaller.

Proponents of globalization insist that as trade and investment move across borders, economic efficiencies raise the standards of living on both sides of the exchange. Developing countries receive the benefits of manufacturing jobs, which, however low paid, are more remunerative than any homegrown options; developed consumer economies receive the boon of cheap goods in return. As Daniel T. Griswold, of the Cato Institute's Center for Trade Policy Studies, argued in a *Philadelphia Inquirer* op-ed piece in February 2004,

> People who live in countries open to the global economy enjoy a higher standard of living, on average, than those trapped behind high-tariff barriers . . . Higher incomes mean a larger, more educated and politically engaged middle class—the foundation of most democracies . . . Those in economically closed nations are nine times more likely to suffer under political tyranny than those in open economies . . . Expanding trade and investment ties creates a more peaceful and hospitable world, where hope for a brighter future can finally replace frustration and envy.

Antiglobalism disputes that sunny picture. Antiglobalists worry that the ubiquity of American pop culture inevitably undermines local cultures—that amoral multinational corporations do damage to both the first world, as they outsource their labor requirements and avoid paying income taxes, and the third world, whose unregulated workers are exploited, and whose unprotected environments are degraded. Thus, Union Carbide (now Dow Chemical) still eludes liability for the deadly accident at Bhopal; Chevron despoils vast stretches of the Amazon rain forests; Coca-Cola turns a blind eye when union leaders attempting to organize Colombian bottling plants are assassinated. Left-wing antiglobalists regard genetically modified crops as a threat to biodiversity and insist that the relentless marketing of packaged junk foods imperils bodies and souls alike. They deplore the International Monetary Fund, the World Bank, and the World Trade Organization for negotiating lopsided "free trade" agreements that they insist amount to economic imperialism. Right-wing antiglobalists worry about the dilution of white, Christian American identity; the exodus of manufacturing jobs; the enrichment of elite, international bankers; and the empowerment of international institutions that they fear could lead to world government.

GREENBACKISM

In 1862, with supplies of gold and silver running dangerously low, the federal government issued paper dollars, printed on one side only in green ink, to finance the Civil War. This currency was not convertible to gold but was considered legal tender for most debts. The bills were gradually withdrawn from circulation after the war. During the Panic of 1873, debtor interests, mostly farmers, demanded that the government print more "soft," or cheap paper, money, which would make it easier for them to pay off their loans. President Grant vetoed a congressional bill to do just this in 1874; in 1876 the national Greenback Party was formed. In the election of 1878 the Greenbacks—now known as the Greenback Labor Party—received over a million votes and sent fourteen congressmen to Washington. As prosperity returned, the appeal of soft money faded. The Greenbacks fared poorly in the general election of 1880 (their candidate; General James Weaver, also backed woman suffrage and a graduated income tax). Greenbackism would become a central issue in the rise of populism later in the nineteenth century; it is also a founding tenet of monetarism.

HELLENISM

In its broadest sense, Hellenism is an admiration or emulation of the art, philosophy, architecture, and culture of Ancient Greece. Historians characterize the years between 323 and 31 BCE (from the death of Alexander the Great to the Roman victory over the Ptolemaic Egyptians at the Battle of Actium) as Hellenistic, because Greek culture spread into the territories they controlled: Egypt through the Ptolemaic dynasty; Syria and Mesopotamia through the Seleucid dynasty; Anatolia through the Attalid dynasty; and Macedonia and Central Greece through the Antigonid dynasty. Greek influence was felt as far afield as northern India and the Caucasus.

In Judaism, Hellenism refers to the widespread adoption of Greek customs and ideas by the Jewish people of Palestine during the Seleucid dynasty. Many Jews took up the Greek language, donned togas, and participated in nude athletic events; some made sacrifices to Greek gods. The philosopher Philo of Alexandria (ca. 13 BCE–ca. 50 CE), who wrote in Greek, attempted to reconcile Judaism with Greek philosophy—as Moses Maimonides (1135–1204) also would, twelve hundred years later, in his *Guide for the Perplexed*. The revolt of the Maccabees, or Hasmoneans, that began in 168 BCE, and which is commemorated by the Jewish holiday Hanukkah, was as much against the Hellenizing tendency among the Jews themselves as it was against the Greek's Syrian proxy Antiochus IV.

IMPERIALISM

The imposition of rule by one nation over another, or over many others. The ancient Egyptians and Mesopotamians built vast empires, as did the Persians, the Greeks, the Romans, and some Chinese dynasties. Though almost constantly at war, the eastern portion of the Roman Empire, which became known as the Byzantine Empire, remained relatively stable throughout the Middle Ages until it was finally overrun by the Turks in 1453. The Muslim Ottoman Empire that superseded it would last for another five hundred years.

The word *imperialism* is generally used today to describe the historical processes, and especially the ideological assumptions, underlying the European colonial empires that developed beginning in the 1400s. At its apogee, the British imperium extended across India, Africa, North America, the Middle East, the South Pacific, and Asia; the Dutch held colonies in the East Indies, South Africa, and briefly in North and South America; the Spanish ruled islands in the West Indies and nations in Central and South America; the French controlled large portions of North America and Africa (and briefly much of Europe during the time of Napoleon); from the late nineteenth century through World War II, Japan built an empire by conquering parts of China, Korea, and the Philippines.

Nationalism, or expansionism—a nation's determination to annex territory and extend its sway as widely as possible—and colonialism often went hand in hand. Mercantilist economic poli-

cies encouraged the development of colonies for tactical and
strategic reasons. Colonies provided a foothold in a rival nation's
territory, protected vital trade routes, and served as bargaining
chips in diplomatic or military games of give and take. Colonies
were useful for economic reasons as well. The mother country
could exploit them as sources of raw materials, precious metals,
and cheap or slave labor, while at the same time forcing them to
serve as captive markets for their own manufactures.

The colonialists assumed they were innately superior to the
indigenous inhabitants of the territories they conquered. This
justified their worst depredations, since lofty notions like liberty,
justice, and the rights of property could hardly be said to apply to
creatures that only qualified as human beings on technical
grounds. In some cases they believed that they were conferring a
vast beneficence upon their subject peoples by introducing them
to Christianity and European institutions, though, like long-
suffering parents, they knew that the only thanks they were likely
to receive for their sacrifices and trouble was a stab in the back.
As Rudyard Kipling wrote when the United States acquired its
first colony, the Philippines, in the Spanish-American War:

> Take up the White Man's burden—
> Send forth the best ye breed—
> Go bind your sons to exile
> To serve your captives' need;
> To wait in heavy harness,
> On fluttered folk and wild—
> Your new-caught, sullen peoples,
> Half-devil and half-child.

By the end of World War II, virtually all of the former colonies of
Europe and Japan had declared independence. With the breakup
of the Soviet Union in the 1990s, the last of the world's great empires had fallen.

Neocolonialists and neoimperialists are still looking for opportunities to invest in cash-poor, resource-rich countries that are
unencumbered with child labor laws, minimum wage rules, or

troublesome OSHA (Occupational Safety and Health Administration) and environmental regulations, and whose officials are happy to look the other way in return for a piece of the profits. But these modern-day conquistadores march under the banners of global corporate brands like Nike, Monsanto, and Shell, not the flags of nations. In their defense, most of these corporations argue that they are raising the living standards of their workers and introducing them to a better way of life.

INTENTIONALISM   *See* Originalism.

INTERVENTIONISM

In foreign affairs, interventionism is the idea that interference with the affairs of another sovereign nation, usually by economic or military coercion, can be justified either by national self-interest, by reference to a higher moral law, or both. Thus, Condoleezza Rice, in a speech before the Manhattan Institute in 2002, declared, "The burden of maintaining a balance of power that favors freedom should be shouldered by all nations that favor freedom. What none of us should want is the emergence of a militarily powerful adversary who does not share our common values." In economics, interventionism is when a state intrudes on the workings of the "free market" by strict regulation, the imposition of tariffs, adjusting the money supply, deficit spending, etc.

Noninterventionism in foreign policy is the belief that a state's "true policy," in the words of George Washington's Farewell Address, should be "to steer clear of permanent alliances with any portion of the foreign world." In economics, it is the idea that laissez-faire should be allowed to prevail.

For much of the twentieth century, Democratic administrations in the United States have tended to be interventionist in both foreign affairs and economic policies. The New Deal and the Great Society were both products of Democratic administrations, Franklin Delano Roosevelt's and Lyndon Johnson's, respectively. The United States entered World War I and World War II during the Democratic administrations of Woodrow Wilson and FDR.

The Korean and Vietnam wars both began during Democratic administrations as well. As the former Republican senator Bob Dole notoriously declared when he was Gerald Ford's running mate in 1976, "If we added up all the killed and wounded in Democrat wars in this century, it would be about 1.6 million Americans, enough to fill the city of Detroit."

Strangely enough, as the twenty-first century begins, the hallmarks of George W. Bush's Republican administration, one of the least bipartisan in history, have been aggressive Wilsonian interventionism abroad and unprecedented deficit spending at home, along with permanent tax cuts that are likely to cause the deficits to grow even larger.

IRREDENTISM

From *Italia irredenta,* literally "unredeemed Italy," a nationalist movement in nineteenth-century Italy that called for the annexation of neighboring Italian-speaking territories controlled by Austria. The term is used today to describe any cross-border disturbances caused by shared ethnicity, language, or culture. Since the Gulf War of 1991, it has been widely noted that Turkey fears the establishment of an independent Kurdistan in northern Iraq, for fear that it will foment irredentism among the Kurds who live within its own borders.

ISLAMISM   *See* Jihadism.

JACKSONISM

The democratic political and social ideas associated with Andrew Jackson (1767–1845), hero of the Battle of New Orleans, and the seventh president of the United States. Jackson stood for extending the right to vote beyond the moneyed class and supported homesteaders in their efforts to enlarge the United States. A staunch champion of small farmers and working men, he won a plurality of electoral votes in the presidential election of 1824, but lost in the House of Representatives to John Quincy Adams. His victory in the bitterly fought campaign of 1828 was seen as a repudiation of Adams and a victory for democracy. The first self-made president (and the first westerner to hold that office), Jackson owed his election to the people rather than the establishment. Though he supported the integrity of the Union when he denounced South Carolina's "nullification" of tariffs, his legacy was marred by his support of Georgia's patently illegal seizure of Cherokee land. The Trail of Tears—the forced march of some fourteen thousand displaced Cherokee to a new reservation in Oklahoma—cost about a third of them their lives.

JACOBEANISM

From Jacobus, the Latin for James. The Jacobean Age coincides with the reign of England's King James I (1603–25). The era is especially notable for its literature: William Shakespeare wrote his last plays in the first decade of the seventeenth century; Ben Jonson (1572–1637) and John Donne (1572–1631) came to prominence; Francis Bacon (1561–1626) and Robert Burton (1577–1640) were active, and the Authorized Version (or the King James Version) of the Bible was completed and published in 1611.

JACOBINISM

The political ideas of the most radical organization that supported and fomented the French Revolution. The Jacobins advocated universal egalitarianism, and condoned violence and terrorism as means to achieve it; when the king was overthrown, they advocated his execution. Their official name was Société des Amis de la Constitution, or Society of the Friends of the Constitution. They were known as the Jacobins because they met in a former Dominican convent that was located on la rue de Saint-Jacques in Paris (Jacobin pigeons are so called because the tufts of feathers around their heads resemble the hoods worn by Dominican friars). After Louis XVI was overthrown, the club changed its name to the Société des Jacobins, Amis de la Liberté et de l'Egalité, or the Society of the Jacobins, Friends of Liberty and Equality. Under the leadership of Maximilien Robespierre (1758–94), they played a key role in the Reign of Terror. The club was banned in 1794 after Robespierre's execution.

JACOBITISM

The belief that England's King James II (1633–1701), who was exiled after the Glorious Revolution of 1688, and his descendants were the rightful heirs to the throne of England. James II of England was also James VII of Scotland. His loyalists lived mostly in Scotland, Wales, and Ireland, although many fellow Catholics in England were sympathetic to his cause. The first serious attempt to restore the House of Stuart was led by James himself, who was decisively defeated at the Battle of the Boyne, in Ireland, in 1690. The last was in 1745, when Charles Edward Stuart (Bonnie Prince Charlie) led an army of exiles and Scotsmen into England and advanced as far as Derby, 120 miles from London, before retreating back into Scotland. On April 16, 1746, his army was routed at the Battle of Culloden. The Cardinal Duke of York, the last Stuart pretender to the crown, died in 1807. He is buried in St. Peter's Basilica in the Vatican.

There is also a Jacobite church in Syria (see Monophysitism).

JEFFERSONIANISM

The ideas most associated with Thomas Jefferson (1743–1826), perhaps the most sophisticated and erudite of the Founding Fathers. Jefferson was a staunch advocate of states' rights, civil liberties, the separation of church and state, and of a strict construction of the Constitution. He believed that an agrarian, rather than an urban industrial economy, would best preserve the character of the United States.

The author of the Declaration of Independence, a vice president and secretary of state and the third president of the United States, Jefferson was a man of contradictions. A slaveholder and the father of mixed-race children, the coiner of the phrase "all men are created equal" wrote extensively about the inherent inferiority of the Negro race. Jefferson was prescient enough to recognize the moral and political dangers that the "peculiar institution" posed to the future of the Republic, but the longer he lived, the less enlightened his views became. Nevertheless, Martin Luther King Jr., in his "I have a dream" speech, would invoke

Jefferson's words about the "inalienable rights" of "life, liberty and the pursuit of happiness" as "a promissory note to which every American was to fall heir."

The coiner of many memorable aphorisms about the dangers of public and private indebtedness, Jefferson lived so far beyond his means that his estate was auctioned off to satisfy his debtors, and his heirs were forced to accept charity. An implacable enemy of centralized government, his most important act as president, the Louisiana Purchase, vastly increased the scope of federal power, not to mention the national debt. During the bitterly partisan years of his presidency, this most subtle and refined of thinkers and writers was as ruthlessly cynical a political operator as this country has ever seen.

In the words of the historian and biographer Joseph Ellis, Jefferson was "the Great Sphinx" of American history. "Coming to terms with Jefferson [means] coming to terms with the most cherished convictions and contested truths in contemporary American culture," Ellis wrote. Jefferson's belief in the moral and political virtues of self-sufficient agrarianism still has a sentimental resonance for many Americans, even if it is no longer—if it ever was—an economic fact. His staunch advocacy of public education, of the "wall" between religion and state, of civil liberties, and his distrust of excessive federal power—especially his "eternal hostility against every form of tyranny over the mind of man"—continue to inspire reverence and controversy today. Paradoxically, his personal foibles only add to his appeal. In Ellis's words, "Jefferson is Jesus, who came to live among us. Washington is Jehovah, aloof and alone in heaven."

JIHADISM

Though often defined as "holy war," the Arabic word *jihad* literally means "striving," as in the Koranic phrase "striving in the path of God." Not all jihads involve combat; the word has no intrinsic relationship to terrorism. Personal jihad is the struggle to purge one's soul of sin and worldly desires, to be righteous. Verbal jihad is to proclaim the word of Islam, and to protest against injustice. Finally, there is physical jihad, which refers to both defensive and offensive warfare. Wanton and unprovoked slaughter are categorically forbidden by Sharia (Muslim law), which declares that women and children and noncombatants are not to be harmed. An unambiguous declaration of war is also called for. Clearly, some orthodox Islamic terrorists are not quite as orthodox as they would have us believe.

In the twentieth century, fundamentalist Islamic thinkers such as the Egyptian Sayyid Qutb (1906–66) and the Palestinian Abdullah Yusuf Azzam (1941–89) taught that no government is legitimate unless it is an Islamic theocracy, ruled according to Sharia. This idea led to *Islamism,* a term which the neoconservative Middle Eastern scholar Daniel Pipes defined in a 1998 article for the Center for Strategic and International Studies as

> an ideology that demands man's complete adherence to the sacred law of Islam and rejects as much as possible outside influence, with some exceptions (such as access to military and medical technology). It is imbued with a deep antagonism towards non-Muslims and has a particular hostility towards the West. It amounts to an effort to turn Islam, a religion and civilization, into an ideology.

The ideology of Islamism that has become intimately intertwined with the obligation of jihad—and jihad, for these Islamists, is no longer hedged with restrictions. All enemies of Islam—and most prominent among those enemies are Islamic people who presume to practice a religion that is moderate, tolerant, and secularized—are fair game. Al Qaeda's Osama bin Laden first called for a jihad against America because after the Gulf War of 1991, U.S. troops were quartered in "the lands of Islam in the holiest of its territories, Arabia." Because of this offense, he said,

> To kill Americans and their allies, both civil and military, is an individual duty of every Muslim who can, in any country where this is possible, until the Aqsa mosque and the Haram mosque are freed from their grip, and until their armies, shattered and

broken-winged, depart from all the lands of Islam, incapable of threatening any Muslim.

Other Islamist groups whose understandings of jihad sanction terrorism against innocent civilians are Laskar Jihad in Indonesia, Harakat ul-Jihad-i-Islami in Kashmir, Palestinian Islamic Jihad, Egyptian Islamic Jihad, and Yemeni Islamic Jihad.

JINGOISM

Extreme nationalism, almost always backed up by a bellicose foreign policy (see chauvinism). The word dates back to the Russo-Turkish War of 1877, when Great Britain threatened to intervene against the czar on behalf of the Ottomans. The word comes from the lyrics to a popular British music hall song of the day:

> We don't want to fight, yet by jingo if we do,
> We've got the ships, we've got the men,
> And got the money too!

KNOW-NOTHINGISM

An anti-Catholic, protemperance, anti-immigration movement that began in New York State, and with the establishment of the Native American political party in 1845, gradually blossomed into a national movement. Its adherents were called Know-Nothings because the leadership and membership roles of its constituent nativist organizations (such as the Order of the Star-Spangled Banner and the Order of United Americans) were closely kept secrets; questions about them were deflected with the answer, "I know nothing."

The party's platform called for drastic limits on immigration from Catholic countries and a twenty-five-year waiting period for naturalization; it advocated banning non-Protestants from teaching school and would have forbidden foreign-born U.S. citizens from holding political office. When a Know-Nothing descendant of Daniel Boone became mayor of Chicago, he fired every city worker who wasn't born in the United States. By the 1850s, with ex-president Millard Fillmore as their standard-bearer, the movement began to score major electoral successes, but when Southerners seized control of the party in 1855 and endorsed a proslavery reso-lution, the resulting schism greatly vitiated its strength. President Clinton's national security adviser Anthony Lake characterized op-ponents of military intervention in Yugoslavia as "neo-Know-Nothing isolationists."

LIBERALISM

From the Latin *liber,* or "free." In the post-Reagan years, how-ever, the American Right has managed to turn the word *liberal* into a devastatingly effective epithet for those elitist, Volvo-driving, latte-sipping, evolution-believing, church-neglecting, nonhunting, gay-coddling, nonsmoking, weak-on-defense scolds who, while they are weakening the moral fabric of America, want you to eat your vegetables and pay higher taxes as they indoctri-nate your children into the latest Politically Correct nonsense and expose them to sex education. The word's defense is its long and complex lineage.

In Protestant theology, Liberalism refers to the idea that Christianity is more than the sum of the dogmas and rituals im-posed by an all-authoritative church: It is a mode of individual, personal spiritual development. The belief that the human condi-tion—and human nature itself—is capable of improvement, a legacy of the Renaissance, not only led to the Enlightenment and the Romanticism of the eighteenth and nineteenth centuries, but it deeply influenced post-Reformation Christianity.

Rather than conventional piety and obedience or the an-guished consciousness of sin, many Protestants came to regard their personal intimations of the Divinity as the highest form of re-ligious feeling. The German theologian Friedrich Schleiermacher (1768–1834) wrote, "I lie on the bosom of the infinite world. At this moment I am its soul, for I feel all its powers and its infi-nite life as my own." For Schleiermacher, Christ was not literally the son of God; rather, he declared, he was a man in whom "the

God consciousness . . . was absolutely clear and determined each moment, to the exclusion of all else, so that it must be regarded as a continual living presence, and withal a real existence of God in Him."

In government and politics, Liberalism is inextricably connected to the rise of mercantilism and capitalism. Just as Protestantism undermined the hegemony of the Catholic Church in Europe, and the horrors of the Thirty Years' War taught the necessity of at least a modicum of religious toleration, the rising merchant class questioned some of the prerogatives that the aristocracy had long taken for granted. Thinkers like John Locke (1632–1704) and Immanuel Kant (1724–1804) posited a human nature that was capable of self-governance. No longer content to be passive subjects of king and church, or to accept their class status unthinkingly, an increasingly powerful new class of self-made thinkers, scientists, and merchants began to think of themselves as subjects in the philosophical sense of the word: as autonomous individuals whose relationship with the state was strictly voluntary, a contractual rather than a filial relationship.

Thus Locke, in his *Second Treatise on Civil Government* (1690), argued that if people invested some of their liberty in their government, it was with the expectation that they would receive a bankable return.

> Men, when they enter into society, give up the equality, liberty, and executive power they had in the state of nature, into the hands of the society, to be so far disposed of by the legislative, as the good of the society shall require; yet it being only with an intention in every one the better to preserve himself, his liberty and property; (for no rational creature can be supposed to change his condition with an intention to be worse).

But if Liberalism is the belief that individual freedom is paramount, Liberalism and democracy are not entirely complementary, especially when the rights and dignity of the individual citizen are broadly defined. Although the primary role of the state in classical Liberalism is to protect private property, there is no guarantee that a democratically elected government won't seek to redistribute wealth by means of a graduated income tax, estate taxes, luxury taxes, and the like, increasing the happiness of the less-privileged majority by granting them some of the privileges and prerogatives of the moneyed few. As noted in the entry on Libertarianism below, as the United States has become more democratic, Liberalism, ironically, has increasingly come to be associated with the welfare state. If Liberals are still understood to support progressive politics and freedom in the personal sphere (the rights of homosexuals to live as they choose; of minority races and religions to avoid discrimination), they are no longer regarded as such staunch protectors of private property.

LIBERTARIANISM

In a nutshell, Libertarianism is the belief "that government is best that governs least," a slogan that is often attributed to Thomas Jefferson (1743–1826) but is actually a quote from Henry David Thoreau's (1817–1862) *Civil Disobedience*. Thoreau, in his turn, was paraphrasing the slogan of the *United States Magazine and Democratic Review*. John Stuart Mill's (1806–1873) *On Liberty* is a classic expression of Libertarian principles.

A more intensively individualistic variant of classical Liberalism, Libertarians embrace the Enlightenment values of the American Declaration of Independence: that "governments derive their just power from the consent of the governed"; that the sole purpose of government is to guarantee the inalienable right of the individual to enjoy "life, liberty, and the pursuit of happiness," and especially the unfettered enjoyment of his or her own private property. The only time a Libertarian can justify a state's use of force against its citizens is when one faction of citizens seeks to deprive the rest of its citizens of their liberty. (The question of how a slave-holding nation could have held this idea to be "self-evident" is one of the great mysteries.)

By the mid-twentieth century, as classical Liberalism came to be associated with the rise of the welfare state, activist foreign policy, public education, the federal income tax, economic and environmental regulations, affirmative action, intrusive morals laws, military conscription, and so on, Libertarians began to distinguish their beliefs from Liberalism's. The popularity of Ayn Rand's novels, which espoused her libertarian philosophy of objectivism; the aggressive advocacy of the free market by Nobel Prize–winning economist Milton Friedman; the publication of the National Book Award–winning *Anarchy, State and Utopia* in 1974 by the Harvard philosopher (and former radical leftist) Robert Nozick; and the increasing influence of think tanks like the Cato Institute all signaled a revival of Libertarianism on the political Right. Another term for those who oppose big government, believing that the state should limit itself to, in Robert Nozick's words, "the narrow functions of protection against force, theft, fraud, enforcement of contracts," is minarchism.

Though most on the Left still envision a continuing role for big government—socialized medicine, massive public works projects, intensive environmental regulation, etc.—Libertarian socialists like Noam Chomsky and the anarchists in the antiglobalist movement share many core principles with right-wing minarchists.

LIKUDISM

The conservative, hawkish political beliefs of the Israeli Likud Party (Likud-Liberalim Leumi, or Unity-National Liberals). Founded in 1973 as a merger of several staunchly Zionist parties, Likud would elect Menachem Begin (1913–1992), the former leader of the anti-British and anti-Arab paramilitary organization the Irgun (Irgun Zvai Leumi, or the National Military Organization), as its first prime minister in 1977. The Likud Party generally took a hard line on national security issues, especially on the issue of retaining control over the territories captured in the 1967 Six-Day War, adamantly opposing Labor's long-standing proposal to trade land to the Palestinians for peace. Ironically, it was Begin who signed the historic Camp David Accords with Egypt's Anwar Sadat (1918–81) in 1978, which required Israel to return the Sinai peninsula to Egypt; though he was awarded the

Nobel Peace Prize for his efforts, Begin's legacy as a peacemaker was destroyed when Israel invaded Lebanon in 1982.

In 2005 the longtime Likudnik Ariel Sharon broke precedent by expelling Israeli settlers from the Gaza Strip and returning it to Palestinian control. Facing resistance from the party, he resigned from Likud and ran for reelection as the leader of a new party, Kadima (Forward). In January 2006 he was felled by a massive stroke; in the summer of 2006, Sharon's successor invaded Lebanon again.

LOCOFOCOISM

A radical faction of the Democratic Party in New York that opposed not only the national bank, as other Jacksonian Democrats did, but state banks and paper money. When they tried to seize control of a meeting at Tammany Hall in 1835, the party regulars turned off the gaslights, hoping to bring the meeting to an end. Undeterred, the radicals lit candles and matches, or locofocos, which gave them their name.

Locofoco was the brand name for a novelty self-lighting cigar that had come on the market the year before. Since the cigar had a friction match embedded in one end, the term would be extended to matches as well. Its etymology is unclear. One suggestion is that it is derived from the Latin words *loco foci* (literally "in the place of fire"); another is that it was a play on the *loco* in *locomotive,* which was presumably mistranslated to mean "self" as in "self-moving." The literal Latin translation of *locomotive* is, in fact, "moving from a place."

LUDDISM

The Luddites were bands of workingmen who rioted and destroyed industrial machinery in England between 1811 and 1816. The movement began in Nottinghamshire when skilled stocking knitters, who had long been paid a fixed price for piecework, destroyed the knitting machines that were driving down the prices of their wares. The military was called out in Lancashire; seventeen Luddites were executed in York, and many more were transported to Australia.

Most historians attribute the unrest to the economic disruptions caused by the Napoleonic Wars. The renowned labor historian E. P. Thompson argued that the disturbances were, in fact, highly organized. The popular view of Luddism as unenlightened, backward-thinking resistance to technological progress, he said, merely perpetuates the propaganda of the time. Actually, Luddism was a considered protest by working people against the inequities of the so-called free market.

The mythical leader of the Luddites, Ned Lud, was probably inspired by a folk tale about a retarded man who followed two children who had been mocking him into their home, and "in a fit of insane rage" destroyed a stocking frame he found there. "By the time his name was taken up by the frame-breakers of 1812," Thomas Pynchon wrote in an essay in the *New York Times Book Review*, "historical Ned Lud was well absorbed into the more or less sarcastic nickname 'King (or Captain) Ludd,' and was now all mystery, resonance and dark fun: a more-than-human presence, out in the night, roaming the hosiery districts of England, possessed by a single comic shtick—every time he spots a stocking-frame he goes crazy and proceeds to trash it."

MANIFEST DESTINY

The quintessence of American expansionism, the idea that America's self-evident moral superiority justified its spread across the continent and at the same time made it inevitable. The phrase was first used in print by the Jacksonian Democratic newspaper columnist John L. O'Sullivan in 1845, when he declared that the United States was entitled to the Oregon Territory in its entirety (it had occupied it jointly with Great Britain since the Treaty of 1818) "by the right of our manifest destiny to overspread and to possess the whole of the continent which Providence has given us for the development of the great experiment of liberty and federated self-government."

The conquest of Indian territories; the annexation of Texas; and at the turn of the century, the Spanish-American War would all be seen as further proofs of America's divine entitlement. The concept of a unique American covenant with Providence is as old as the "City on a Hill" sermon of 1630 by the Pilgrim John Winthrop (often quoted by Ronald Reagan), which invoked Moses' farewell to the Israelites as they prepared to enter and possess their own promised land.

MANORIALISM

Also known as seigneurialism. In feudalism, the upper classes traded fealty and military service to their superiors for control of their own territories. At the bottom of the social hierarchy, the peasantry rented land from the lord (or in France, the *seigneur*) of a manor, or a rural estate—the smallest administrative unit in the feudal state. In addition to rent (usually paid in labor and/or a portion of the proceeds of the land), the peasants paid the lord for the use of a mill, granaries, wine and cider presses, and the like, as well as for grazing and hunting privileges; in return, the lord administered local justice and policed the land.

Not all manors were controlled by lords; the church owned some, as did kings and higher nobility. Not all peasants were renters, either—some of them were granted land that was heritable, while others worked strictly for wages on land that was owned outright by the manor (demensne land).

MAOISM

The military, social, and political philosophy of Mao Tse-tung (or Zedong) (1893–1976), one of the key founders of the People's Republic of China. A brilliant military strategist and a revolutionary since his early youth, Mao simultaneously fought the Japanese and the Kuomintang (the Chinese Nationalist Party led by Chiang Kai-shek) throughout the 1930s and 1940s, moving with his guerrilla army among the rural people "as a fish swims in the sea," in his famous saying. "When the enemy advances," he wrote, "withdraw; when he stops, harass; when he tires, strike; when he retreats, pursue." In 1949, as Chiang Kai-shek and his followers retreated to Taiwan, Mao was named chairman of both the People's Republic and the Communist Party. He held the latter position until his death.

Maoism, or Mao Zedong Thought, as it is called in China, began as a variant of Marxist-Leninism. Recognizing that China was lacking in a sufficiently developed urban proletariat, Mao set about to transform the peasantry with forced collectivization. His Great Leap Forward forced farmers to adopt the same pseudoscientific agricultural methods that Stalin favored (known as Lysenkoism, after the Marxist scientist who devised them): Dams, canals, and other massive infrastructure projects were undertaken with forced labor, and peasants were ordered to produce steel in furnaces in their backyards. It was an unqualified disaster; millions died in the resulting famines.

By the early 1960s, China and the Soviet Union were bitter enemies (Mao regarded Khrushchev's disavowal of Stalinism as a betrayal of the revolution), and Mao had been reduced to a figurehead in his own country. Refusing to be sidelined, Mao launched a cult of personality. As many as a billion copies of *Quotations from Chairman Mao*, or *The Little Red Book,* as it was known in the West, were distributed. In his fawning foreword to the volume, the soon-to-be disgraced Lin Biao, who would die in a plane crash in 1971 (his official obituaries accused him of attempting to overthrow Mao), described the chairman as

> The greatest Marxist-Leninist of our era. He has inherited, defended and developed Marxism-Leninism with genius, creatively and comprehensively and has brought it to a higher and completely new stage . . . Therefore, the most fundamental task in our Party's political and ideological work is at all times to hold high the great red banner of Mao Tse-tung's thought, to arm the minds of the people throughout the country with it and to persist in using it to command every field of activity.

The Cultural Revolution, which was launched in 1966, pitted the Red Guards, mostly cadres of students, against the party elite and the intelligentsia, at the cost of millions more lives. As a strict ideology, Maoism did not survive its creator. "Socialism with Chinese Characteristics," as propounded by Mao's successor, Deng Xiaoping (1904–97), would fuel China's rise as an emerging industrial power.

The hallmarks of Maoism—relentless propaganda, a rural guerrilla movement that proletarianizes the peasantry, ideological purity, and especially the ruthless certainty, in the chairman's words, that "political power comes out of the barrel of a gun"— are still evident in contemporary revolutionary movements in Peru, the Philippines, India, and Nepal.

MENSHEVISM   *See* **Bolshevism.**

MINARCHISM   *See* **Libertarianism.**

MONROE DOCTRINE

First articulated in President James Monroe's (1758–1831) State of the Union Address in 1823, which was written with considerable input from his secretary of state, John Quincy Adams (1767–1848), the Monroe Doctrine declared that while the United States would not take sides in ongoing European conflicts, it would regard any attempt to establish new colonies on the American side of the Atlantic (or interference in the affairs of former colonies) as an act of hostility, "dangerous to our peace and safety." Though it would be many years before the United States had the military power to back it up, the doctrine was reaffirmed in the 1840s by James Polk when he warned Great Britain and Spain away from Oregon, California, and Mexico. In 1904, Theodore Roosevelt appended the Roosevelt Corollary to the doctrine, in which the United States granted itself the power to preemptively "exercise international police power" over sovereign nations in the Western Hemisphere in the event of chronic or dangerous "wrongdoing or impotence" that might tempt European powers to intervene.

MUGWUMPISM

Probably a corruption of *mugguomp,* an Algonquian word for "war chief." The term came into wide use during the presidential election of 1884 when Charles A. Dana of the *New York Sun* derided Republicans who had abandoned their party's candidate, James Blaine, to support the reform-minded Democrat Grover Cleveland as "little mugwumps"; they defiantly adopted it as an honorific. In 1911, Ambrose Bierce's ironical *Devil's Dictionary* defined *mugwump* approvingly as "one who is afflicted with self respect and addicted to the vice of independence," but the word's negative connotations proved more lasting. In the 1930s the politician Albert J. Engel famously declared that "a mugwump is one of them boys who always has his mug on one side of the political fence and his wump on the other." Neomugwump is sometimes used today as a pejorative for socially liberal or otherwise independent Republicans (also known as RINOs, or Republicans in name only).

MULTILATERALISM   *See* Unilateralism.

NATIONALISM

"Patriotism," wrote the French statesman Charles de Gaulle, "is when love of your own people comes first; nationalism, when hate for people other than your own comes first." *Nationalism* is defined as the belief that the chief attribute of one's identity—and the focus of one's moral obligations—derives from membership in a particular nation. *Ethnocentrism,* the belief that one's own language, culture, and blood are superior to others', is different from nationalism because it's not tied to a place. The Hebrews of the Old Testament, whose peoplehood and attachment to a particular territory were sealed by a covenant with God, were probably the first nationalists in recorded history; the Athenian Greeks were nationalistic as well. In the Middle Ages, ties to the universal church, to empire, and especially to one's feudalistic superior diluted national identity. As kings were able to centralize their power in the sixteenth and seventeenth centuries, as mercantilism supplanted feudalism, and finally, as liberal ideas about the social contract and the state took hold, nationalism began to assert itself as a powerful new political force.

In the nineteenth century, the disparate independent states that constituted Germany and Italy unified; the United States conquered its indigenous inhabitants, spread out across the North American continent, and then fought a Civil War to maintain its national identity; Ireland pressed for independence from Britain (which was increasingly hard pressed to maintain its empire in Africa, India, and the Middle East); and the Ottoman and Austro-Hungarian empires began to fracture under the pressure of nascent nationalist movements.

Literally hundreds of new nations appeared in the wake of the world wars and the collapse of the Soviet Union in the twentieth century. The last century also saw the rise (and fall) of the most extreme form of nationalism, Fascism, and the use of genocidal ethnic cleansing on an unprecedented scale against the Jews and the Gypsies by the Nazis, against the Tutsi in Rwanda, the Muslims in Bosnia, the Armenians in Turkey, and the Mayans in Guatemala, to name only a few instances.

NAZISM

The racist, expansionist, fascistic, and genocidal doctrines and policies of Adolf Hitler's (1889–1945) Nationalsozialistische Deutsche Arbeiterpartei (National Socialist German Workers Party), Germany's sole political party from 1934 to 1945, which bears the chief responsibility for the greatest bloodletting in the history of the world. The word *Nazi* is formed from the first and fifth syllables of *Nationalsozialistische*.

Hitler's beliefs about German racial superiority; his fanatic hatred of Jews, the Romanys (Gypsies), and Slavs; and his quest for German lebensraum (living space, which required the conquest and elimination of lesser peoples) are well documented in his memoir, *Mein Kampf*; his many speeches; official pronouncements; letters; and other documents. Nietzsche and Wagner are both obvious sources for his neopagan, Nordic weltanschauung, though Nietzsche was far from a proto-Nazi. For all of his extravagantly anti-Christian and anti-Jewish utterances, Nietzsche also spoke of the Jews with undisguised admiration and of anti-Semites with contempt. In *Beyond Good and Evil,* he described the Jews as "the strongest, toughest, and purest race living in Europe," and suggested, in the same passage—one which Hitler certainly never quoted—"that it would perhaps be useful and fair to banish the anti-Semitic bawlers out of the country." Hitler was influenced as well by a number of lesser, mostly forgotten racist thinkers, such as Wilhelm Marr (1819–1904).

A senior Nazi official and tireless expositor of its official ideology was Alfred Rosenberg (1893–1946), the author of *The Myth of the Twentieth Century,* a book he conceived as a "sequel" to the racialist classic by Wagner's son-in-law Houston Stewart Chamberlain (1855–1927), *The Foundations of the Nineteenth Century.* The second best-selling book in Nazi Germany after *Mein Kampf,* Rosenberg's book expounded "the belief, incarnate with the most lucid knowledge, that Nordic blood represents that mystery which has replaced and overcome the old sacraments." Rosenberg was tried and hung by the International Military Tribunal at Nuremberg.

NEOCONSERVATISM

Irving Kristol, one of the godfathers of neoconservatism, famously quipped, "A conservative is a liberal who has been mugged by reality." (Tom Wolfe's memorable rejoinder in his best-selling *The Bonfire of the Vanities* is "a liberal is a conservative who has been arrested.") Kristol was one of a number of formerly liberal or even radical members of the intelligentsia who moved sharply to the right in the late 1960s and early 1970s, alienated by the increasingly strident anti-American and anti-Zionist rhetoric of the New Left and the militancy of black separatists who had begun to eclipse the old guard of the civil rights movement. Writing in magazines like the *Public Interest* (edited by Kristol and Daniel Bell) and in *Commentary* (edited by Norman Podhoretz), they expressed profound skepticism about the social engineering efforts of the welfare state. Staunch in their support for

Israel, they disavowed the isolationism and anti-interventionism engendered by the perceived failure of the Vietnam War. In contrast to traditional conservatives and libertarians, they were not opposed to big government per se; they didn't shy from deficit spending or monetarist intervention when it was necessary to stimulate the economy. Many of them remained liberal in their attitudes about abortion, civil liberties, and women's rights.

Though the novelist and social critic Gore Vidal famously accused Norman Podhoretz and his wife, Midge Decter, of being fifth columnists for Israel, some of neoconservatism's most influential figures, such as Jeane Kirkpatrick, Pat Moynihan, and Michael Novak, were not Jewish. Many of the architects of George W. Bush's invasion of Iraq were identified with neoconservatism. The conservative pundits John Podhoretz and William Kristol are two of its founders' sons. High-ranking State and Defense Department officials and advisers like Richard Perle, Paul Wolfowitz, Elliott Abrams, and Douglas Feith have all been associated with neoconservative think tanks, such as the Project for the New American Century and the American Enterprise Institute. In 2004, Katrina vanden Heuvel, editor of the liberal journal the *Nation,* facetiously defined neoconservatives as "nerds with Napoleonic complexes."

NONORIGINALISM　*See* Originalism.

ORANGEISM

The cause of the Orangemen, members of the fraternal organization called the Orange Institution, or the Orange Order, which was founded by Protestants in 1795 in Ulster to resist the movement for Catholic emancipation and to support English control of Ireland. Its name is taken from England's King William III, or William of Orange, who defeated the dethroned Catholic King James II at the Battle of the Boyne in 1690. Every July 12, the anniversary of the victory, its members don orange sashes and march in parades, often provoking riots when they pass through Catholic neighborhoods.

ORIGINALISM

The belief that judicial interpretation of laws, either statutes or the Constitution, should be guided by their authors' explicit intentions. In the words of the conservative American legal scholar Robert Bork, whose nomination for the Supreme Court was rejected by the Senate in 1987:

> If the Constitution is law, then presumably its meaning, like that of all other law, is the meaning the lawmakers were understood to have intended. If the Constitution is law, then presumably, like all other law, the meaning the lawmakers intended is as binding upon judges as it is upon legislatures and executives. There is no other sense in which the Constitution can be what article VI proclaims it to be: "Law . . ."

Originalism encompasses several interpretative philosophies. A textualist is an originalist who accords especial weight to the structure and language of the law, on the assumption that its authors' intentions can never be gleaned with absolute certainty. Intentionalists do just the opposite; they maintain that if the literal language of the law is anachronistic or otherwise imprecise, a careful, disinterested review of the historical, political, and legal context in which the law was originally framed and enacted will reveal its original purpose.

Strict constructionism is related to originalism but is not identical to it—even the most conservative jurists acknowledge that some constitutional principles were deliberately left vague and inchoate. Arguably, a strict constructionist can legitimately interpret something like due process of the law, for example, with reference to our contemporary rather than our historical understanding of the phrase. As Thomas Jefferson framed the issue in a letter to James Madison, "No society can make a perpetual constitution, or even a perpetual law. The earth belongs always to the living generation. They may manage it then, and what proceeds from it, as they please, during their usufruct."

Two years before he was appointed to the Supreme Court, William Rehnquist (1924–2005), then an assistant attorney

general, ventured a starkly political (some might say cynical)
generalization about strict constructionists in a memo to President Richard Nixon:

> A judge who is a "strict constructionist" in constitutional mat-
> ters will generally not be favorably inclined toward claims of ei-
> ther criminal defendants or civil rights plaintiffs—the latter two
> groups having been the principal beneficiaries of the Supreme
> Court's "broad constructionist" reading of the Constitution.

Nonoriginalists fall into two camps. A pragmatist gives substantial weight to precedent when formulating an opinion, also
considering its possible consequences. If an originalist interpretation of the Constitution would promote instability or otherwise
result in harm to the polity, a pragmatist might choose a different
one. Natural law theorists adjudicate with regard to a higher
moral law, rather than precedent, intention, or consequences.

Article 1, section 8, clause 3 of the Constitution, the Commerce Clause, which grants Congress the right "to regulate Commerce with foreign Nations, and among the several States, and
with the Indian Tribes," has been a particular bone of contention
between strict constructionists and nonoriginalists. The conservative Supreme Court in the 1930s struck down many of Roosevelt's
New Deal programs with the argument that they interfered with
issues that were strictly intrastate; *United States v. Lopez* (1995)
revolved around the issue of whether Congress's Gun-Free School
Zones Act of 1990, which made it a federal crime to possess an illegal firearm within a school zone, fell within Congress's right to
regulate commerce.

OWENISM
The utopian social, political, and philosophical ideas of Robert
Owen (1771–1858), which ranged from the obligation to provide
safe working conditions for factory workers to the elimination of
money and the wholesale reorganization of society under com-
munalist conditions. A self-made man, Owen became a success-

ful cotton manufacturer while still in his twenties. In 1800 he purchased his father-in-law's mills in New Lanark, Scotland, and turned it into a model town, providing clean, safe working conditions, good housing and schools, and nonprofit stores for his employees—and raising his profits in the process.

Owen campaigned for the Factory Act of 1819, which banned outright the employment of children under age nine, and mandated no more than a twelve-hour working day for children between ages nine and sixteen. But these incremental reforms failed to satisfy him. Believing that human character is a product of its environment, Owen sought to totally transform society and mankind. He moved to the United States in the 1820s and purchased the thirty-thousand-acre holdings of the Harmony Society, a celibate, socialist Christian community. There he founded the community of New Harmony, Indiana, which, as a self-sufficient, agricultural/manufacturing cooperative, was intended to be a showpiece for Owen's utopian ideas.

Mired in dissension (the banning of money was a particular point of contention), the community disbanded after only a few years, though New Harmony remained a center of progressive thinking throughout much of the nineteenth century. Several of Owen's children continued to live in Indiana after he returned to England; his son Robert Dale Owen (1801–77) was an early activist for birth control and women's rights, as well as an abolitionist and a spiritualist. As a U.S. congressman, he helped create the Smithsonian Institution. Owen's son Richard (1810–1890) was a geologist and the first president of Purdue University.

PALEOCONSERVATISM

The term *paleoconservative* is used to distinguish the anti-big-government, anti-immigration, isolationist, free-market-capitalist, anti-affirmative-action, traditionally moralistic, Goldwaterite ideas of the Old Right, or classic conservatism, from the globally interventionist, domestically activist view of government espoused by neoconservatism. Paleoconservatives like the former Nixon speechwriter, pundit, and failed presidential candidate Pat Buchanan hearken back to the anti–New Deal, America First ideologues of the 1920s and 1930s, such as the aviation hero and Nazi sympathizer Charles Lindbergh (1902–74) and the radio priest Father Charles Coughlin (1891–1979).

"Who are the neoconservatives?" Buchanan asked in March, 2003, in his magazine the *American Conservative,* Figuratively pounding the podium, he answered his own question:

> The first generation were ex-liberals, socialists, and Trotskyites, boat-people from the McGovern revolution who rafted over to the GOP . . . Almost none came out of the business world or military, and few if any came out of the Goldwater campaign. The heroes they invoke are Woodrow Wilson, FDR, Harry Truman, Martin Luther King, and Democratic Senators Henry "Scoop" Jackson (Wash.) and Pat Moynihan (N.Y.) All are interventionists who regard Stakhanovite support of Israel as a defining characteristic of their breed.

PAN-AFRICANISM   *See* Afrocentrism.

PERONISM

The ideology of Juan Domingo Perón (1895–1974), also called Justicialismo, after the political party Partido Justicialista (Party of Social Justice), which Perón led. President of Argentina from 1946 to 1955, when he was excommunicated by the church and overthrown by the army, and again from 1973–1974, after his return from exile in Franco's Spain, Perón began his political career as a pro-Fascist colonel in the Argentine army in the early 1940s. He rose to prominence as secretary of labor and social welfare (he won the allegiance of Argentine workers by enacting generous welfare policies), minister of war, and vice president. The hallmarks of Peronism were a populist cult of personality, extreme nationalism, anti-imperialism (he was particularly hostile to the United States), authoritarianism (freedom of the press was nonexistent; his police force was liberally staffed with ex-Nazis), and economic policies that he described as occupying a "third position" between capitalism and communism, in which both industries and labor unions were nationalized. Perón's second wife, Eva, was virtually his copresident for much of his first term (she died of cancer in 1952); a former actress and a wildly popular speaker, she organized the mass demonstrations that led to his release from prison after his arrest in 1945. Perón's third wife, Isabella, briefly ruled the country after his death in 1974.

PHALANGISM

A Maronite Christian, nationalist political party in Lebanon (also known as the Kataeb Party) founded in 1936 by Pierre Gemayel (1905–1984) and inspired by the Falangist movement in Spain. Gemayel's son Bashir (who sought to expel the Palestinians from Lebanon and possibly make peace with Israel) was elected president of the republic in 1982 and almost immediately assassinated; his brother Amine followed him into office, until he went into exile in 1988.

POPULISM

From the Latin *populus*, or "the people." Any political movement or rhetorical style that appeals to the interests of the common folk, the average man, as opposed to the aristocracy, the plutocracy, or any other elite. Populism can be left wing or right wing. In recent American presidential elections, the leftists Jesse Jackson, Al Sharpton, and Howard Dean were often labeled populists. George Wallace's presidential campaigns of the late 1960s and early 1970s and Pat Buchanan's in the 1990s all incorporated tropes from the America Firsters of the 1930s, inveighing as they did against elite academics and the media, globally minded Wall Streeters and multinational corporations, homosexuals, immigrants, and, implicitly, international Jewry.

The Populist Party of the 1890s grew out of the greenbackism of the 1860s and 1870s. In the presidential campaign of 1892, the Populists won more than a million votes as a third party by appealing to the farmers of the south and the west and the industrial workers of the big cities. Their platform called for the adoption of silver and paper money, government ownership of transportation and communication networks, direct election of senators, a graduated income tax, and an eight-hour working day. The Democratic Party absorbed most of the Populists when it nominated William Jennings Bryan (1860–1925) as its presidential candidate in 1896.

REGENCY ERA

The nine years between 1811 and 1820 when the future king George IV of Britain and Hanover (1762–1830) ruled on behalf of his mentally ill father, George III (1738–1820). The era is often extended backward and forward a decade to include the Napoleonic Wars and George IV's official reign. Perhaps because Jane Austen's (1775–1817) best-known novels were published during this time period, it is a favorite setting for popular romance novels today. The archetypal dandy Beau Brummell (1778–1840) figures in many of these entertainments.

REPUBLICANISM

From the Latin *res* and *publica,* "public thing." In its broadest sense, republicanism is the belief that a state's sovereignty resides in its citizens (in historical times they were likely to be native-born men of property), who in turn elect representatives to govern it for the public good. Usually the state's power is strictly limited by an explicit or implicit constitution. Though republicanism is often antimonarchical, as it was in France and the United States, England's constitutional monarchy is considered a form of republicanism as well, though its king or queen originally shared power with both an elected and a hereditary legislature.

Today the Republican Party is one of the two major political parties in the United States; the other is the Democratic Party. During the presidency of Thomas Jefferson, the Anti-Federalist Party became known as the Republican Party. By about 1820, it would be called the Democratic Republican Party, and by the time Andrew Jackson became president in 1829, it had shortened its name to the Democratic Party. Its rival was the Whig Party. Abolitionist opponents of the Kansas-Nebraska Act of 1854 organized a new Republican Party; Abraham Lincoln was its successful presidential candidate in 1860.

It wasn't until the populist movement captured the Democratic Party in the 1890s that the Republican Party began to identify itself as the party of conservatism. Under Theodore Roosevelt, the party would be associated with aggressive expansionism and robust resistance to the depradations of monopolies and trusts. By the 1930s, the Republicans had become isolationist and were opposed to Franklin Roosevelt's expansion of the government under the New Deal; in the post–World War II years, they would identify themselves as the party of big business and smaller government.

Richard Nixon's victorious "southern strategy" in 1968—in which the former "party of Lincoln" reached out to southern voters who were disaffected by the Democrats' championship of civil rights—laid the groundwork for the party's ascension in the 1980s and 1990s under Ronald Reagan and the two George Bushes. The Republican Party's two major constituencies today are not always in accord—the representatives of business and wealth advocate for less government; social conservatives would like to see the federal government expand its scope of interference into citizens' private lives.

THE RESTORATION

Charles II (1630–85), who assumed the English throne in 1660 after the Protectorate of Oliver Cromwell (1599–1658) had run its course, was sometimes called the Merry Monarch. Not only was he an inveterate gambler and womanizer, he was also a generous patron of science and the arts.

The Royal Society was officially founded in 1660 by Christopher Wren (1632–1723), Robert Boyle (1627–91), Robert Hooke (1635–1703), and other distinguished scientists; the poet John Dryden (1631–1700), the diarist Samuel Pepys (1633–1703), and the religious writer John Bunyan (1628–88) were all active during this era. Theaters, which had been closed during the interregnum, reopened; Restoration comedies by playwrights such as George Farquhar (1678–1707), William Congreve (1670–1729), and William Wycherley (1640–1716) were notable for their fast-paced, complex plots, their cynicism, and their scandalous bawdiness. Though the royal succession was interrupted again when James II (1633–1701) was deposed in the Glorious Revolution of 1688, the era is generally considered to have continued until about 1700.

RUGGED INDIVIDUALISM

A catchphrase for the unfettered, entrepreneurial spirit of American capitalism, tempered by the privations of frontier life and inspired by its limitless horizons. In one of his presidential campaign speeches, Herbert Hoover (1874–1964) gave the Republican Party credit for dismantling the temporarily centralized economy of World War I and restoring the freedom, vitality, and prosperity of free enterprise:

> We were challenged with the choice of the American system, rugged individualism, or the choice of a European system of diametrically opposed doctrines—doctrines of paternalism and state socialism. The acceptance of these ideas meant the destruction of self-government through centralization of government; it meant the undermining of initiative and enterprise upon which our people have grown to unparalleled greatness.

But Hoover (who also once said, "The only trouble with capitalism is capitalists. They're too damned greedy.") added that he was by no means advocating that the United States government discontinue its "public works for purposes of flood control, of navigation, of irrigation, of scientific research or national defense." Neither, he insisted,

> do I wish to be misinterpreted as believing that the United States is free-for-all and the devil-take-the-hindmost. The very essence of equality of opportunity is that there shall be no domination by any group or trust or combination in this republic

whether it be business or political. It demands economic justice
as well as politics and social justice. It is no system to laissez
faire.

SAINT-SIMONISM

The beliefs of Henri de Saint-Simon (1760–1825), elucidated
posthumously by his followers. The father of French socialism,
Saint-Simon envisioned a new society led by an elite of enlightened scientists, engineers, and industrialists whose reorganization
of labor along scientific lines would result in "spontaneous harmony"; he also promoted a secular humanist New Christianity, in
which scientists would serve as priests. As a teenager, Saint-Simon
fought in the American Revolution on the side of the colonists; he
sat out the French Revolution but made a fortune speculating in
real estate; he was penniless, however, by the time he was forty. A
teacher of Auguste Comte (1798–1857), Saint Simon engendered
ideas that played a large role in the development of positivism.

SANSCULOTTISM

Radical ideas—egalitarianism, confiscatory taxes on the rich—espoused by lower-class supporters of the French Revolution and
their most radical leaders during the days of mass protests between 1792 and 1795. The sansculottes dressed in cloth working-
man's trousers (*pantalons*), as opposed to the silk knee breeches
favored by the upper classes (their name translates literally as
"without knee breeches"). Their chief spokesmen were the political journalist Jacques-René Hébert (1757–94), who was guil-
lotined during the Reign of Terror, and the leader of the *enragés*
(literally "madmen") faction of the movement, the ex-priest
Jacques Roux (1752–94), who committed suicide before he could
be beheaded.

SECTARIANISM   *See* Communalism.

SEIGNEURIALISM   *See* Manorialism.

SEXISM

Legal, institutional, personal, or linguistic discrimination based solely on gender (almost always the female gender). The first recorded use of the word *sexist* in this context is in 1965, in a speech by Pauline Leet of Franklin & Marshall College, in which she declared of an adversary who justified the exclusion of women poets from an anthology because of their rarity:

> You are taking a position analogous to that of the racist. I might call you in this case a "sexist" who says that since so few Negroes have held positions of importance . . . their exclusion from history books is a matter of good judgment rather than discrimination.

The first recorded use of the word *sexism* was by Caroline Bird in 1968, who wrote: "Sexism is judging people by their sex where sex doesn't matter." A pamphlet called "Freedom for Movement Girls—Now!" published by the Southern Student Organizing Committee in 1969, noted that the word

> *Sexist* . . . is short, precise, instantly understandable. It has a sharp, vicious sound; and it inherits the ugly overtones of *racist*. It is potentially a word of power. *Male chauvinist* and *male chauvinism* should be dropped and *sexist* and *sexism* adopted throughout the Movement.

The movement to purge the English language of its implicit gender bias—substituting *police officer* for *policeman,* for example, or avoiding gender-specific pronouns by using the passive voice and plurals, even when they are ungrammatical or awkward—has generally taken hold in recent years, much to the consternation of some political and cultural conservatives, who can frequently be heard deploring the effort as yet another example of political correctness run amok.

SOCIAL CONSTRUCTIONISM   *See* Culture Studies.

SOCIALISM

In general use, socialism is the opposite of capitalism. In socialist economies, the means of production are either controlled by or directly owned by the state, which also takes responsibility for the delivery of social services, such as medicine, education, charity, and retirement benefits. In capitalist economies, these functions are left to the private sector. In practice, the differences between capitalism and socialism are not so clear-cut. Most private enterprise systems offer some form of socialized or subsidized medicine; virtually all of them provide education and pensions. Since the impact of Keynesian economic theory (John Maynard Keynes, 1883–1946), even the most ardently capitalist governments micromanage their economies to some extent.

Throughout the Christian era there have been communalistic sects and communist movements, for instance, the Levellers in seventeenth-century England. There is considerable historical and scriptural evidence that the early Christian communities held their goods in common. The Industrial Revolution spawned a number of utopian socialist schemes, such as Fourierism, Saint-Simonism, and Owenism. By the 1840s, Karl Marx (1818–83) and Friedrich Engels (1820–95) were advocating communism or scientific socialism, in which revolutionary class struggle was not only an inevitability, but a necessity for reestablishing society on a just basis.

Though Marx deplored his utopian and "gradualist" rivals, who imagined that capitalist economies would voluntarily reform themselves, the notion of "evolutionary" socialism took hold throughout Europe. In Britain, the Fabian Society, founded in 1884, would become the basis of the Labor Party. In the United States, the moderate Socialist Party split off from the radical Socialist Labor Party. In Russia there was conflict between the Mensheviks and the Bolsheviks. With the Russian Revolution in 1917, revolutionary and democratic socialism divorced each other for good.

SPENGLERISM

The ideas of Oswald Spengler (1880–1936), German author of *The Decline of the West* (1926) and other books. *The Decline of the West* posits an organic view of culture and history, in which the great civilizations of the world (Spengler concentrated on eight: the Babylonian, the Egyptian, the Chinese, the Indian, the Aztec, the Hellenic, the Arabian, and the Western), each with a unique worldview, pass in succession through cycles of growth, maturation, decay, and death.

> This—the inward and outward fulfillment, the finality, that awaits every living Culture—is the purport of all the historic "declines," amongst them that decline of the Classical world which we know so well and fully, and another decline, entirely comparable to it in course and duration, which will occupy the first centuries of the coming millennium but is heralded already and sensible in and around us today—the decline of the West. Every Culture passes through the age-phases of the individual man. Each has its childhood, youth, manhood and old age . . .

The Western civilizations, which Spengler characterized as Faustian because of their desire for the unobtainable, were already in their decadent phase, he argued. One sure sign of that was the rise of the bourgeoisie and democracy. To Spengler, the aristocracy represented the highest aspirations of the culture; democracy he found merely materialistic.

The first volume of *Decline of the West* was published in 1918, the second in 1920; though their academic reception was mixed (Max Weber called him "a very ingenious and learned dilettante"), their popular impact was enormous, especially in Germany. Though Spengler voted for Hitler, he didn't share his anti-Semitism. After he was introduced to the führer in 1933, he was said to have remarked that Germany didn't need "a heroic tenor but a real hero." Shortly before his death he predicted that the Reich would cease to exist within ten years.

STAKHANOVISM

Soviet propaganda campaign named after a thirty-year-old coal miner. In 1935, during Stalin's second Five-Year Plan, Aleksei Grigorievich Stakhanov dug a staggering 102 tons of coal in six hours, vastly exceeding his quota; soon after, his name and likeness were plastered across billboards and magazines and attached to competitions and training programs. Emphasizing hard work, organizational efficiency, and unconditional loyalty to the fatherland, Stakhanovism also included "market" incentives. Stakhanovite pieceworkers received a higher rate of pay when they surpassed their quotas, and were awarded preferences in housing; widely distributed newsreels showed them driving the new cars they received as gifts. For most Soviet workers, Stakhanovism was just another name for the dreaded capitalist speedup, when workers were compelled to produce more work for less pay.

STALINISM

The political ideology and methods of Joseph Stalin (1879–1953), the leader of the Soviet Union from 1922 to 1953. Stalinism is usually used as a pejorative—in his lifetime, by his Trotskyite enemies; after his death, by his successor Nikita Khrushchev (1894–1971). In a secret speech to a closed session of the Twentieth Party Congress in 1956, Khrushchev formally repudiated Stalin's "extreme methods and mass repression . . . not only against actual enemies, but also against individuals who had not committed any crimes against the Party and the Soviet government."

In 1924, Stalin advanced the thesis of "Socialism in One Country," in which he argued that rather than fomenting worldwide revolution and then seeking assistance from more industrialized allies, Russia should instead become economically self-sufficient, a goal he attempted to accomplish by forced collectivizations and a series of ultra-ambitious Five-Year Plans.

In 1933 he argued that the more successful the class struggle, the greater the resistance to be expected from surviving exploiters, some of whom would surely worm their way into the

heart of the party and attempt to subvert it from within. The only
defense was mass arrests, bloody purges, and brutal repression of
dissent—which not incidentally consolidated his personal power.

STRAUSSIANISM

Pertaining to the teachings (and more often to the conservative
politics of some of his better-known acolytes) of the German-
born political philosopher Leo Strauss (1899–1973). The author
of *On Tyranny, Natural Right and History, Persecution and the Art
of Writing* and *What is Political Philosophy?* and a longtime member of the faculty of the University of Chicago, Strauss
emphasized the moral dimensions of politics. An admirer of
Socrates, Strauss took the Athenian gadfly's antidemocratic sentiments seriously; his hermeneutical readings (close interpreta-
tions that treat texts as though they were written in code) of
philosophical texts often revealed a hidden "esoteric" dimension
intended only for an elite readership.

One of Strauss's best-known students was Allan Bloom
(1930–92), the author of the 1980s blockbuster *The Closing of the
American Mind* (and the model for the title character in Saul Bel-
low's late novel *Ravelstein*). Paul Wolfowitz, Richard Perle, Irving
and William Kristol, and a number of other influential conservatives are self-described Straussians as well.

STRICT CONSTRUCTIONISM   *See* Originalism.

SYNDICALISM   *See* Anarcho-syndicalism.

TEXTUALISM   *See* Originalism.

TORYISM   *Also see* Whiggism.

From an Irish word for "outlaw," *Tory* was at first a derogatory
name for the supporters of the Catholic James II's succession to
the throne; later it was extended to those who supported the divine right of kings and state control of religion. Though as a political party the Tories accepted the principle of constitutional

monarchy after the Glorious Revolution of 1688 (which, indeed, was accomplished with their participation), they were less hostile to the king's prerogatives than the Whigs, and they remained associated with the country gentry. Since they were less involved in trade than the Whigs, they tended to oppose England's involvement in European wars. The Jacobite uprisings in the first half of the eighteenth century did tremendous damage to the party, but it returned to power under William Pitt the Younger (1759–1806) and remained indomitable until the Reform Act of 1832 broke its hold on the House of Commons, after which it was absorbed into the newly formed Conservative Party.

During the American Revolution, loyalists to the Crown were called Tories. The conservative pundit George Will describes himself as a Tory because "I trace the pedigree of my philosophy to Burke, Newman, Disraeli and others who were more skeptical, even pessimistic, about the modern world than most people are who today call themselves conservatives."

TOTALITARIANISM

Benito Mussolini (1883–1945) coined the term *totalitario* to describe the absolute nature of the Italian state under Fascism: "All within the state, none outside the state, none against the state." In totalitarianism the police, the military, the academy, the media are all subordinated to the ruler, who, in turn, directs all of his or her efforts to attaining a transcendent goal. In the case of the Fascists, this goal was nationalistic: Italy sought to restore the lost glories of the Roman Empire; in Hitler's case, it was to eliminate the Jews and restore the Germanic race to its rightful rulership of Europe. Stalin's Communistic totalitarianism was dedicated to the eventual defeat of capitalism. "Totalitarianism," wrote the philosopher Hannah Arendt, in *The Origins of Totalitarianism* (1951), "Strives not toward despotic rule over men but toward a system in which men are superfluous."

In 1979, in an article in *Commentary,* the conservative Democrat Jeane Kirkpatrick, who would become President Ronald Reagan's ambassador to the United Nations, made a case for distinguishing between authoritarian and totalitarian regimes (a notion, though not original with her, that would become known as the Kirkpatrick Doctrine). Authoritarian regimes, she said, were essentially selfish; they only sought power over the bodies of their subjects and were content to merely enrich themselves.

> Traditional autocrats leave in place existing allocations of wealth, power, status, and other resources, which in most traditional societies favor an affluent few and maintain masses in poverty. But they worship traditional gods and observe traditional taboos. They do not disturb the habitual rhythms of work and leisure, habitual places of residence, habitual patterns of family and personal relations.

Totalitarian regimes such as those that ruled the Soviet Union and China, however, served a transformative ideology: They sought not just to rule their subjects but, vampirelike, to transform their minds and souls. Not only were authoritarian regimes the lesser of two evils, Kirkpatrick concluded, their corruption made them unstable and amenable to gradual reform, so it made tactical and moral sense to form alliances with them against totalitarian states. Thus the Reagan administration's generous support for illiberal, nondemocratic governments and movements like the Islamist mujahideen in Afghanistan, the Contras in Nicaragua, the apartheid regime in South Africa, and so on. Ironically, the Evil Empire of the Soviet Union ceased to exist within Kirkpatrick's lifetime (she died in December 2006); the Islamists are now America's most implacable foes.

TROTSKYISM
After Leon Trotsky (1879–1940), whose relentless advocacy of world revolution earned him the enduring enmity of Stalin.

Born Lev Davidovich Bronstein in Russia, he became a Marxist in 1896 and was arrested soon after. He escaped from Siberia in 1902 and, traveling under the name of Trotsky (which he'd borrowed from the warden of a prison in Odessa), made his way to London. He worked with Lenin on the revolutionary journal

Iskra, flirted with Menshevism, and in 1905 returned to Russia, where he was swiftly rearrested. After he escaped from Siberia for a second time, he lived in Vienna, Switzerland, France, and New York. Upon Nicholas II's overthrow, he returned to Russia to become a leading member of the Bolshevik Party. Under Lenin, he served as the people's commissar for foreign affairs and the commissar for war.

Trotsky held that communism could not take hold in an undeveloped country like Russia unless, by fomenting proletarian revolutions throughout the world, it gained economic allies. This put him at odds with Lenin's successor Stalin, who had relegated world revolution to the back burner. "After the victorious proletariat of one country has consolidated its power and has won over the peasantry for itself," Stalin wrote in his book *Problems of Leninism,* "It can and must build up the socialist society." Expelled from the Politburo in 1926 and from the USSR in 1929, Trotsky resumed his global peregrinations, moving to Turkey, France, Norway, and finally to Mexico City, where he was assassinated, probably by a Soviet agent, in 1940.

UNILATERALISM

In foreign affairs, unilateralism is when a nation adopts a policy or commits an action toward another country without the expectation of a specific quid pro quo (as in Ariel Sharon's withdrawal of Israeli settlers and soldiers from Gaza in 2005), or without regard to other countries' opinions. Thus the left-wing newspaper *The Guardian* excoriated President George W. Bush's decision to skip the Johannesburg summit on the environment in 2002 as another instance of "the Bush doctrine of go-it-alone unilateralism, in which America pursues its own interests first—with an avowed aversion to any multilateral efforts to make the world a better place."

The right-wing journal the *National Review* takes the opposite stance, reminding its readers that:

> Unilateralism, a word presumed to have negative connotations, is a favorite of those who wish to heap shame on the U.S. for its

carelessness of the feelings of other nations . . . It's time to quit paying attention to those who have made unilateralism into an insult. To the extent that every rational nation acts in its own interests, we are all unilateralists. We cannot surrender as lost a term that has served American policy so well for over 200 years.

Bilateralism refers to trade agreements or treaties between two countries, for instance the SALT I and SALT II treaties between the Soviet Union and the United States. *Multilateralism* is when a group of countries cooperate together to make war or for mutual defense, to establish international norms, or to promote international trade—the principle behind organizations like the United Nations and the World Trade Organization, alliances like NATO, and agreements like the Geneva Conventions on the Laws of War and the Kyoto Accords to reduce global warming.

UTOPIANISM

In an op-ed piece in the *Wall Street Journal* about the interventionism that has characterized the administration of George W. Bush, David Rieff worried that the

> "Hard Wilsonians" of the Bush administration . . . and their liberal interventionist interlocutors are suffering from a terrible hubris, a terrible utopianism about not just the use of force, but about the promise of democracy itself. The right at least used to scorn utopianism, as a folly of liberalism and the left. Communism, it was said, taught one where utopianism led. And yet, what has the administration's policy been if not utopian?

A compound of two (or possibly three) Greek words, *ou* and/or *eu,* meaning "no" and "good" respectively, and *topos,* or "place," Utopia literally means "no place" or "good place." The word was coined by Sir Thomas More in 1516, as the name of an ideal island paradise (and the title of his book describing it), which unlike the tumultuous England of Henry VIII, was nonmaterialistic, just, and enlightened in every way. More's imaginary country bears marked similarities to Plato's *Republic.* With its strict morality and superb organization, it is reminiscent of an enlightened monastic order as well.

Today utopianism (as in David Rieff's "terrible utopianism" above) is usually a pejorative for unrealistically idealistic schemes for political or social reform. Owenism, for instance, was a victim of its utopianism; it came to grief in New Harmony, Indiana, in the 1820s, when its members found themselves unable to transcend the desire for money.

A *dystopia* (a word coined by John Stuart Mill), literally a "sick place," is the opposite of a utopia. Mill's elder Jeremy Bentham had used the word *cacotopia,* or "bad place," to mean the same thing. Just as utopian thinkers dream of mankind at its best, dystopians brood about how much worse things can get. Aldous Huxley's *Brave New World* (1932), a searing account of a future society shaped by genetic engineering and mind-altering drugs, and dedicated to the pursuit of spiritually empty hedonism, and George Orwell's *1984* (1949), which brought the horrors of Stalinism home to a future England, are literary classics. Dystopias are also a staple of the science fiction genre, which is replete with stories about robots revolting against their human masters, iron-fisted dictators who dominate entire star systems, and grim visions of the atavistic, Hobbesian hell that awaits the survivors of an imminent nuclear or ecological catastrophe.

VICTORIANISM

Anything relating to the reign of Britain's queen Victoria (1819–1901), whose coronation was in 1837, or to the arts, literature, and politics of the era. In a time of unprecedented prosperity and expansion, Britain became thoroughly industrialized during the sixty-four years of Victoria's reign: Railroads, telegraphs, and telephones altered the landscape and people's perceptions of time and place (much as the Internet is doing for us today), and the visible structural ironwork in bridges, train stations, and the Crystal Palace blended engineering and estheticism. Mass production brought fine furniture and decorative bric-a-brac within the means of the middle class. Though the dominant styles were Gothic, especially in masculine domains, such as dark-paneled libraries and smoking rooms, and rococo in female preserves, such as the frilly, beflowered upholstery in ladies' dressing rooms, eclecticism reigned. The comparatively plain austerities of the Arts and Crafts movement, spearheaded by the socialist William Morris (1834–96), arose in reaction to this excess.

The Victorian era is also identified with a characteristic attitude of moral certainty. "Earnestness," "self-reliance," and "propriety," were the self-characterizations of those who identified themselves with those virtues. Social critics, such as the novelist Charles Dickens (1812–70), the journalist Henry Mayhew (1812–87), and the poet Matthew Arnold (1822–88), who took a darker view of things, used words like *sanctimonious, smug,* and *hypocritical.* Victorians idealized motherhood and the family, partially in imitation of Queen Victoria's deliriously happy marriage to her consort Albert, but prostitution ran rife in their cities. Social Darwinists and conservative churchmen found common cause in excoriating the underclass's deplorable morality while refusing them charity in order to strengthen their characters.

There were fault lines running just beneath the surface of Victorian complacency. If the era is distinguished by its outward propriety, we need to remember that Marxism and Darwinism both came of age during Victoria's reign. As Walter Houghton wrote in his classic history *The Victorian Frame of Mind* (1957):

> As one prophet after another stepped forward with his program of reconstruction, the hubbub of contending theories, gaining in number as the century advanced . . . created a climate of opinion in which quite apart from any specific doubts, the habit of doubt was unconsciously bred. One had an uneasy feeling, perhaps only half-conscious, that his beliefs were no longer quite secure.

WHIGGISM

Probably a shortened form of *whiggamore,* a term of uncertain origin in Scottish Gaelic that means "cattle driver" or "cattle thief." The name was derisively applied to Scottish Presbyterian and English opponents of the succession of James II. The king's supporters, in turn, were known as Tories (see Toryism), an Irish epithet for "outlaw." After James was deposed in the Glorious Revolution of 1688, both parties accepted the notion of a consti-tutional monarchy in which the king's prerogatives would be sharply limited by a powerful Parliament. Still, the Tories tended to be the party of the old aristocracy, while the Whigs were asso-ciated with religious dissenters and the increasingly populous middle class.

During the American Revolution, the terms were used to de-note loyalists to the Crown (Tories) and supporters of Indepen-dence (Whigs). The Whig Party was formed in America in 1834 as a coalition of forces opposed to Andrew Jackson (1767–1845); two of its most notable standard-bearers were Henry Clay (1777–1852) and Daniel Webster (1782–1852).

The Whig Interpretation of History (1931), by the English historian and philosopher of history Herbert Butterfield, criti-cizes

> the tendency of many historians to write on the side of Protes-tants and Whigs, to praise revolutions provided they have been successful, to emphasize certain principles of progress in the past and to produce a story which is the ratification if not the glorification of the present.

The Victorian historian Thomas Macaulay epitomized this retro-spectively triumphalist tendency. His multivolume *History of England from the Accession of James II* (1848–61) purports to demonstrate how the "history of our country during the last hun-dred and sixty years is eminently the history of physical, of moral, and of intellectual improvement."

WILSONIANISM

After Woodrow Wilson (1856–1924), the twenty-eighth president of the United States, who entered World War I to fight "a war to end all wars," and, with the Treaty of Versailles, attempted to negotiate a "peace without victory." In a speech to a joint session of Congress on January 8, 1918, Wilson elaborated the Fourteen Points that would establish a "just and lasting peace" in Europe:

1) The abolition of secret treaties
2) Freedom of the seas
3) The removal of economic barriers between nations
4) Disarmament (to a point consistent with safety)
5) Self-determination for colonized countries
6) Revolutionary Russia to be allowed to develop independently
7) The end of the occupation of Belgium
8) Alsace-Lorraine to be returned to France
9) Italy's borders returned to their pre-1915 shape
10) Individual countries of the former Austro-Hungarian Empire allowed to develop independently
11) Occupation of the Balkan states to end and Serbia given access to the Adriatic
12) Sovereignty for the Turks and other nations in the former Ottoman Empire
13) Establishment of a free Poland with access to the sea
14) The establishment of a multilateral association of nations that would adjudicate the peace

Though Wilson was awarded the 1919 Nobel Peace Prize, his efforts to recast American diplomacy in such an idealistic, visionary mold were successfully resisted by Americans and Europeans alike.

ZIONISM

The modern political movement to establish a Jewish homeland in Palestine. Shaken by the spectacle of the Dreyfus affair, the Vienna-educated Theodor Herzl (1860–1904), a secular lawyer, journalist, novelist and playwright, argued in *The Jewish State* (1896) that Diaspora Jews would be subject to anti-Semitism until they established and relocated to their own nation: "The Jews have but one way of saving themselves—a return to their own people and an emigration to their own land."

At Basel, in 1897, Herzl organized the World Zionist Congress, which rejected Britain's offer of a homeland in Uganda, and argued about the nature of a Jewish state in Palestine. Would it be socialist and secular or theocratic? How would it be funded? The biochemist Chaim Weizmann (1874–1952), who took over leadership of the Zionist movement after Herzl's death, obtained the Balfour Declaration from Britain in 1917, in which the foreign secretary declared:

> His Majesty's Government views with favor the establishment in Palestine of a national home for the Jewish people, and will use their best endeavors to facilitate the achievement of this object, it being clearly understood that nothing shall be done which may prejudice the civil and religious rights of existing non-Jewish communities in Palestine or the rights and political status enjoyed by Jews in any other country.

Though Jewish emigration to Palestine increased in the following decades, its Arab population was adamantly opposed to dividing their territory with their new Jewish neighbors. In 1939, the British issued a white paper that backed away from the Balfour Declaration, calling instead for the gradual creation of an independent state "in which Arabs and Jews share government in such a way as to ensure that the essential interests of each community are safeguarded." In the meantime, Jewish immigration was to be sharply curtailed.

The timing was disastrous. Just as millions of European Jews were being forcibly displaced and murdered, a possible refuge was declared off limits. The Zionist movement split on the question of how to deal with the dual problems of Britain and the Arabs, some reluctantly accepting the notion of an Arab/Jewish partition, others insisting that large-scale Jewish immigration—"facts on the ground" (a phrase Moshe Dayan coined decades later to describe the Jewish settlements in Arab territories captured in 1967)— would force the issue in their favor. In 1947, Great Britain handed the problem over to the newly formed United Nations, which proposed that Palestine be partitioned into Arab and Jewish territories, with Jerusalem and Bethlehem jointly administered. War broke out between the Jewish state and its Arab neighbors in 1948, and has continued on and off through the present day.

In 1975, the UN Security Council issued Resolution 3379, which declared, "Zionism is a form of racism and racial discrimination"—an almost unbearable irony for a nation that was founded as a refuge from racist persecution. Though the resolution was formally revoked in 1991, the accusation is often repeated.

Philosophy
& the Arts

⟨✍⟩

ABSTRACT EXPRESSIONISM

Also called action painting or the New York School, abstract expressionism (the term was coined by the critic Robert Coates in the *New Yorker* in 1946) encompasses a wide range of work by artists who gravitated to New York City from the far-flung capitals of Europe and the rural United States in the 1920s and 1930s, and rose to prominence in the postwar years. What they had in common was the desire to capture the ineffable: the churnings of their subconsciouses, their intimations of the sublime. Jackson Pollock (1912–56), the most famous of the abstract expressionists, dripped, poured, and spattered his paints—his canvases were as explosive and complex and as baffling to middlebrow tastes as the bebop improvisations of Charlie Parker and Dizzy Gillespie. "Today painters do not have to go to a subject matter outside of themselves," Pollack explained. "Most modern painters work from a different source. They work from within."

Unlike the surrealists, expressionists, symbolists, Dadaists, and cubists who preceded them, the abstract expressionists did not claim to record or represent their inner visions—rather, they enacted and perpetuated them. "The canvas began to appear to one American painter after another as an arena in which to act—rather than as a space in which to reproduce, re-design, analyze, or 'express' an object, actual or imagined," wrote the critic Harold Rosenberg (1906–78) in *ARTnews* in 1952. "What was to go on the canvas was not a picture but an event." Rosenberg's writings did much to popularize the movement, which shifted the center of the art world from Europe, especially Paris, to the United States.

In addition to Pollack, some of the best-known abstract expressionists were Arshile Gorky (1904–48), Philip Guston (1913–80), Helen Frankenthaler (b. 1928), Willem de Kooning (1904–97), Lee Krasner (1908–84), Robert Motherwell (1915–91), Barnet Newman (1905–70), Mark Rothko (1903–70), Frank Stella (b. 1936), Clyfford Still (1904–80), and Franz Kline (1910–62).

AESTHETICISM   *See* Symbolism.

ARISTOTELIANISM

In general use, Aritotelianism denotes an inductive, empirical approach to the world, as opposed to the deductive idealism of Platonism. If Plato saw the physical world as a transient, imperfect manifestation of universal, immortal ideas, Aristotle derived his ideas from the world itself. Aristotelians are more earthy and practical than Platonists.

Aristotle (384–322 BCE) studied under Plato, tutored Alexander the Great, and founded the Lyceum in Athens (also known as the Peripatetic school because of his habit of walking while teaching). Although he is reputed to have written many dialogues, only fragments of them have survived. Most of the writings attributed to him that have come down to us are probably lecture notes; they cover logic, ethics, metaphysics, epistemology, physics, biology, meteorology, mathematics, psychology, rhetoric, dialectics, aesthetics, and politics.

In logic, Aristotle was the first to write about the deductive inference or the classic syllogism (all men are mortal, Socrates is a man, therefore Socrates is mortal). Aristotle's ethics revolve around the pursuit of happiness, which he understands as a being's desire to fulfill its essential nature. For humans, happiness is achieved both in solitary contemplation and in the social world. Aristotle studied nature empirically, but like Plato, he understood it in teleological terms, which means that he assumed that the nature of an organism could be defined in terms of its ultimate goals. Unlike his teacher, however, Aristotle concluded that forms exist in the real world, that the quality of "treeness," for example, inheres in particular trees; for Aristotle there is no transcendent realm where the disembodied essences of trees reside.

The Roman philosopher Boethius (ca. 480–ca. 524), the Persian scholar Avicenna (980–1037), and the Andalusian Arab Averroës (1126–98) translated Aristotle into Latin and wrote commentaries on his works; through them, he came to the attention of Albertus Magnus (ca. 1200–80) and his student Thomas Aquinas (ca. 1225–74) who, along with other Scholastic thinkers, would attempt to reconcile Aristotelian rationalism with Christian dogmas. Aquinas's five proofs of God, with their Unmoved Mover and First Cause, are deeply indebted to Aristotle's metaphysics:

1) Motion proves the existence of an Unmoved Mover.
2) Effects prove the existence of a First Cause.
3) Contingency proves the existence of a Necessary Being.
4) Degrees of perfection prove the existence of a Most Perfect Being.
5) Design proves the existence of a Designer.

Aristotle's vision of the cosmos—earth centered, with the sun, the moon, the planets, and the stars revolving about it in nested spheres—would be the normative view of astronomy until Copernicus; his nonanthropomorphic conception of God as an abstract intelligence that is the First and Final Cause of the world but not actively engaged with it anticipates deism.

ART NOUVEAU   *See* Symbolism.

ATOMISM
In its most general sense, atomism is the belief that the physical world is compounded out of minute, indivisible particles. Logical atomism is a corollary of Bertrand Russell's (1872–1970) analytic

realism. It proposes that the world can be logically reduced to discrete facts that exist independently of our perceptions of them. Psychological atomism is the epistemological position, associated with David Hume and John Locke, that consciousness is a collection of individual perceptions and ideas that stand in various relationships to each other.

Physical atomism (the basis of Epicureanism) is the philosophical system developed by the pre-Socratic Greek philosophers Leucippus (birth and death unknown) and his student Democritus (460–370 BCE) as a response to Parmenides (birth and death also unknown). Anticipating Plato and in some ways Buddhism, Parmenides had argued that the so-called real world of birth and death, growth and decay, illness and confusion—the world that we experience on an everyday basis—is an illusion; that true being is indivisible and unchanging. Leucippus and Democritus argued that the world is made up of myriads of Parmenidean units: irreducible, immortal "atoms," moving in a void and assuming various temporary combinations. The world that we perceive as solid and real, just as in Parmenides, is anything but—it is merely a contingent convergence of atoms. As Democritus wrote in one of the few fragments that have come down to us, we make assumptions about our world that aren't necessarily true. We agree that anchovies taste salty and honey tastes sweet, for example, but how do we know that what I experience as salty you might not experience as sweet? Convention compels us to use same names for products and their attributes, but the essence of existence eludes our senses.

> By convention sweet is sweet, by convention bitter is bitter, by convention hot is hot, by convention cold is cold, by convention color is color. But in reality there are atoms and the void. That is, the objects of sense are supposed to be real and it is customary to regard them as such, but in truth they are not. Only the atoms and the void are real.

ATONALISM

Literally, music that is composed without reference to the major and minor scales. Traditional post-Renaissance music in the West is based on tonality—a hierarchical organization of harmonies around a tonic note (keys), major and minor (or diatonic) scales consisting of five whole tones and two sharps or flats, and relatively fixed notions of consonance and dissonance. In the eighteenth and nineteenth centuries, and especially in the Romantic era, composers introduced more and more accidentals (notes that aren't in a key's diatonic scales) and dissonant harmonies into their compositions, vastly enlarging their tonal and expressive palettes.

By the early twentieth century, composers such as Anton Webern (1883–1945), Charles Ives (1874–1954), Alban Berg (1885–1935), and Arnold Schoenberg (1874–1951) had abandoned traditional tonality altogether—instead of the seven notes of the diatonic scale, they used all twelve notes in the octave. Another name for atonality is twelve-tone or dodecaphonic music.

Traditional harmony contains an implicit organization—whenever the music returns to the tonic, tension is resolved and the listener has a feeling of coming home; minor keys sound sad, and major keys happy. Serialism was conceived as a new organizing principle in which certain sequences of tones must be played through before any of them can be repeated. The results can be incredibly expressive, but in general, composers and critics have found it more compelling than audiences. The anthropologist Claude Lévi-Strauss (b. 1908) compared serial music to

> A sailless ship, driven out to sea by its captain, who is privately convinced that by subjecting life aboard to the rules of an elaborate protocol, he will prevent the crew from thinking nostalgically either of their home port or of their ultimate destination.

AUGUSTANISM   *See* Classicism.

AUTEURISM

The auteur, or author, theory of cinema was first propounded in 1954 by a young ex-con and aspiring filmmaker named François Truffaut (1932–84), who in later years would become internationally acclaimed as the director of such movies as *The Four Hundred Blows, Jules and Jim,* and *Day for Night.* Writing in the journal *Cahiers du Cinéma,* Truffaut proposed a *politique des auteurs,* a method of analyzing movies not just for the content of their stories, the skill of their actors, and the spectacle of their scenery but for their uniquely personal style—as if they had been "authored" by a single person rather than stamped out by a studio assembly line. The credit for authorship was usually ascribed to directors, occasionally to a producer or a charismatic star like Humphrey Bogart, but almost never, ironically, to the screenwriters.

Truffaut, of course, recognized that most Hollywood and French movies were mere commodities. But some American directors, such as Howard Hawks, Alfred Hitchcock, and John Ford, whom most critics (and studio executives) regarded as skilled hacks, as well as undoubted artists like Jean Renoir, actually wielded their cameras like pens. Through their framing shots and the rhythms of their cuts, through the performances they coaxed out of their actors and the music and cinematography they oversaw, they imposed a highly personal style on their movies. Jean-Luc Godard, Éric Rohmer, and Claude Chabrol—all of whom went on to become famous directors themselves—also promoted auteurism in the pages of *Cahiers du Cinéma.*

Auteurism has undoubted shortcomings as a critical method: While underestimating the collaborative nature of moviemaking, it perhaps overestimates the integrity of directors—even the most brilliant of them have turned out movies that were devoid of style or quality. Even so, it provides indispensable perspective on the movies of such multitalented star/writer/director/musicians as Charlie Chaplin, Woody Allen, and Clint Eastwood. It might also

be the only critical theory ever whose inventors and chief proponents were significant creative artists themselves.

BAUHAUS *See* **Modernism.**

CHROMOLUMINARISM *See* **Impressionism.**

CLASSICISM
In its broadest sense, classicism is a taste for the "best" exemplars
of an art form (in Latin, *classicus* means "of the first rank"). A classic can thus be anything—a play, a poem, a heavy metal ballad—
that is generally deemed to be great, outstanding, or definitive.
Classicism is also used to mean the opposite of Romanticism—
classicism is decorous, formal, restrained, traditional, and impersonal, while Romanticism is unruly, licentious, subversive, and
egoistic. More narrowly, classicism refers to the Greek and Roman
writers of antiquity and to the aesthetic rules they espoused. Plays
that conform to the three unities of action, place, and time, that
Aristotle espoused in his *Poetics*, and that meet the criteria below
are considered classical as well.

> An imitation of an action that is serious, complete, and of a cer-
> tain magnitude; in language embellished with each kind of artis-
> tic ornament, the several kinds being found in separate parts of
> the play; in the form of action, not of narrative; through pity and
> fear effecting the proper purgation of these emotions.

Jean Baptiste Racine (1639–99), Pierre Corneille (1606–84), Ben
Jonson (1572–1637), and John Dryden (1631–1700) are all classic tragedians in the Aristotelian sense. Poets, satirists, and essay-
ists who follow Horace's (65–8 BCE) advice in his *Ars Poetica*:

> Make the Greek authors your supreme delight;
> Read them by day, and study them by night

are classical as well. Alexander Pope (1688–1744), along with his
contemporaries Jonathan Swift (1667–1745), Joseph Addison
(1672–1719), and Richard Steele (1672–1729), appear in literary

anthologies under the rubric of Augustanism or neoclassicism. Horace himself was a classicist, or Hellenist, as were the vast majority of Romans in the age of the historical Augustus (63 BCE–14 CE).

Classical music is a catchall term for "art music"; the classical era in music is bracketed between the baroque and the Romantic eras. Along with that of many other lesser composers, the classical music of Franz Joseph Haydn (1732–1809), Wolfgang Amadeus Mozart (1756–91), and the early Ludwig van Beethoven (1770–1827) was less polyphonic, more rhythmically complex, and more chromatic than baroque music; the most characteristic musical forms of the era were the sonata, the symphony, and the string quartet.

In the visual arts, neoclassicism refers to a movement, inspired by the Enlightenment and the French Revolution, that stripped paintings of their rococo floridity and sensuality, offering in their stead severe, linearly coherent compositions, classical themes, and archaeologically accurate costumes and settings that were meant to evoke the martial virtues of Republican Rome (and by implication Revolutionary France). *The Oath of the Horatii* (1785) by Jacques-Louis David (1748–1825) has all the hallmarks of the style; other important neoclassicists were Jean-Auguste-Dominique Ingres (1780–1867) and Pierre-Paul Prud'hon (1758–1823).

CONFETTISM   *See* Impressionism.

CONSTRUCTIVISM
In its general sense, constructivism refers to the practice of "building" abstract art out of separate, distinguishable components, often industrial materials such as plastic or steel. In revolutionary Russia, constructivism was a movement in art, architecture, and graphic and industrial design spearheaded by Aleksandr Rodchenko (1891–1956), El Lissitzky (1890–1941), Vladimir Tatlin (1885–1953), Varvara Stepanova (1894–1958), Naum Gabo (1890–1977), and Antoine Pevsner (1886–1962). They referred to their work as "constructions" instead of "compositions" to eliminate what they regarded as the elitist distinction between the arts and industry. They also believed that artists were obliged to aid the

revolution by producing practical items and propaganda. Rodchenko designed newspaper kiosks; Tatlin a coverall for workers; Lissitzky many famous revolutionary posters.

The brothers Gabo and Pevsner (Gabo was a pseudonym) remained true to abstraction. Both of them split from the movement in the early 1920s and immigrated to Europe, where they became involved in International Constructivism, a movement that included László Moholy-Nagy (1895–1946), Ben Nicholson (1894–1982), and Willi Baumeister (1889–1955). Moholy-Nagy and many other constructivists would become involved with that bastion of modernist industrial design, the Bauhaus (see Modernism).

Closely related to Constructivism is neoplasticism, the spiritual and aesthetic theories of the artist and theosophist Piet Mondrian (1872–1944), who sought to render the underlying unity of existence in his wholly abstract, starkly geometrical paintings. "As a pure representation of the human mind," he wrote, "art will express itself in an aesthetically purified, that is to say, abstract form. In the straight line and the clearly defined primary colour."

CUBISM

An epochal movement in modern painting and sculpture that flourished between 1907 and 1914 and was spearheaded by Pablo Picasso (1881–1973) and Georges Braque (1882–1963). Among the many other painters who worked in the cubist idiom were Juan Gris (1887–1927), Robert Delaunay (1885–1941), and Fernand Léger (1885–1955), as well as the sculptors Jacques Lipchitz (1891–1973) and Alexander Archipenko (1887–1964).

Influenced by the geometric formalism of the late paintings of Paul Cézanne (1839–1906) and African masks and sculpture, cubism abandoned traditional perspective and pictorialism, rendering its subjects in two dimensions from multiple points of view. To the extent that cubism was representational, it depicted objects as they are consciously processed by the mind, rather than unthinkingly perceived. Cubism's first phase, known as analytical cubism, produced mostly austere and monochromatic paintings; in its more decorative second phase, synthetic cubism, the colors were more brilliant, and many of the paintings incorporated collage. Around 1912, the surrealist poet Guillaume Apollinaire (1880–1918) analogized the colorful nonrepresentational paintings of Delaunay, Léger, Francis Picabia (1879–1953), and Marcel Duchamp (1887–1968) to music, grouping them together in a movement that he termed Orphism (after Orpheus, the legendary musician of Greek mythology).

CULTURE STUDIES

A multidisciplinary academic field that utilizes sociology, literary theory, anthropology, philosophy, literary and political theory, semiotics, and original popular texts (novels, films, television shows, cartoons, pop music) to analyze the structure, attitudes, and beliefs of a culture or subculture, almost always in the developed world, usually with an attentive eye toward issues of gender, sexuality, race, ethnicity, and class. The book *Bodies of Inscription: A Cultural History of the Tattoo Community,* by Margo DeMello (Duke, 2000) is an example of culture studies, as is Regina Spellers's essay "The Kink Factor: A Womanist Discourse Analysis of African American Mother/Daughter Perspectives on Negotiating Black Hair/Body Politics," reprinted in the volume *Understanding African American Rhetoric* (Routledge, 2003).

At the heart of culture studies is the notion of social constructionism, a theory that was elaborated in *The Social Construction of Reality: A Treatise in the Sociology of Knowledge* (1966), by Peter L. Berger and Thomas Luckmann, and which has become one of the principal tenets of postmodernism. Like its cousin deconstructionism, social constructionism maintains that what we think of as objective "facts" and "knowledge" are inevitably inflected by the social context in which they are embedded. This is an enormously useful insight when it comes to understanding race, gender, and power, and it certainly suggests that many of the prevailing views in the social sciences should be taken with a grain of salt. However, it is something of a red herring when it is applied to the objective sciences, such as mathematics and physics. The cutting-edge Lacanian feminist critic Luce Irigaray, for example, wrote:

> Every piece of knowledge is produced by subjects in a given historical context. Even if that knowledge aims to be objective, even if its techniques are designed to ensure objectivity, science always displays certain choices, certain exclusions, and these are particularly determined by the sex of the scholars involved.

Had Irigaray confined her observation to scientists' presuppositions and prejudices that were specific to gender—say, the reluctance of epidemiologists to acknowledge suspiciously high incidences of breast cancer in certain locales, or the egregious claims by psychologists (and a former president of Harvard University) about women's innate disabilities in the realm of abstract reasoning—it wouldn't be controversial. But instead, Irigaray went on to make the mind-boggling claim that by privileging "the speed of light over other speeds that are vitally necessary to us," $E=mc^2$ is a "sexed equation."

In 1996, Alan Sokal, a professor of physics at New York University, submitted an article to the journal *Social Text* entitled "Transgressing the Boundaries: Toward a Transformational Hermeneutics of Quantum Gravity." Packing it with quotations from cutting-edge theorists, jargony buzzwords, and elementary errors that a scientifically literate editor should have immediately spotted, he put forward the outrageous assertion that " 'physical reality,' no less than social 'reality,' is at bottom a social and linguistic construct"; concluding that Euclid's pi and Newton's gravity,

> formerly thought to be constant and universal, are now perceived in their ineluctable historicity; and the putative observer becomes fatally de-centered, disconnected from any epistemic link to a space-time point that can no longer be defined by geometry alone.

The article—a patchwork of deliberate nonsense—was not only accepted and published, it was featured in a special issue of the magazine as a rejoinder to criticisms of social constructionism that had been advanced by some prominent scientists. When Sokal revealed his hoax, it was widely covered in the media. The point he wanted to make wasn't that social constructionism is entirely without merit, but that mathematics and physics set definite limits to the claims of epistemological relativism. At the very least, he insisted, you should have some idea about what you're talking about if you're going to write responsibly about science.

CYNICISM

School of philosophy founded by Antisthenes (ca. 444–ca. 371 BCE) in Athens. Its name comes from the Greek word *kunikos,* which means "doglike" and probably originated as a term of opprobrium (which the Cynics cheerfully appropriated). Though Antisthenes styled himself a follower of Socrates, the Cynics were as much beatniks and performance artists as thinkers. Stripping life to its naked essence, they disdained the hypocritical and artificial forms of civilization, such as bodily privacy and courtesy, and followed nature's laws instead, which they took to be supremely rational and virtuous.

The Cynics flaunted their asceticism. Antisthenes' famous pupil Diogenes of Sinope (ca. 404–323 BCE) was said to have lived in a tub; according to an anecdote in *The Lives of Eminent Philosophers*, by his namesake Diogenes Laertes (who lived in the third century CE), when he saw a child drinking from his hands, Diogenes threw his cup away, declaring, "A child has beaten me in plainness of living." When he was noticed masturbating in the marketplace, he supposedly remarked that he "wished it were as easy to relieve hunger by rubbing an empty stomach." Plato was said to have described him as "A Socrates gone mad."

> He was great at pouring scorn on his contemporaries. The school of Euclides he called bilious, and Plato's lectures a waste of time, the performances at the Dionysia great peep-shows for fools, and the demagogues the mob's lackeys. He used also to say that when he saw physicians, philosophers and pilots at their work, he deemed man the most intelligent of all animals; but when again he saw interpreters of dreams and diviners and those who attended to them, or those who were puffed up with

conceit of wealth, he thought no animal more silly. He would continually say that for the conduct of life we need right reason or a halter.

It was Diogenes who lit a lamp in broad daylight because he was searching for an honest man.

DADAISM

An international movement of artists and poets that began in Zurich in 1915 and swiftly spread to Paris, Barcelona, Berlin, New York, Cologne, and Hanover. Born out of disgust for the bourgeois value system that brought about World War I, the Dadaists espoused a deliberately provocative antiaesthetic; nihilism, illogic, absurdity, and deliberate ugliness were their weapons of choice. The name Dada was by some accounts chosen at random from a French dictionary (in French *dada* is a child's word for "hobbyhorse"); *da da* also means "yes, yes" in Rumanian, the native language of the poet Tristan Tzara (1896–1963). The Dada Manifesto of 1916 was proclaimed in Zurich by the German poet Hugo Ball (1886–1927); in retrospect it anticipates the yippie antics of Abbie Hoffman and Jerry Rubin in the 1960s: "How can one get rid of everything that smacks of journalism, worms, everything nice and right, blinkered, moralistic, europeanised, enervated?" Ball asked. "By saying dada."

Tristan Tzara's Dada Manifesto of 1918 has a Blakean intensity; its incantatory peroration eerily foreshadows the epic poem *Howl* (1956), by Allen Ginsberg (1926–97):

> DADA . . . to respect all individualities in their folly of the moment, whether serious, fearful, timid, ardent, vigorous, decided or enthusiastic; to strip one's church of every useless and unwieldy accessory; to spew out like a luminous cascade any offensive or loving thought, or to cherish it—with the lively satisfaction that it's all precisely the same thing—with the same intensity in the bush, which is free of insects for the blue-blooded, and gilded with the bodies of archangels, with one's

soul. Liberty: DADA DADA DADA;—the roar of contorted pains, the interweaving of contraries and all contradictions, freaks and irrelevancies: LIFE.

In New York City, Dada's spirit was less anguished and more ironic and playful—Marcel Duchamp (1887–1968) defaced a reproduction of the *Mona Lisa* with a mustache and goatee; his notorious found sculpture *Fountain* was a urinal signed by "R. Mutt." By the mid-1920s, Dadaism had evolved into surrealism; decades later its influence can still be felt in the "accidental" effects of the abstract expressionists, the found objects and subversive spirit of pop art, and the antiformalism of conceptual art.

Other important artists and poets who were identified with the Dada movement were Hans Arp (1887–1966), Man Ray (1890–1976), Georg Grosz (1893–1959), Francis Picabia (1879–1953), Kurt Schwitters (1887–1948), and Louis Aragon (1897–1982).

DECADENCE   *See* **Symbolism.**

DECONSTRUCTIONISM   *See* **Structuralism.**

DIVISIONISM   *See* **Impressionism.**

DUALISM   *See* **Monism.**

EMPIRICISM
From the Greek word *empeirikos* ("experienced"), empiricism is the philosophical idea that direct personal experience, either information from the senses or introspective reflection upon one's own mind, is the sole source of knowledge. (Logical positivism is a radical form of empiricism.) Though most empiricists will admit some a priori (Latin for "before experience") knowledge—in other words, truths that are accepted at face value as "givens," at least in the realms of mathematics and logic—they regard any conclusions derived from deductive reasoning as opposed to physical evidence with deep skepticism. A thoroughgoing empiri-

cist would rephrase the statement "All elephants are large" in a conditional form—something like "All of the elephants that we have ever observed, and that have ever been reported by other observers, are large. This by no means rules out the possibility that a mouse-sized elephant has yet to be seen."

Ironically, since its premises seem so earthbound, empiricism can lead to radical idealism, the belief that only ideas are real, and hence to radical doubt. How do I know that other people aren't merely figments of my imagination, that I'm not really a disembodied brain in a jar in a laboratory somewhere dreaming about a world in which elephants are big? How do I know that anything besides me even exists? (See solipsism.)

Empiricism is opposed to rationalism (from the Latin *rationalis*, "belonging to reason"), which is the belief that the world is organized in a consistent and logical enough way that general truths can safely be deduced by pure reason. For instance, when an astronomer observes a "wobble" in a star's light, he or she might conclude—confident that the laws of physics are universally applicable—that it is caused by the gravitational attraction of an orbiting planet that is too small to be seen.

EPICUREANISM
The teachings of the philosopher Epicurus (341–270 BCE), who founded a school in his garden outside the walls of Athens. At the heart of Epicureanism is its acceptance of the main tenets of Democritus's atomism. Since the universe, and all life within it, is a product of accidental and temporary agglomerations of irreducible atoms, and since death is merely oblivion, and the gods, though they exist, are completely aloof from the human realm, true wisdom, the Epicureans concluded, consists in the pursuit of pleasure.

"The Garden" accepted students for more than four centuries; by the early Christian era, its teachings had been dispersed throughout the classical world. Philodemus of Gadara (ca. 110–ca. 40 BCE), for example, who taught the Roman poet Virgil (70–19 BCE), had studied at the Garden; Seneca (3 BCE–65 CE), Cicero

(106–43 BCE), Plutarch (46–127), and Lucretius (94–49 BCE) all had much to say about Epicureanism.

Epicureanism was anathema to the Christians because of its thoroughgoing materialism, so few of its texts (and almost none of Epicurus's many writings) have survived. In his letter to Menoeceus (preserved by Diogenes of Laertes and included in his *Lives of the Philosophers*), Epicurus wrote:

> The wise man does not deprecate life nor does he fear the cessation of life . . . And even as men choose of food not merely and simply the larger portion, but the more pleasant, so the wise seek to enjoy the time which is most pleasant and not merely that which is longest.

The Epicureans' hedonism was far from a sensual debauch, however.

> By pleasure we mean the absence of pain in the body and of trouble in the soul. It is not an unbroken succession of drinking-bouts and of revelry, not sexual lust, not the enjoyment of the fish and other delicacies of a luxurious table, which produce a pleasant life; it is sober reasoning, searching out the grounds of every choice and avoidance, and banishing those beliefs through which the greatest tumults take possession of the soul. Of all this the beginning and the greatest good is wisdom.

Much as some groups of early Christians did, Epicureans withdrew into self-sufficient communities that admitted rich and poor and women and slaves on an equal basis.

ESSENTIALISM   *See* Nominalism.

EUPHUISM
A rarely used rhetorical term (pronounced *YOU-few-ism*) that means "ornately flowery writing." The word comes from *Euphues, or the Anatomy of Wyt* (1578) and *Euphues and His England* (1580), by the notoriously florid Elizabethan writer John Lyly (ca. 1553–1606). His hero's name was derived from the Greek word

euphues, which means "well endowed by nature." Euphuism is not to be confused with euphemism (from the Greek *euphēmos,* or "sounding good"), which is the substitution of a delicate or deliberately obfuscatory locution for words deemed disturbing, vulgar, or harsh. Thus "passed away" or "expired" stands in for "died," "passed gas" is substituted for "farted," and "conjugal relations" supersedes "fucked." Words of Latinate rather than Anglo-Saxon origin are generally preferred in polite conversation.

EXISTENTIALISM

Philosophical and literary movement that flowered in Europe in the years after World War II, but whose roots extended back into the nineteenth century, and particularly into the thought of Søren Kierkegaard (1813–55) and Friedrich Nietzsche (1844–1900). At the heart of existentialism is the famous formulation by Jean-Paul Sartre (1905–1980) that "existence precedes essence."

Everybody knows intuitively *that* they exist—it is the *why, how,* and *what* of being that are so problematic. In a world in which religion, nation, social class, and custom no longer provided secure identities, people felt empty, oppressed, and panicked. If there is no God, if human history and life serve no grand, transcendent purpose, then aren't all our strivings absurd? Sartre's novel *Nausea* describes its protagonist's terrible epiphany when he sees the world as so much naked, undifferentiated being. No *what* or *how* or *why*—just a terrifying, sickening *is.*

> Usually existence hides itself. It is there, around us, in us, it is *us,* you can't say two words without mentioning it, but you can never touch it . . . And then all of a sudden, there it was, clear as day: existence had suddenly unveiled itself. It had lost the harmless look of an abstract category: it was the very paste of things, this root was kneaded into existence. Or rather the root, the park gates, the bench, the sparse grass, all that had vanished: the diversity of things, their individuality, were only an appearance, a veneer. This veneer had melted, leaving soft, monstrous masses, all in disorder—naked, in a frightful, obscene nakedness.

If there is a liberatory quality to this revelation—if existence is a blank slate, there's nothing to stop you from writing your own rules on it, living by your own values—it also engenders terrible anxiety.

"Dread is the dizziness of freedom which occurs when . . . freedom . . . gazes down into its own possibility, grasping at finiteness to sustain itself," wrote Kierkegaard. For Kierkegaard, Christianity provided the solution—not the rote recitations of a church's conventional creeds, but an authentic, personal leap of faith, in despite of doubt, in despite of this faith's apparent absurdity. Nietzsche, too, had wrestled with the problem of nihilism—what should we believe in when we no longer believe in God? His answer was the Overman—a new sort of man who embraced his freedom rather than feared it, and (contra Kierkegaard) created his own morality. "What is the ape to man?" wrote Nietzsche. "A laughingstock or a painful embarrassment. And man shall be just that for the Overman: a laughingstock or a painful embarrassment."

This notion of pure contingency, of existence stripped of the attributes and values that custom attributes to it, had been a topic of study since the turn of the century. Edmund Husserl (1859–1938) was the founder of phenomenology, the philosophical and psychological study of the ways that the mind interacts with the world, and even more important, how the mind interacts with itself, how we become conscious of what we are conscious of. Martin Heidegger (1889–1976) had been Husserl's student, but he would ban his former professor, whose parents had been Jewish, from the library of Freiburg University when he was its rector, and erase Husserl's name from the dedication of his most famous book, *Being and Time*. His Nazi sympathies aside, Heidegger also faulted Husserl for sidestepping an essential philosophical problem: what it *means* to be "an entity whose what [essence] is precisely to be and nothing but to be."

Heidegger reasoned that a person discovers his "whatness," as opposed to his or her mere "isness" (a philosophical term for this is *quiddity,* from the Latin *quid* or "what"), by deliberate engagement in the world: by embedding oneself in social and religious and political institutions and taking certain actions. As difficult as it is to commit oneself to any project when one knows that no matter how hard one strives, death will always be one's ultimate fate (Heidegger used the word *nothingness* to describe this feeling of disassociation and futility; Sartre, *absurdity*), the necessity to do so is one of the burdens of being human.

But our freedom is not unlimited. Another difficulty of the human condition, the existentialists noted, is the problem of other people. We can never see ourselves objectively except vicariously, through somebody else's eyes. This is the origin of shame, and it is vividly illustrated in Sartre's play *No Exit*, in which a group of characters who hate each other are trapped in a confined space for eternity. "Hell is other people," one of them declares. And even if one can escape the censorious gaze of the "other," one's choices are still circumscribed by one's historical and social circumstances. "Bad faith" (Sartre's term) is what results when the role you choose to inhabit is incompatible with your authentic self. Up until 1934, Heidegger dedicated his authentic self to realizing "the inner truth and greatness of National Socialism." Sartre threw himself into Marxism.

Other important existentialist thinkers and writers were Albert Camus (1913–60), José Ortega y Gasset (1883–1955), Sartre's romantic partner Simone de Beauvoir (1908–86), Miguel de Unamuno (1864–1936), Karl Jaspers (1883–1969), Gabriel Marcel (1889–1973), Maurice Merleau-Ponty (1908–61), and Martin Buber (1878–1965).

Existential psychotherapy deals specifically with the anxiety of feeling alone in the world, the difficulty of making authentic life choices, and the fear of death. Rollo May (1909–94), Victor Frankl (1905–97), Ernest Becker (1924–74) and Irvin D. Yalom (b. 1931), the best-selling author of *Love's Executioner* (1989), are some of the important theorists and practitioners in this field.

EXPRESSIONISM

Not a formal artistic movement so much as an aesthetic and psychological tendency, *expressionism* is used to characterize paintings, sculptures, woodcuts, drawings, plays, novels, films, and poems that distort reality in order to express an artist's personal feelings and visions. Expressionist art has the emotional immedi-acy—and often the psychedelic, hallucinatory quality—of night-mares. The terrifying panoramas of hell created by the Dutch painter Hieronymous Bosch (1450–1516) may have been painted in the Gothic era, but they have decided expressionist tendencies, as do the engravings of grotesque monsters in Francisco de Goya's (1746–1828) series of *Caprices*. The haunting, dreamlike stories of Franz Kafka (1883–1924), filled with faceless persecutors, bizarre metamorphoses, and an anguished sense of alienation and guilt, are expressionist. The self portraits of Vincent van Gogh (1853–90), electric with incipient madness and pain, are expressionis-tic in effect, as were the carnivalesque faces of the mob in *Christ's Entry into Brussels,* by the Belgian painter James Ensor (1860–1949). The unclassifiable architecture of Antonio Gaudi (1852–1926)—part folk art, part art nouveau, part neo-Gothic—has expressionist qualities as well. Egon Schiele (1890–1918), Edvard Munch (1863–1944), Chaim Soutine (1894–1943), and Oskar Kokoschka (1886–1980) are other major expressionists.

Three German art movements in the last century were broadly expressionistic: Die Brücke, Der Blaue Reiter, and Neue Sach-lichkeit. Die Brücke (the Bridge) was a community of painters and woodcut artists based in Berlin and Dresden in the first decade of the twentieth century; its members included Emil Nolde (1867–1956), Ernst Ludwig Kirchner (1880–1938), Otto Mueller (1874–1930), and Erich Heckel (1883–1970). Der Blaue Reiter (the Blue Rider) was a multinational group of artists who worked in Munich between 1911 and 1914; they took their name from a painting by Wassily Kandinsky (1866–1944); other members in-cluded Paul Klee (1879–1940) and Franz Marc (1880–1916). Neue Sachlichkeit, or "the new matter-of-factness," was the name given to a group of postexpressionistic German artists who came to prominence during the Weimar Republic in the 1920s. They in-cluded Otto Dix (1891–1969) and George Grosz (1893–1959), whose bitingly fierce caricatures were sometimes characterized as veristic expressionism, and Max Beckmann (1884–1950).

Some of August Strindberg's (1849–1912) plays are considered expressionistic, as are a few early works of Eugene O'Neill (1888–1953). A number of German playwrights, such as Benjamin Franklin Wedekind (1864–1918), Georg Kaiser (1878–1945), and Ernst Toller (1893–1939) wrote expressionist plays in the teens and twenties; Wedekind's *Lulu* was the basis for the opera of the same name by Alban Berg (1885–1935). Expressionist films, such as Robert Wiene's *The Cabinet of Dr. Caligari* (1919), F. W. Murnau's *Nosferatu* (1922), and Fritz Lang's *Metropolis* (1927), with their bizarre, otherworldly sets; oblique points of view; and weird Weltanschauungs, have had a lasting impact on the medium.

FAUVISM

Short-lived French art movement in the first decade of the twentieth century whose chief exponents were Henri Matisse (1869–1954), Georges Rouault (1871–1958), André Derain (1880–1954), Kees van Dongen (1877–1968), and Maurice de Vlaminck (1876–1958). Noticing a classical statue of a youth surrounded by some of their canvases at the Salon d'Automne in 1905, the critic Louis Vauxcelles quipped, "C'est Donatello dans la cage aux fauves!" ("It is Donatello in a cage of wild animals!")

Fauvist canvases weren't shocking for their content but for the intensity of their colors and the flattened simplicity of their forms. Perspectiveless fauvist landscapes featured orange, yellow, and blue trees against pink skies; human forms were rendered as simple geometries. Amélie Matisse was painted with a green stripe running down her face in a 1905 portrait by her husband. Less a theory or a school than a style, fauvism anticipated expressionism and cubism. Matisse, however, remained true to the style for most of his long career.

FORMALISM

In general usage, formalism is a characterization of an aesthetic production whose surface or style is more important than its explicit content. If a painting's colors, paint strokes, and compositional features are more noticeable than the objects it ostensibly represents, it might be called formalist; a novel would be considered formalist if the music of the language or its structure was more important than its plot and characters. A hallmark of modernism, abstract paintings are formalist by definition, as are Gertrude Stein's tautological poems, like "a rose is a rose is a rose."

Earthbound Marxist critics, who regarded art primarily as a medium for propaganda, deplored formalism as so much bourgeois decadence. Thus, D. Diamond in the 1943 *Communist Review:*

> Lenin demanded realism in art and more than once stood out against the petit-bourgeois, idealistic aesthetic tendencies among which formalism occupied the leading role. Later formalism went over to active opposition, and open warfare against Marxism.
>
> To all these tendencies in question of art, the Party has posed the Leninist slogan of art as a weapon of socialist education, of art joined to the masses, of art as a means of understanding and remaking the world.

Russian formalism is a school of literary theory that emerged in Moscow and St. Petersburg around 1915 that attempted to establish a scientific basis for understanding what made literary texts literary (their "literariness"). Victor Shklovsky (1893–1984), one of its leading proponents, advanced the concept of *ostranenie* or "making strange" (also called defamiliarization). "Art is a way of experiencing the artfulness of an object," he wrote, "The object is not important." This idea was key to the New Criticism as well—John Crowe Ransom (1888–1974) wrote extensively about the ways that the constraints of poetic forms (specifically rhyme and meter) created an ontologically distinct form of discourse; lyric poetry said things that prose never could.

The formalists distinguished *syuzhet,* or "plot"—the novelist's mode of unfolding the events of a narrative—from *fabula,* or "story," the whos, whats, and wheres that give a novel texture. The critic Boris Tomashevsky (1890–1957) used the term *motif* to refer to the elements of plots: "bound" motifs were essential, "free" motifs were added at the author's discretion. The enormously influential linguist Roman Jakobson (1896–1982) was a member of the circle early on; he moved to Prague in the 1920s and finished his long career at Harvard. Jakobson's interest in Saussurean linguistics aligns his later work with structuralism.

FUTURISM

Anti-Romantic, protofascist artistic movement founded in Italy in 1909 that glorified industry, noise, violence, and revolt against every form of tradition. Futurism's manifesto, written by the poet F. T. Marinetti (1876–1944), who would join Mussolini's political movement as early as 1919, exuberantly declared that

> the splendor of the world has been enriched with a new form of beauty, the beauty of speed.
>
> Except in struggle, there is no more beauty We will glorify war—the world's only hygiene . . . We will destroy the museums, libraries, academies of every kind, will fight moralism, feminism, every opportunistic or utilitarian cowardice.

Futurist poetry aspired to "burst the sentence's steampipe, the valves of punctuation, and the adjectival clamp"; futurist paintings by artists such as Umberto Boccioni (1882–1916), Giacomo Balla (1871–1958), Gino Severini (1883–1966), and Carlo Carrà (1881–1966) adapted cubist techniques to render motion and "express the plastic equivalents of the sounds noises and smells found in theaters, music-halls, cinemas, brothels, railway stations, ports, garages, hospitals, workshop." The painter Luigi Russolo (1885–1947) wrote a manifesto heralding an "Art of Noise"; he created a variety of musical instruments that he utilized in multimedia performances (none of them have survived). Fiercely iconoclastic and mad for publicity, the futurists anticipated the *épater le bourgeois* spirit (the desire to scandalize the middle classes) if not the politics of the Dadaists.

The short-lived Russian cubo-futurist movement included such important poets as Velimir Khlebnikov (1885–1922), Alexei Kruchenykh (1886–1968), and Vladimir Mayakovsky (1893–1930), as well as the painter Kasimir Malevich (1878–1935).

Inspired by the writings of the mystical mathematician P. D. Ouspensky (1878–1947), and by his long-standing desire to "free art from the burden of the object," Malevich went on to spearhead the short-lived suprematist movement, for which he painted purely abstract geometrical compositions, sometimes minimally colored. *White on White,* completed in 1918, was his last suprematist statement—it pictured a tilted white square on a slightly lighter-colored background. Many of the leaders of Russian constructivism were Malevich's students.

IDEALISM

In philosophy, the notion that ideas have an independent, transcendental existence apart from the concrete things, actions, or qualities they are associated with. An idealist might say, for example, that *good* is not merely an attribute of a specific virtuous act, or an adjective used to describe its subjective quality, but a real, separable thing, accessible to the mind if not the senses. The Platonic notion of forms is perhaps the best-known instance of philosophical idealism (somewhat paradoxically, the Scholastics called this realism as opposed to nominalism), but idealism is a feature of modern philosophy too. Immanuel Kant (1724–1804) was an exponent of transcendental idealism, which declared that things in themselves are inaccessible to us because they are always mediated by our minds; G. W. F. Hegel (1770–1831) believed that what we think of as the real world is nonetheless the historical unfolding of a vast, divine idea.

In art, idealism is the tendency to apply aesthetic, rather than realistic, criteria in representation—the artist renders his subjects as his sensibility or the reigning aesthetic orthodoxy of the day mandates that they *should* appear rather than how they do. Thus, Leonardo's *Vitruvian Man*, inspired by a text by the Roman architect Vitruvius (ca. 80 BC–ca. 25 BC), illustrates how the proportions of the human body form a microcosm of the universe. The perfectly proportioned statues of Greek antiquity or, for that matter, the impossibly slim, big-busted, spandex-clad heroines of super-hero comics are further instances of idealism in art, as are the wholly abstract, sublime images of a modern artist like Barnett Newman (1905–70).

In human behavior and ethics, an idealist is someone who aspires to the highest moral and spiritual standards (see Quixotism); often they put themselves at a disadvantage by assuming that others are as high-minded as they are. An idealist can be a moral monster as well. T. E. Lawrence, in *The Seven Pillars of Wisdom* (1922, 1926), wrote of a soldier/scientist of his acquaintance: "He was logical, an idealist of the deepest and so possessed by his convictions that he was willing to harness evil to the chariot of good." Robespierre during the Reign of Terror in France in the 1790s, Stalin's murderously idealistic apparatchiks in the 1930s, and Pol Pot's minions in Cambodia in the 1970s gladly shed buckets of their countrymen's blood to realize their visions of a revolutionary paradise.

Materialism, as opposed to idealism, is the notion that the physical world is all there is. Dialectical materialism, or Marxism, is a mirror image of Hegel's objective idealism—to Marx, history is a process driven not by the interplay of ideas but by conflicts engendered by money, greed, and power. A thoroughgoing Darwinian believes that the origins and attributes of life (including human intelligence) can be adequately explained by natural processes—thus, the well-known zoologist and writer on evolution, Richard Dawkins, declared that "Darwin made it possible to be an intellectually fulfilled atheist." Phillip E. Johnson, a prominent polemicist for intelligent design, triumphantly quoted Dawkins's words in *The Boston Review* in 1997, offering them up as proof positive that "protecting materialism is what Darwinism is mainly about, and protecting Darwinism is what evolutionary biology is mainly about."

IMAGISM

Short-lived movement in modern English and American poetry, beginning about 1912, that likened poetry to sculpture. A statement of principles in the first imagist anthology, edited by Ezra Pound (1885–1972), declared their preference for the language of common speech, insisted on the freedom to use free verse or whatever cadence they wished, to write about whatever they wished, and most of all:

- To present an image (hence the name *imagist*). We are not a school of painters, but we believe that poetry should render particulars exactly and not deal in vague generalities, however magnificent and sonorous. It is for this reason that we oppose the cosmic poet, who seems to us to shirk the real difficulties of his art.
- To produce poetry that is hard and clear, never blurred nor indefinite.
- Finally, most of us believe that concentration is of the very essence of poetry.

Among the leading imagists were Amy Lowell (1874–1925), T. E. Hulme (1883–1917), and H.D., or Hilda Doolittle (1886–1961). The objectivists, whose work was first featured as a group in 1931 in the magazine *Poetry*, were highly influenced by imagism and Ezra Pound. They included William Carlos Williams (1883–1963), Charles Reznikoff (1894–1976), and Louis Zukofsky (1904–78).

IMPRESSIONISM

An enormously popular artistic movement in French painting that began as an avant-garde revolt against French academicism in the mid-1860s. An outgrowth of realism—the leading realist Édouard Manet (1832–83) would adopt many of impressionism's themes and techniques in his own paintings—the impressionists eschewed the polished surfaces and the stylized historical, classical, or mythological subjects favored by the Academy; when their paintings were rejected by the Académie des Beaux-Arts, they organized their own salons. Utilizing a brilliant pallette and boldly textured brush strokes that called attention to their paintings as paintings, rather than as windows into an idealized, static world, the impressionists' subjects were homely land and seascapes, farmhouses, gardens, and ordinary people at work and play. Their canvases were often painted outdoors, capturing the evanescent play of light and shadow as they had actually been observed at a particular moment in time—their subjects were their own sense impressions, rather than things themselves. The movement's name came from a journalist's scathing comments on Monet's 1872 painting *Impression: Sunrise* in the satirical review *Le Charivari:* "When I beheld the work I thought that my glasses were dirty, what did this canvas mean? . . . The picture had neither up nor down . . . Impression! Of course, it makes an impression."

Some of the principal French impressionists were Claude Monet (1840–1926), Pierre-Auguste Renoir (1841–1919), Camille Pissarro (1830–1903), Berthe Morisot (1841–95), Edgar Degas (1834–1917) and Alfred Sisley (1839–99). The American painter Mary Cassatt (1844–1926) was a significant impressionist as well.

In 1886, Georges Seurat (1859–1891) completed his monumental painting *Sunday Afternoon on the Island of La Grande Jatte.* Two years in the making, he had painted and sketched some sixty studies in preparation for the work, which was rendered in tiny dots of pure color. This technique, called pointillism (also divisionism and confettism), was inspired by the optic studies and color theories of such scientists as the chemist and art restorer Michel-Eugène Chevreul, and Ogden Nicholas Rood, who explained how the eye blends closely juxtaposed colors. Seurat devised his own artistic science, chromoluminarism, in which lines and colors are utilized to create specific emotional effects. The critic Félix Fénéon (1861–1944) coined the term *neoimpressionism* to describe the works of Seurat and his followers, who included Camille Pissarro for a time, his son Lucien (1863–1944), and Paul Signac (1863–1935).

In 1910, the English painter and critic Roger Fry (1866–1934) curated an exhibition in London called Manet and the Post-Impressionists (Fry coined the term), which illustrated how Vincent van Gogh (1853–90), with his anguished emotionality; Paul Gauguin (1848–1903), with his symbolic and spiritual depth; and Paul Cézanne (1839–1906), with his emphasis on pure form (his paintings were already inspiring the cubists), had extended the affective and technical repertoire of impressionism.

Maurice Ravel (1875–1937), Claude Debussy (1862–1918), and other composers of atmospheric, evocative music in this period are called impressionists; the novels of the American writers

Stephen Crane (1871–1900) and Henry James (1843–1916) are sometimes characterized as impressionistic as well. Henry James famously defined a novel as "in its broadest sense, a personal, a direct impression of life."

INTERNATIONAL STYLE   *See* Modernism.

LACANISM

The psychological, philosophical, and linguistic theories espoused by the French psychoanalyst Jacques Lacan (1901–81). Though his influence as a clinician has been fairly limited (perhaps not surprisingly, since he argued that the true goal of his practice was analysis rather than cure), his theories were widely adopted by structuralist and poststructuralist literary theorists starting in the late 1960s, after the publication of his famous book *Ecrits* (1966).

Lacan's idea that the phallus is the chief signifier of male authority, and that boys enter into society driven by a fear of castration, while girls begin their journey away from the family with the sense that they are "lacking" something, may seem implicitly inimical to feminism, but many feminists, perhaps most famously Lacan's student Luce Irigaray, have been drawn to his theories. Perhaps Lacan's best-known idea is the mirror phase in a child's development—the critical moment, which occurs between the ages of six and eighteen months, when a child recognizes his or her reflection in the mirror. This marks the inception of the process of individuation, which paradoxically begins with a subject's recognition of itself as an object, an "other." According to Lacan, the ego is constructed out of intersubjective, relational experiences with parents, teachers, and authority figures; with objects of desire; and especially with the phenomenological self, which can only experience itself reflexively. Language, too, is an intersubjective experience—words don't have any intrinsic meaning when considered in isolation; they acquire their meanings from the contexts they're embedded in: their syntactical and associational relationships to other words, and the words, gestures, or expressions that an interlocutor uses when he or she responds to them. "A psychoanalyst," Lacan wrote, "is not an explorer of an unknown continent, or of great depths; he is a linguist." Despite language's slippery, decentered qualities, Lacan allowed that people do agree on certain "master-signifier" (emotion-laden concepts like love, patriotism, and religion which, though unfathomable in and of themselves, are accepted on an a priori basis) that function as archetypes and symbols, providing a modicum of social and psychological cohesion. Though Jacques Derrida famously deplored Lacan's notion of language as insufficiently deconstructive, the two had much in common (including their gnomic, often impenetrable prose styles and cultish followings). But if Lacan has his acolytes, he also has his detractors. Noam Chomsky is reputed to have dismissed him as an "amusing and perfectly self-conscious charlatan."

LOGICAL POSITIVISM *See* Positivism.

MATERIALISM *See* Idealism.

MELIORISM
From the Latin *melior* ("better"), the philosophic position that the world is gradually improving, if not by divine plan then by the efforts of humanity. A product of Enlightenment faith in scientific, technological, and moral progress, the word was coined by the Victorian novelist and thinker George Eliot (1819–80), who wrote, "I will not answer to the name of optimist, but if you like to invent Meliorist, I will not say you call me out of my name." In a similar vein, the novelist and poet Thomas Hardy (1840–1928) once declared, "People call me a pessimist; and if it is pessimism to think . . . that 'not to be born is best,' then I do not reject the designation . . . But my pessimism, if pessimism it be, does not involve the assumption that the world is going to the dogs . . . On the contrary, my practical philosophy is distinctly meliorist."

In *Pragmatism: A New Name for Some Old Ways of Thinking* (1907), William James proposed that we live in "a world not certain to be saved, a world the perfection of which shall be conditional merely, the condition being that each several agent does its own 'level best.' " In other words, whether God does or doesn't exist, human beings are obliged to do all in their power to make the world a better place. "You see that pragmatism can be called religious," James concluded, "if you allow that religion can be pluralistic or merely melioristic in type." In Judaism the idea that God, however omnipotent in his own sphere, may require human assistance in this world, is called *tikkun olam* ("repairing the world"); in Christianity this idea is sometimes referred to (usually pejoratively) as finite godism.

MINIMALISM

In sculpture and painting, the word *minimalism* began to be used in the 1960s to describe radically simple and austere compositions that were often composed of repetitive elements. The famous *Bird in Space* sculptures of Constantin Brancusi (1876–1957) anticipate the minimalist esthetic, as did the abstract expressionist canvases of Barnett Newman (1905–70). The works of Ad Reinhardt (1913–67), Frank Stella (b. 1936), Donald Judd (1928–94), Dan Flavin (1933–96), Sol LeWitt (b. 1928), and Robert Rauschenberg (b. 1925) are often described as minimalist.

In literature, writers as different as Samuel Beckett (1906–89), Raymond Carver (1938–88), Bret Easton Ellis (b. 1964), and Joan Didion (b. 1934) have been called minimalists—it is more of a descriptive adjective than a genre (though for many years at *Esquire* magazine and the book publisher Alfred A. Knopf, the influential editor Gordon Lish [b. 1934] was known to champion writers whose work had a minimalist ethos).

Musical minimalism was a more coherent movement in art music that came to enjoy significant popular success. The experimental composer and conceptual artist John Cage (1912–92), whose compositions include *4′33″*, which consists of four and a half minutes of silence, was a forerunner of the minimalists, as was the street musician Louis "Moondog" Hardin (1916–99), who anticipated many of the motifs, tropes, and hypnotic, trancelike features of the music as it developed in the 1960s and 1970s. Other influences were Javanese gamelan music, Indian ragas, the eccentric variety of Impressionism of Erik Satie (1886–1925), the trance-inducing Australian Aboriginal didgeridoo, the modal jazz of John Coltrane (1926–67), and African drumming and chants. The hallmarks of minimalist music are repetition, drones, the use of silence, and the absence of complex harmonic and melodic development. La Monte Young (b. 1935), Steve Reich (b. 1936), Philip Glass (b. 1937), Terry Riley (b. 1935), and John Adams (b. 1947), are some of the leading composers whose works have been called minimalist; the dancer/singer/filmmaker/choreographer Meredith Monk (b. 1942) has also composed and recorded music in the minimalist idiom.

MODERNISM

Catchall term for the varieties of avant-garde expression that arose in the early years of the twentieth century and continued until roughly the 1950s. In the visual arts, modernism encompasses the variety of international movements—symbolism, expressionism, postimpressionism, cubism, constructivism, futurism, Vorticism, Orphism, surrealism, Dadaism, suprematism, neoplasticism, fauvism, etc.—that subverted, sidestepped, ignored, or transcended traditional pictorialism. To the modernist, the art object is no longer a mirror of this world or a window into an idealized realm; it is a thing in itself. If it does refer to something beyond its own surface, its content is more likely to be metaphysical, psychological, or political than mimetic.

The architectural and industrial designs that were pioneered by the Bauhaus school, founded by the architect Walter Gropius (1883–1969), epitomized modernism (the furniture designer Marcel Breuer [1902–81] and the typographer Herbert Bayer [1900–85] were both associated with Bauhaus as well). Gropius, Mies van der Rohe (1886–1969), who led the Bauhaus from 1930 until 1933, when it was closed by the Nazis; and Le Corbusier (1887–1965) designed many clean, functional, glass-clad buildings in what came to be known as the International Style. Art deco and art moderne designs, and Frank Lloyd Wright's (1867–1959) late buildings, like the Solomon R. Guggenheim Museum in New York City, were less austere, but their gleaming exteriors and sleek geometries still epitomized a machine-age aesthetic.

Modernist music challenged conventional notions of tonality and melody and classical form; modern dance abandoned the traditional forms of academic ballet for a more expressive (and athletic) repertory of movements. Modernist poetry embraced the compact lyricism of imagism and the densely allusive, fractured, collagelike formalism of *The Waste Land* of T. S. Eliot (1888–1965). In fiction, James Joyce (1882–1941), Virginia Woolf (1882–1941), William Faulkner (1897–1962), and Marcel Proust (1871–1922) exploded the traditional novel. Instead of the omniscience of the traditional disembodied narrator (or the earnest confidences of a first-person narrator), they reproduced their characters' often unreliable streams of consciousness. The plots of their books (when they had plots) unfolded out of sequence and were presented from multiple points of view; many modernists depicted the intimate details of their characters' lives with an unusual degree of candor—Joyce's Leopold Bloom defecates, micturates, and masturbates in full view of the reader. Style—whether the polylingual babble of James Joyce's *Finnegans Wake* (1939) or the stripped down simplicity of Ernest Hemingway's (1899–1961) taciturn prose—was always paramount.

If the hallmarks of modernism were high seriousness, ardent intellectualism, a religious desire for transcendence, and an elitist disdain for popular taste, postmodernism, which emerged in the 1950s and 1960s, is playful and often camp. The high modernists had seen themselves as the new priests of a fallen world, reverently shoring up its fragments against the ruins; postmodernism is a creature of television and the Internet, where everybody gets to be famous for fifteen minutes and irony is the antidote to angst. Postmodernism is postexistential in that it takes the sense of life's randomness and meaninglessness for granted, and deconstructive in that it takes aporia (a critical term much beloved by deconstructionists that literally means "difficulty" or "impasse" in Greek; they use it to describe the inevitable collapse of any text into self-contradiction) as its very method.

The pop art of the 1960s embraced images from advertising and commerce; conceptual artists like Jeff Koons (b. 1955) incorporate pornography and kitsch into their deliberately provocative creations. Form no longer follows function in architecture; buildings are a pastiche of styles: the Chippendale pediment atop the ATT Building, designed by Philip Johnson (1906–2005), pokes fun at the glass and steel boxes beside it in the New York City skyline; Robert Venturi's *Complexity and Contradiction in Architecture* (1966) called for a "both/and" style, which "can include elements that are both good and awkward, big and little, closed and open, continuous and articulated, round and square, structural and spatial."

In music, the recording studio is no longer the passive recipient of sound but a musical instrument in its own right—a whole art form, hip-hop, is based on sampling and dubbing. High modernists might have disparaged rap music for its commercial vulgarity, its pandering to the lowest common denominator, or critiqued it for its false consciousness, its failure to recognize that its valorization of violence and sexism and bling makes it complicit in the oppression of the very social class that performs and consumes it; postmodernists cheerfully emulate its spirit in their own endeavors.

Postmodernist literature is wildly allusive (and self-referential); the novels of Thomas Pynchon (b. 1937), Kurt Vonnegut (b. 1922), David Foster Wallace (b. 1962), Italo Calvino (1923–85) and Don DeLillo (b. 1936) play with time and space and causality; they're abuzz with the ambient noise of pop culture and, at the same time, hyperaware of themselves as artifacts—the author is explicitly or implicitly present in their texts as the man behind the curtain.

If *modernism* is an umbrella term that embraces a huge swath of culture and time, *postmodernism* is less useful. It's more of a buzzword in that it describes a particular (but by no means universal) tendency in contemporary art. Don DeLillo's *White Noise* (1985) epitomizes many of the attitudes of postmodernism, for example, but the same author's *Underworld* (1997) is as high modern as James Joyce's *Ulysses* (1922).

MONISM

In philosophy, theology, and mysticism, the position that everything is ultimately reducible to a single substance or can be explained by a single principle is called monistic. Thus the pre-Socratic philosopher Parmenides asserted that an eternal, indivisible "One" is the sole reality and that the world we live in—the world of change, motion, generation, and plurality—is an illusion. In Hinduism, Brahma is the ultimate ground of being; in mystical Judaism it is Ein Sof, the infinite aspect of God; in Neoplatonism it is the Godhead, from which the temporal world is manifested in stages, like water cascading down a fountain. An atheistic materialist, who believes that there is no such thing as spirit or soul, that ideas and feelings are simply electrochemical stimuli in the brain, may be characterized as a monist; Marxist economic determinism is certainly a form of monism.

Opposed to monism are the positions of dualism, which reduces the world to two competing principles, and pluralism, which allows for many. Manichaeanism, the Persian religion that arose in the early centuries of the Christian era, described a cosmos divided between the forces of Darkness and Light; this is a classically dualistic formulation, as are Plato's conceptions of matter and form. Some Gnostic systems combine elements of monism and dualism. They are dualistic in that they believe that the material world was created and ruled by a lesser divine being called Demiurge, who only pretends to be God; they are monistic in that they believe that the enlightened soul can find its way out of this debased, inferior realm and merge with the real God. The philosopher René Descartes (1596–1650) posited an essential dualism between bodies and minds, and suggested that the pineal gland might be the bridge that enables these opposite modes of being to interact.

Pluralism argues that the truth lies in a variety of disparate systems and explanations. As the philosopher William James (1842–1910) put it,

> Everything you can think of, however vast or inclusive, has on the pluralistic view a genuinely "external" environment of

some sort . . . Things are "with" one another in many ways, but nothing includes everything, or dominates over everything. The word "and" trails along after every sentence. Something always escapes. "Even not quite" has to be said of the best attempts made anywhere in the universe at attaining all-inclusiveness. The pluralistic world is thus more like a federal republic than like an empire or a kingdom. However much may be collected, however much may report itself as present at any effective center of consciousness or action, something else is self-governed and absent and unreduced to unity.

A scientist who pragmatically accepts that quantum and Newtonian mechanics may not ever be reconciled in an as-yet-undiscovered grand unified theory, but continues to make use of both of them to solve different sorts of problems, is a pluralist; a scientist who stakes everything on discovering the holy grail of a "theory of everything" is a frustrated monist.

MYCTERISM
A rarely used rhetorical term to characterize a disdainful, sneering comment. It is derived from the Greek word *mykter*, which means "nose," probably because the speaker wrinkles up his nose as he delivers his devastating mot. Another anatomically derived word is *supercilious*, meaning "patronizing" or "arrogant," which comes from the Latin *superciliosus*, or raised eyebrow.

NATURALISM
In painting and sculpture, the attempt to capture natural forms as they really appear, rather than according to classical ideals or abstract geometries. In philosophy, the rejection of supernaturalism (magic, religion, mysticism, Platonic forms) as an explanation for natural phenomena or as a category of being. Naturalism is not a school of thought per se (though it bears marked similarities to positivism)—as an adjective, it is broad enough to be applied to as diverse a group of thinkers as Bertrand Russell (1872–1970), Aristotle (384–322 BCE), Friedrich Nietzsche (1844–1900), John

Locke (1632–1704), William James (1842–1910), and the contemporary moral philosopher John Rawls (1921–2002). Western science is naturalistic by definition.

The school of naturalism in literature includes such American writers as Frank Norris (1870–1902), Theodore Dreiser (1871–1945), Stephen Crane (1871–1900), William Dean Howells (1837–1920), and James T. Farrell (1904–79); and in France, Edmond (1822–96) and Jules de Goncourt (1830–70), Guy de Maupassant (1850–93), and especially Émile Zola (1840–1902), who is considered to be literary naturalism's leading theorist. In his essay "On the Experimental Novel," he declared that naturalism "consists simply in the application of the experimental method to the study of nature and of man." The novelist, Zola continued, must

> possess a knowledge of the mechanism of the phenomena inherent in man, to show the machinery of his intellectual and sensory manifestations, under the influences of heredity and environment, such as physiology shall give them to us, and then finally to exhibit man living in social conditions produced by himself, which he modifies daily, and in the heart of which he himself experiences a continual transformation.

Naturalists assumed that environment and heredity were the chief determinants of human character (no great believer in religion or the soul, Zola once declared, "Civilization will not attain to its perfection until the last stone from the last church falls on the last priest"); the naturalists' gritty, darkly pessimistic novels portrayed, with an almost clinical detachment, the sordid, often tragic destiny of "human beasts," in Zola's phrase, trapped in a Darwinian jungle and helplessly in thrall to the conditions of their lives and births. The social and economic determinism of naturalism, along with its preoccupation with the lower classes, made it highly compatible with the socialist realism that the Soviet Union would mandate its writers to produce in the 1930s.

In drama, naturalism attempted to bring a new realism to the stage, from the costumes and scenery to the actors' performance styles, and, of course, the content of the plays. Maxim Gorky

(1868–1936), who would go on to become the director of the Union of Soviet Writers, wrote:

> The characters of the drama should act independently of the volition of the dramatist in accordance with the law of their individual natures and social environment; they must follow the inspiration of their own destiny, and not that of any other destiny arbitrarily imposed by the author.

The Moscow Art Theater, cofounded in 1897 by Konstantin Stanislavsky (1863–1938) and Vladimir Nemirovich-Danchenko (1859–1943), presented highly influential productions of plays by Anton Chekhov (1860–1904) and Maxim Gorky himself. August Strindberg's (1849–1912) *Miss Julie* (1888) is a classic of dramatic naturalism.

NEOCLASSICISM   *See* Classicism.

NEOPLASTICISM   *See* Constructivism.

NEW CRITICISM

An influential approach to literary criticism whose name came from *The New Criticism* (1941), a collection of critical essays by the poet and teacher John Crowe Ransom (1888–1974). Ransom also drafted the "Statement of Principles" for the 1930 anthology *I'll Take My Stand*, which defended the pastoral, philosophical values of an idealized South against the materialistic, antiaesthetical North, and gave birth to the short-lived fugitive agrarian movement.

Influenced by logical positivism and opposed to the prevailing biographical criticism of the day, in which the facts of an author's life were marshaled to illuminate his or her writings, the New Criticism flourished between the 1930s and 1960s. Eschewing the affective (impressionistic descriptions of how a literary work makes the critic feel), historical (documentation of the ways that it relates to the historical context in which it was produced), and intentional (speculation about what its author was trying to say) fallacies of the prevailing modes of criticism, New

Criticism approached literary texts instead as autotelic objects (something that has no purpose or meaning beyond itself). T. S. Eliot (1888–1965) was the first to use this philosophical term in regard to poetry.

For Ransom and his coterie, meaningful critical analysis focused exclusively on a work's formal structure, its use of irony, the texture and semantics of its language, its use of symbolism and metaphor—in short, on its verbal architecture. Their approach worked splendidly with lyrical poetry, less so with larger forms like social novels and plays. *Understanding Poetry* (1938), the textbook by Ransom's students Cleanth Brooks (1906–94) and Robert Penn Warren (1905–89), introduced generations of undergraduates to the New Criticism; other important proponents of the method were W. K. Wimsatt (1907–75), Yvor Winters (1900–68), Allen Tate (1899–1979), Kenneth Burke (1897–1993), R. P. Blackmur (1904–65), William Empson (1906–84), and I. A. Richards (1893–1979). Structuralist and deconstructionist hermeneutics are in many ways an elaboration and extension of New Critical principles; culture studies and the New Historicism are something of a reaction to them.

NEW HISTORICISM

A school of criticism that concentrates on the historical context of literary works. While informed by the methods, interests, and philosophical positions of the post–structuralists, the New Historicism rejects the pure formalism of the New Criticism and deconstruction to examine, in Stephen Greenblatt's words, the "mutual permeability of the literary and the historical." Greenblatt, the author of the bestselling *Will in the World: How Shakespeare Became Shakespeare* (2004), which speculates that Shakespeare's family were underground Catholics, as well as many scholarly books, is a distinguished Renaissance scholar who teaches English literature at Harvard University. Generally acknowledged to be the founder and chief exponent of the critical movement, he wrote *Practicing New Historicism* (2000) with the Victorian scholar Catherine Gallagher

(b. 1945). Other notable New Historicists are Marjorie Garber (b. 1944), Stephen Orgel, and Harold Veeser.

NIHILISM

From the Latin *nihil,* "nothing." In philosophy, the term denotes a radical skepticism, a denial that anything can be known with absolute certainty. Ivan Turgenev's novel *Fathers and Sons* (1862), which included the character Bazarov the Nihilist, brought the term into common use; it became associated with the nascent revolutionary movement of the same name in Russia, which sought to destroy all forms of authority—religious and political—by violent means (Czar Alexander II was assassinated by Nihilists in 1881). The Nihilists were vague about what sort of society they would construct upon the ruins of the old one, other than that it would be based on rational, scientific principles. "I describe what is coming, what can no longer come differently: *the advent of nihilism,*" wrote Friedrich Nietzsche (1844–1900) in his posthumously published *The Will to Power.* "For some time now, our whole European culture has been moving toward a catastrophe . . . restlessly, violently, headlong, like a river that wants to reach the end, that no longer reflects, that is afraid to reflect."

NOMINALISM

In medieval philosophy, the denial of the existence of universals or Platonic forms. A nominalist would say that there is no such thing as a "universal" table, for example—there are only individual tables. The word *table* may be a universal, but it is only a name, not a real thing. Another name for this idea is essentialism.

A Platonist would argue that when we perceive a table, what we're really seeing is an imperfect imitation of the ideal form of a table that exists elsewhere, in another world. The table that we see in front of us, the "real" table, as we are accustomed to think of it, is not real at all. Although the nomenclature is confusing, this Platonic or idealist position is called exaggerated realism, although what's "real" is not the concrete table that you can eat your dinner at but its invisible, otherworldly ideal. Another way of thinking about this is the idea that "tableness" is a real quality that actually exists independently of any existing tables.

A conceptualist would say that the ideal model or form of the table *does* exist, but only in our minds. The particular concrete table that we see is a percept; the generalized table that we mentally relate it to is the concept. Finally, a moderate realist, and this describes the position of the great Scholastic thinker Thomas Aquinas (1225–74), who was profoundly influenced by Aristotle, would say that universals do exist, but they are immanent in things—the ideal table, for example, is instantiated (made real) by any particular table—it is the source of its "tableness." Universals also exist in our minds and in the mind of God—in fact, it is through these universals that we come to have knowledge of God.

OBJECTIVISM   *Also see* Imagism.

The libertarian philosophy espoused by the novelist and screen-writer Ayn Rand (1905–82), which she set out at length in her book *The New Intellectual* (1961). In her own words, objectivism holds that

1) Reality exists as an objective absolute—facts are facts, independent of man's feelings, wishes, hopes or fears.

2) Reason . . . is man's only means of perceiving reality, his only source of knowledge, his only guide to action, and his basic means of survival.

3) Man—every man—is an end in himself, not the means to the ends of others. He must exist for his own sake, neither sacrificing himself to others nor sacrificing others to himself. The pursuit of his own rational self-interest and of his own happiness is the highest moral purpose of his life.

4) The ideal political-economic system is laissez-faire capitalism . . . The government acts only as a police-man . . . it uses physical force only in retaliation and

only against those who initiate its use, such as criminals or foreign invaders . . . there should be (but, historically, has not yet been) a complete separation of state and economics, in the same way and for the same reasons as the separation of state and church.

Occasionalism

A metaphysical theory that relies on God to resolve the mystery of physical causality in a world in which mind and matter are intrinsically incompatible. How can our immaterial minds influence our material bodies and other objects and vice versa? If matter is by definition inert, how can it be made to move? The Persian philosopher Abu Hamid Muhammad ibn Muhammad al-Ghazali (1058–1111), a Sufi mystic and the author of the polemic *Incoherence of the Philosophers*, which emphatically rejected Aristotle, Plato, and all other rationalistic, non-Islamic thinkers, proposed that Allah was the answer. What appear to be causes and effects are illusions—they are merely an occasion for Allah to intervene and impose his will on the world. When I pass you the salt, it is not I who is making the saltshaker travel across the table. God wills it to move; I am only his instrument.

Western philosophers didn't begin to grapple with this problem until the seventeenth century, after René Descartes (1596–1650) proposed that matter and mind are completely incompatible—what became known as Cartesian dualism—but he wasn't able to satisfactorily account for their interactions. He suggested that the pineal gland provided a bridge between the material and the immaterial aspects of being, but *how* it did so, and how something material could also be immaterial, was left up in the air. Arnold Geulincx (1624–69) argued that if one doesn't know how a thing is done, then one hasn't done it. Since he doesn't know how or even if his mind controls his body, "I am therefore a mere spectator of this machine. In it I form naught and renew naught, I neither make anything here nor

destroy it. Everything is the work of someone else." That someone else, of course, is God.

Nicolas Malebranche (1638–1715) proposed a God that
worked through laws, but at the same time was intimately and essentially involved with every aspect of creation:

> When you set yourself to raise your arm, this mental act of
> yours can't possibly cause any event in the world of matter, but
> it is the *occasion* for God to hoist your arm. The relationships
> of occasional causes to efficacious causes are encoded in gen-
> eral laws that God has prescribed for himself. He has done this
> so as to make himself recognizable through his works, and also
> to confer on his work a uniformity of action that makes the
> parts hang together and saves it from being confused, irregular,
> and unintelligible.

ORIENTALISM   *Also see* **Postcolonial theory.**
In its original sense, Orientalism referred to the scholarly study
of the history, culture, and art of the East: India, Asia, the Levant.
Thus the French scholar Eugène Burnouf (1801–52), who translated Old Iranian and Sanskrit texts, and Max Müller (1823–
1900), the German philologist who oversaw the translations of
essential Hindu, Zoroastrian, Buddhist, Taoist, Confucian, Jain-
ist, and Islamic texts that were compiled in the fifty-volume
Sacred Books of the East between 1879 and 1910, were Orientalists. Orientalism can also refer to Western imitations or adaptations of Asian motifs in painting, architecture, and the decorative
arts—another name for this is *chinoiserie*. Eighteenth-century
Delft pottery incorporates decorative elements from Ming vases;
formal gardens often included pagodas and other Asian touches.
Ingre's *La Grande Odalisque* (1814) mines the East for its exoticism; Whistler's compositions were influenced by Hiroshige and
other Japanese woodblock artists.

Since 1978, when the Palestinian scholar Edward Said
(1935–2003) published his seminal book *Orientalism,* the word
has taken on a pejorative, imperialistic connotation. "Oriental-

ism," Said wrote, "Is a style of thought based upon an ontological and epistemological distinction made between 'the Orient' and (most of the time) 'the Occident.'"

> Thus a very large mass of writers, among whom are poets, novelists, philosophers, political theorists, economists, and imperial administrators, have accepted the basic distinction between East and West as the starting point for elaborate theories, epics, novels, social descriptions, and political accounts concerning the Orient, its people, customs, 'mind,' destiny, and so on . . . Orientalism can be discussed and analyzed as the corporate institution for dealing with the Orient—dealing with it by making statements about it, authorizing views of it, describing it, by teaching it, settling it, ruling over it: in short, Orientalism as a Western style for dominating, restructuring, and having authority over the Orient.

ORPHISM   *See* Cubism, Pythagoreanism.

PHENOMENALISM

In epistemology, the notion that physical objects do not exist in and of themselves, but as logical constructions made out of "bundles" of sense data. Thus a rubber ball isn't the object that a child is playing with, but the sum of its sensuous qualities as they are assembled in the mind: its roundness, its softness, its redness, its "bouncyness," etc. The main proponents of this radically empiricist point of view were A. J. Ayer (1910–89), C. I. Lewis (1883–1964), and Ernst Mach (1838–1916). David Hume (1711–76), the Scottish philosopher, wrote in his *A Treatise of Human Nature* that "I may venture to affirm to the rest of mankind that they are nothing but a bundle of or collection of different perceptions, which succeed each other with an inconceivable rapidity and are in a perpetual flux and movement."

PHENOMENOLOGY   *See* Existentialism.

PLATONISM

The moral, political, metaphysical, cosmological, scientific, and mathematical ideas of the ancient Athenian philosopher Plato (ca. 428–347 BCE). Plato was a student of Socrates and the teacher of Aristotle. The Academy, the school he founded in a suburb of Athens named after the mythical hero Academos, accepted students until the Roman emperor Justinian closed it in 529 CE. The author of innumerable philosophical dialogues such as *The Republic, The Apology, The Symposium,* and *The Phaedo*, which are also highly regarded for their literary qualities, Plato is perhaps best remembered for his idealistic, mystical epistemology, which was memorably contrasted with Aristotle's empiricism in this much-cited comment of the English poet Samuel Taylor Coleridge (1772–1834):

> Every man is born an Aristotelian or a Platonist. I do not think it possible that anyone born an Aristotelian can become a Platonist; and I am sure that no born Platonist can ever change into an Aristotelian. They are two classes of man, beside which it is next to impossible to conceive a third. The one considers reason a quality or attribute; the other considers it a power . . . Aristotle was, and still is, the sovereign lord of the understanding—the faculty judging by the senses. He was a conceptualist, and never could raise himself into that higher state, which was natural to Plato, and has been so to others, in which the understanding is distinctly contemplated, and, as it were, looked down upon from the throne of actual ideas, or living, inborn, essential truths.

We are all of us Falstaffs or Hamlets, Don Quixotes or Sancho Panzas, Little Nells or Molly Blooms. The great mystics and visionaries are Platonists; rulers and soldiers are Aristotelians. Platonists are soulful and transcendent, Aristotelians matter-of-fact and earthy.

Plato's famous allegory of the cave explains his notion of ideal forms. Imagine, he says, a group of people who have spent their entire lives chained in a cave, watching shadows cast upon the walls by the world outside. How would they ever know that the dim images they perceive are not all there is? That is how an unenlightened person perceives and understands the world. Truth, which Plato identifies with reality, is the eternal realm of the ideas, a realm that is not accessible to the sense. A real-world tree is a dull, flawed reflection of the ideal form of a tree; just as a real world instance of Justice or Beauty is only a pale shadow of their corresponding forms. The supreme form is the idea of Good, and this is the hardest to apprehend:

> The prison-house is the world of sight . . . my opinion is that in the world of knowledge the idea of good appears last of all, and is seen only with an effort; and, when seen, is also inferred to be the universal author of all things beautiful and right, parent of light and of the lord of light in this visible world, and the immediate source of reason and truth in the intellectual; and that this is the power upon which he who would act rationally, either in public or private life must have his eye fixed.

If Aristotle, an empiricist, used his senses and his mind to inductively derive the truth from the world around him, Plato deduced a higher realm of pure ideas. To Aristotle, the mind was a tool; to Plato it was a vehicle of transcendence. If this sounds vaguely Gnostic, it's not a coincidence. One of the scrolls found at Nag Hammadi contained a portion of *The Republic* in a Coptic translation.

PLURALISM   *See* **Monism.**

POINTILISM   *See* **Impressionism.**

POSITIVISM
School of philosophy, also known as Comteism after its founder Auguste Comte (1798–1857), that rejects all metaphysical speculation, arguing that only objective, scientific knowledge—of concrete things, relationships, and causes and effects that can be accurately observed and precisely measured—is meaningful. Comte is also the founder of sociology, a term that he coined.
   Logical positivism is a twentieth-century school of epistemology developed by the Vienna Circle of philosophers that gravitated

around Moritz Schlick (1882–1936). Inspired by the early writings of Ludwig Wittgenstein (1889–1951), logical positivists test knowledge against the verifiability principle, which holds that a statement can only be said to have meaning if it is tautological (in which case its meaning derives from its own terms) or if it can be confirmed by empirical observation. The English philosopher A. J. Ayer (1910–89) was one of the best-known proponents of logical positivism.

POSTCOLONIAL THEORY

An academic field that crosses many disciplines—philosophy, history, economics, science, politics, anthropology, psychology, cultural studies, and especially literature and literary theory—to study the lingering aftermath of colonialism as it is manifested both in newly independent countries and in the Western powers who formerly occupied them. Everything from a mainstream novel by an African writer—the Nigerian writer Chinua Achebe's *Things Fall Apart,* for example—analyses of discredited scientific theories about tropical disease, legal studies about Union Carbide's efforts to avoid liability for the disaster in Bhopal, to the most rarified philosophical "discourse on modes of alteriority" can fall under the rubric of postcolonial theory. Edward Said's *Orientalism* is considered to be the founding text of the field; Frantz Fanon's (1925–61) books are canonical as well. Gayatri Chakravorty Spivak (b. 1942) and Rey Chow are prominent in the field today.

Not all postcolonial literature is about conflicts between whites and blacks, East and West, or the first and third worlds. Colonialism is the deeper subject of many books from the antipodes. Peter Carey's *True History of the Kelly Gang* (2001), the imagined confessions of a historical nineteenth-century Australian outlaw, has much to say about the enduring conflicts between the poor Irish transports who peopled the continent and their English overlords. Matthew Kneale's *English Passengers* (2000), the multilayered, tragicomic story of, among other things, the last Tasmanian aborigine and the ironic fate of an English racial theorist, is saturated with postcolonial themes. A significant body of postcolonial studies is specific to the literature of Canada, such as Margaret Atwood's *Alias Grace,* published in 1997. Canada is at once a former colony of England, an expropriator of lands inhabited by indigenous people, a conqueror of French territory, and, in modern times, an uneasy neighbor of a superpower, the United States.

POSTMODERNISM   *See* Modernism.

POSTSTRUCTURALISM   *See* Structuralism.

PRAGMATISM

The philosophical stance that practical efficacy provides a standard for judging the truth, value, or propriety of a proposition or a course of action—in other words, that what works best is what's right.

Utilitarianism's ethical standard—that which provides the greatest good for the greatest number—is a pragmatic one; as is the scientific notion of contingent truth—that a scientific law applies only so long as it yields consistent results and until it is successfully challenged. In 1906, William James (1842–1910) lectured on "What Pragmatism Means":

> The term is derived from the same Greek word *pragma,* meaning action, from which our words 'practice' and 'practical' come. It was first introduced into philosophy by Mr. Charles Peirce in 1878 . . . Mr. Peirce, after pointing out that our beliefs are really rules for action, said that, to develop a thought's meaning, we need only determine what conduct it is fitted to produce: that conduct is for us its sole significance. And the tangible fact at the root of all our thought-distinctions, however subtle, is that there is no one of them so fine as to consist in anything but a possible difference of practice. To attain perfect clearness in our thoughts of an object, then, we need only consider what conceivable effects of a practical kind the object may involve—what sensations we are to expect from it, and what reactions we must prepare. Our conception of these effects, whether immediate or

remote, is then for us the whole of our conception of the object,
so far as that conception has positive significance at all.

In a different context, James declared that "on pragmatistic principles, if the hypothesis of God works satisfactorily in the widest
sense of the word, it is true." Peirce (1839–1914), whose epistemology had more in common with logical positivism's, and who
regarded James's as entirely too subjective, began to call his philosophy pragmaticism, to better distinguish his views.

Other notable pragmatists are John Dewey (1859–1952),
George Herbert Mead (1863–1931), and F. C. S. Schiller (1864–
1937).

PRECISIONISM

Interwar movement in American painting influenced by cubism and
futurism in which generally urban or industrial subjects were rendered realistically, but with especial attention to their geometrical
form. The principal artists were Charles Demuth (1883–1935),
Charles Sheeler (1883–1965), and George Ault (1891–1948). Georgia O'Keefe's (1887–1986) cityscapes are precisionist. The paintings,
which have a clean, almost sterile quality, are influenced by photog-
raphy as much as by Picasso; O'Keefe's husband, the photographer
Alfred Stieglitz (1864–1946) was a major influence. Precisionists are
sometimes called cubist realists.

PRE-RAPHAELITISM

A neomedieval artistic and literary movement in nineteenth-
century England. The Pre-Raphaelite Brotherhood was founded
in 1848 by the maverick English painters John Everett Millais
(1829–96), William Holman Hunt (1827–1910), Dante Gabriel
Rossetti (1828–82), James Collinson (1825–81), and the sculptor
Thomas Woolner (1825–92) in reaction to what they regarded as
the sentimentality and mannerism of contemporary art. Strongly
influenced by Romantic poetry and the criticism of John Ruskin
(1819–1900), they sought to "sympathize with what is direct and
serious and heartfelt in previous art, to the exclusion of what is

conventional and self-parading and learned by rote." By "previous art" they meant paintings dating from before the time of Raphael (1483–1520), who they believed had introduced sterile academicism into painting.

Though John Ruskin praised them individually and as a group, writing that "the Pre-Raphaelites are wholly sincere and natural," and in another context, that Rossetti's paintings in particular heralded "the dawn of a new era in art, in a true unison of the grotesque with the realistic power," their faux medievalism was not to every critic's taste. Charles Dickens savaged Millais' *Christ in the House of His Parents* as "mean, odious, revolting and repulsive." By 1853 the brotherhood had dissolved and the artists gone their separate ways.

Starting around 1856, Rossetti, Edward Burne-Jones (1833–98), William Morris (1834–96), and several other artists revived the movement, which would become the nucleus for both art nouveau and the Arts and Crafts movement. Some poets who also adopted the Pre-Raphaelite aesthetic and its medieval subjects were Dante Rossetti's sister, Christina Rossetti (1830–94), and Algernon Charles Swinburne (1837–1909).

PYTHAGOREANISM

Founded by Samos of Pythagoras in Southern Italy around 525 BCE, the school of Pythagoras combined the secretive, cultic, visionary aspects of Greek mystery religions, especially Orphism, with sober philosophical, musical, astronomical, and mathematical inquiry.

The Orphists were an ancient cult supposedly founded by the legendary musician Orpheus. They believed that human bodies were fashioned by Zeus from the ashes of the vanquished Titans but that human souls contained aspects of Dionysius, the god of wine. Through ecstatic experiences and purification rites, people could purge themselves of their earthly nature—a process that took many lifetimes. At the end of the cycle of incarnations, the purified soul would be reunited with its divine source.

Pythagoreans believed that the world was reducible to pure

number (like the ideal forms of the Platonists). Just as musical intervals conformed to mathematical ratios—shorten a string by half and the tone it produces is an octave higher—so does the underlying order of the universe. The notion of the "music of the spheres" originated with the Pythagoreans; the Pythagorean theorem, which states that "the area of the square built upon the hypotenuse of a right triangle is equal to the sum of the areas of the squares upon the remaining sides" (perhaps better known in its algebraic form, $a^2 + b^2 = c^2$), was likely Pythagoras's personal discovery.

Pythagoreanism enjoyed a revival in the first centuries of the Christian era. The first-century philosopher Apollonius of Tyana believed that he was a reincarnation of Pythagoras. Apollonius's contemporary, the mathematician Nichomachus of Gerasa, was a Pythagorean, as was Numenius of Apamea, a Syrian syncretist who lived in the second century and was believed to be a major influence on Plotinus (205–270 CE), the founder of Neoplatonism.

RADICAL IDEALISM   *See* **Empiricism.**

RATIONALISM   *See* **Empiricism.**

REALISM   *Also see* **nominalism, naturalism, socialist realism.**
In its broadest, most simplistic, and unqualified philosophical sense, realism is the commonsensical (but epistemologically problematic) idea that the world exists independently of our perceptions of it—that the proverbial tree in a forest has a being and identity in and of itself, whether or not someone is looking at it or thinking about it or describing it in one or another language. Should that tree fall, it would make a sound. Obviously, this is different from Platonic realism, which is concerned with the independent existence of universals.

Though modern science is broadly understood to be a naturalistic, materialistic, and realistic enterprise that formulates its theories based on real-world observations and experiments, Heisenberg's uncertainty principle has called this into question at least in the quantum realm, where subatomic particles paradoxically exist as both particles and waves until they are measured. Once a particle's position is determined, the direction it is moving can only be conjectured statistically, in terms of probabilities. And if we know a particle's direction, we can only conjecture its position. In this case, an object's inherent qualities seem to depend upon its observer's biases and choices rather than its fixed, intrinsic qualities. Einstein refused to believe that indeterminacy, even in the restricted world of very tiny things, was the way that things are; that henceforth science would be required to partition off one realm of the world from the laws of cause and effect and settle for knowing the odds of an outcome rather than the outcome itself. This is what he meant when he famously said, "God does not play dice." He assumed that the problem was in the nature of the theory, rather than the objects themselves, that some day either a different model of the world or better equations would be developed that would work at both the quantum and the macrolevel. In his autobiography, he went on to say,

> I still believe in the possibility of a model of reality—that is, of a theory which represents things themselves and not merely the probability of their occurrence. I am . . . firmly convinced that the essentially statistical character of contemporary theory is solely to be ascribed to the fact that this theory operates with an incomplete description of physical systems.

In politics and international affairs, *realism* has the same meaning as the German word *realpolitik*: amoral, hardheaded policies based on actualities rather than ideals. A political realist deals with existing facts on the ground rather than aspirations. *Realism* defines international relations as the push and pull of military power. Thus a realist seeks to achieve peace by forming opportunistic alliances that maintain a stable balance of power. During the administration of Richard Nixon, his Secretary of State Henry Kissinger, an astute student of Klemens Wenzel von Metternich's (1773–1859) diplomatic efforts to keep the Hapsburg empire afloat in the nineteenth century, concluded that the United States could gain leverage in its relations with the Soviet Union if it opened up relations with Communist China. The fact that Mao's dictatorship was as inimical to America's ideals as Brezhnev's was irrelevant. George W. Bush's war on terror walks a tightrope between pragmatic realism, in the name of which the United States sends suspected terrorists overseas to be tortured by its less fastidious allies and, with its high-minded aspirations to export Democratic values, Wilsonian idealism.

In the arts, realism rejects classical subjects and visual conventions, and presents the world as the artist sees it. Nineteenth-century French realist paintings depicted ordinary people in recognizable settings rather than heroes and gods in idealized landscapes. Gustave Courbet's (1819–77) *L'Origine du monde,* a graphic depiction of a reclining woman's vagina, takes this tendency to a provocative extreme; Édouard Manet's (1832–83) *Olympia* was infamous for its monumental depiction of a nude reclining woman who looked more like a prostitute than a fanciful odalisque from the pages of *The Arabian Nights.* Impressionism, in which artists attempted to reproduce their own subjectivity, blurring and distorting images as they saw them, was a natural outgrowth of realism.

Literary realism, which also reached its peak in the nineteenth century, is typified by the works of George Eliot (1819–80) in England, Honoré de Balzac (1799–1850) in France, Leo Tolstoy (1828–1910) in Russia, and William Dean Howells (1837–1920) in the United States. Realist novels fostered verisimilitude in their story lines; their characters existed in a recognizable social and political milieu.

RELATIVISM

In epistemology, the view that all truths are subjective—that my idea of a truth (say, that dead people can't talk to the living) will not necessarily be held by someone else who is a product of a different belief system. Epistemological relativism maintains that ideas are manufactured by language, history, and cultural conventions and cannot be held to any objective, universal standards. Even mathematical or geometrical absolutes are relative according to this point of view; conceivably, another civilization could exist for which two plus two equals three.

In ethics and morality, relativism is the notion that ideas of the good and the bad, the just and the unjust, the desirable and the undesirable differ from place to place and people to people, and that moral judgments should thus be withheld. A moral relativist might thus declare that while he or she believes that it is wrong for a grownup to have sex with young children, someone from a different culture might reasonably believe otherwise. A moral absolutist, say an heir to the monotheistic Judeo-Christian tradition, would declare idolatry and incest abhorrent no matter where they were encountered, because the prohibitions against them were issued by the all-powerful, one God. A moral relativist would tolerate them as expressions of legitimate cultural differences. Practices like sex slavery, female circumcision, and ethnic cleansing have been known to test the forbearance of even the most committed of relativists, who are perhaps neither as numerous nor as influential as their opponents make them out to be.

In April 2005, Cardinal Ratzinger (who would shortly become Pope Benedict XVI) delivered a homily before the College of Cardinals in which he contrasted a steadfast faith in Christ and church with the pernicious pluralism of the day:

> The small boat of thought of many Christians has often been tossed about by these waves—thrown from one extreme to the other: from Marxism to liberalism, even to libertinism; from collectivism to radical individualism; from atheism to a vague religious mysticism; from agnosticism to syncretism, and so forth . . . Having a clear faith, based on the Creed of the Church, is often labeled today as a fundamentalism. Whereas, relativism, which is letting oneself be tossed and "swept along by every wind of teaching," looks like the only attitude (acceptable) to today's standards. We are moving towards a dictatorship of relativism which does not recognize anything as for certain and which has as its highest goal one's own ego and one's own desires.

RENAISSANCE HUMANISM   *See* Humanism.

ROMANTICISM

An intellectual and aesthetic movement that began in the late eighteenth century in Europe as a reaction against the rationalism of the Enlightenment and the aristocratic formality of neoclassicism, Romanticism exalts both individual genius as it is manifested in the lone artist and the collective creativity of the anonymous bards and fabulists of folk literature. In late medieval times, the word *romantic* referred to literature that was written in the vernacular (in Romance languages) as opposed to Latin (the language of learning). In the seventeenth century, *romance* took on the derogatory connotations of the bizarre and the fantastical; by the eighteenth century, the word was used to describe the quality of gentle melancholy or sentimentality. Both qualities were present in the gothic fiction—Horace Walpole's *The Castle of Otranto* (1765), Ann Radcliffe's *The Mysteries of Udolpho* (1794), Matthew Lewis's *The Monk* (1796)—that was increasingly in vogue by the close of the eighteenth century; a literature of sensation and exoticism that would reach its zenith in Mary Shelley's *Frankenstein* (1818) and Edgar Allan Poe's (1809–49) horror stories.

The German poet, scholar, and critic August von Schlegel (1767–1845) was probably the first to use Romanticism as the antithesis of classicism; his brother Friedrich (1772–1829) also ventured a definition of Romantic poetry: "Romantic poetry is a progressive, universal poetry . . . Poetry alone is infinite . . . and recognizes as its first law that the freedom and originality of the poet should not suffer under a law itself."

Madame de Staël (1766–1816), already a devotee of Jean-Jacques Rousseau (1712–78), whose ideas about the "noble savage" and man's innate goodness would influence many Romantic writers, did much to popularize the Schlegels' ideas in France. August Schlegel's translations of Shakespeare's plays created a sensation in Germany and inspired more translations across the Continent. Shakespeare's dramatic intensity, the simultaneous earthiness and loftiness of his language, his indifference to the classical unities, and the singular mystery of his origins—

an unlettered glover's son and actor, who somehow made himself the conduit for sublime inspiration—enthralled the Romantics.

The Sorrows of Young Werther, the story by Johann Wolfgang von Goethe (1749–1832) of a passionate, anguished youth who takes his life after the woman he loves rejects him, provided Europe with a prototype of the Romantic artist: a figure of volcanic sensibility with an alarming susceptibility to what a contemporary psychologist would no doubt diagnose as a borderline personality disorder. The disquieting details of the private lives of Percy Bysshe Shelley (1792–1822) and Lord George Gordon Byron (1788–1824) lend some teeth to this supposition.

Both English and German Romantics were much taken with James Macpherson's (1736–96) adaptations of Ossian's ancient Celtic poetry (the fictional Werther translates some of his work); the "boy poet" Thomas Chatterton (1752–70), who forged a cycle of medieval poems at age twelve, is sometimes considered England's first Romantic poet. His astonishing youth, his outsider status, and his untimely suicide—a trifecta of Romantic ideals— gave him iconic status.

The manifesto of English Romanticism was the introduction to *Lyrical Ballads* (1800), in which William Wordsworth (1770–1850) defined the poet as:

> A man speaking to men . . . endowed with more lively sensibility, more enthusiasm and tenderness, who has a greater knowledge of human nature, and a more comprehensive soul, than are supposed to be common among mankind; a man pleased with his own passions and volitions, and who rejoices more than other men in the spirit of life that is in him; delighting to contemplate similar volitions and passions as manifested in the goings-on of the Universe, and habitually impelled to create them where he does not find them.

And poetry as:

> The breath and finer spirit of all knowledge; it is the impassioned expression which is in the countenance of all Science . . .

Poetry is the first and last of all knowledge—it is as immortal as the heart of man.

Romantic poetry is oracular and inspired—it is a species of knowledge, a revelation, whether it is William Blake's (1757–1827) visionary prophecies, John Keats's (1795–1821) lyrical odes, William Wordsworth's "great emotion recollected in tranquility," the transgressive irony of Byron's *Don Juan,* Ralph Waldo Emerson's (1803–82) austerely abstract transcendentalism, or Walt Whitman's (1819–92) exuberantly democratic and unabashedly erotic *Song of Myself.*

A strong strain of pantheism and paganism runs through Romanticism, which sees intimations of the divine in nature. Romantic painters like Caspar David Friedrich (1774–1840) painted sublime landscapes, as did Thomas Cole (1801–48) and Frederic Church (1826–1900) of the Hudson River school. Though spirituality was an essential ingredient of Romanticism, so were its liberatory tendencies, whether in the practice of free love, the defiance of social conventions and class barriers, the abhorrence of hypocritical religiosity, or in the larger sense of national liberation—and even chauvinistic nationalism. The theories of the German Johann Gottfried von Herder (1744–1803) on the unique spirit of a nation that he called the *volksgeist* tread perilously close to racism. "The most natural state therefore is one people with a natural character," he wrote. "Nothing seems more obviously opposed to the purpose of government than the unnatural enlargement of states, the wild mixing together of different human species and nations under one scepter." Nazism, with its cult of the *volk* and the superman, its love of grandiloquent spectacle and its bogus historicity, was in some ways a bastard outgrowth of Romanticism.

If Romanticism celebrated nature and rural simplicity, it also encouraged a cult of hero worship. The piano virtuoso and composer Franz Liszt (1811–86), as has often been noted, was the prototype of a rock star, as was the swashbuckling Lord Byron. Napoléon Bonaparte (1769–1821) had been considered a Romantic hero until the establishment of the First Empire in 1804. Ludwig van Beethoven

(1770–1827)—another tempestuous, larger-than-life Romantic genius—had called his Third Symphony, which he was still composing in 1804, his Bonaparte Symphony. When he heard that Napoleon had crowned himself emperor, he angrily struck his name from it and published it as the *Eroica*, which, according to its new inscription, was "composed to celebrate the memory of a great man," presumably Napoleon the liberator.

Other notable Romantic composers are Hector Berlioz (1803–69), Frédérick Chopin (1810–49), Anton Dvoκák (1841–1904), and Peter Ilyich Tchaikovsky (1840–93). All of them expanded music's harmonic and tonal vocabulary, and employed larger and larger orchestras to maximize the expressiveness of their music, which was often programmatic and poetic, and drew liberally on folk music for its themes. Richard Wagner's (1813–83) operas, with their overpowering nationalism, extravagant sets, stormy emotionality, and eccentric mysticism, were perhaps the apotheosis of Romantic spectacle.

SCHOLASTICISM   *See* **Aristolelianism.**

SECESSIONISM   *See* **Symbolism.**

SERIALISM   *See* **Atonalism.**

SESQUIPEDALIANISM
See **Antidisestablishmentarianism.**

SOCIAL DARWINISM   *See* **Darwinism.**

SOCIALIST REALISM
Socialist realism was the blatantly propagandistic genre of art and literature preferred by the Soviet regime. Innumerable plays, films, novels, and stories that praised Stalin's governance while illustrating the irresistible processes of dialectical materialism and the ultimate victory of the proletariat in the class struggle were produced by order of the state; Vladimir Krikhatsky's painting *The First Trac-*

tor, in which a group of agricultural workers gather to admire their collective's new tractor, is a classic exemplar of the genre.

Though the avant-garde had continued apace in the early years of the Russian Revolution, by the 1930s formalism (artistic works in which surface or style is more important than representational, narrative, or ideological content) had been officially condemned as decadent and bourgeois. The Union of Soviet Writers, headed by the celebrated author, journalist, and revolutionary Maxim Gorky (1868–1936), resolved that the guiding spirit of Soviet art would henceforth be socialist realism. "Socialist realism is not some set of tools that are handed out to the writer for him to make a work of art with," A. I. Stetsky, the manager of the Culture and Leninist Propaganda Section of the Central Committee of the Communist Party of the USSR, disingenuously assured the members of the Writer's Union in 1934. "Socialist realism can best be shown in those works of art which Soviet writers produce."

To the Soviets, artists were simply another species of worker, their output ideally contributing to the transformation of the citizenry into the New Soviet Man. "The production of souls is more important than the production of tanks," Stalin declared at a gathering of writers in 1932. "And therefore I raise my glass to you, writers, the engineers of the human soul." The socialist realist style was exported to most of the Socialist Republics; the expatriate Czech writer Josef Skvorecky appropriated Stalin's phrase as the ironic title of one of his novels.

Mikhail Bulgakov (1891–1940) was one of the many Soviet writers whose work was too humanist, bourgeois, or subversive to pass muster with the authorities; for the last decade of his life he was unable to publish at all. In *The Master and Margarita,* a novel that he wrote in secret, and which miraculously found its way into print during the 1960s, he brutally satirized the bureaucracy of the Congress of Soviet Writers and the opportunism of the writers who shamelessly abased themselves to stay in print.

SOCRATICISM

A rarely used term for the ethics, epistemology, and pedagogical method of the Athenian philosopher Socrates. Born in 470 BCE, Socrates was executed in 399 BCE for the crimes of promoting atheism and corrupting the young. Plato (ca. 428–348 BCE), who studied with Socrates, included him as a character in most of his dialogues; he is perhaps best remembered for saying that "an unexamined life is not worth living" and "the only true wisdom consists of knowing that you know nothing." Aristophanes (446–388 BCE) portrayed Socrates in his play *The Clouds* as a Sophist, which was not at all the case. Socrates did not teach for money, nor did he instruct his students in rhetoric.

As portrayed by Plato and recorded by Xenophon (427–355 BCE) in his *Memorabilia,* Socrates' chief preoccupations were the nature of knowledge, the soul, morality, and a just government. Socrates' method of arriving at the truth was the relentless questioning of all received opinions (thus the Socratic method in pedagogy, in which a teacher asks questions rather than lectures). Socrates' challenges to conventional thinking made him, in his own words, something of a gadfly on the body of the state; though he goaded it to think clearly about itself, he also annoyed it no end. Though his execution probably had as much to do with the treasonous and subversive activities of his students Alcibiades and Critias as with his own controversial teachings, he is remembered and celebrated as a martyr for his intellectual ideals.

SOLIPSISM

The reductio ad absurdum of radical empiricism, the philosophical conviction that experience is the only source of true knowledge, taken to such an extreme that the only experience that's considered certain is one's own thoughts. A solipsist (from the Latin *ipse,* "self," and *solus,* "alone") has reached the conclusion that no one but him- or herself exists. Thus the speaker of Sylvia Plath's poem "Soliloquy of the Solipsist" muses about how the neighbors don't realize that "if I choose to blink/they die." Comedian Sarah Silverman has a routine in which she illustrates the incredible self-centeredness of the solipsist. She says she will never forget the horror of September 11; that was the day she learned that soy lattes were extremely high in calories.

Though solipsism is most often associated with post-Cartesian philosophy, the idea dates back to the Sophist Gorgias (ca. 483–378 BCE). In his work *On Nature, or the Non-Existent,* he put forth three propositions:

1) Nothing exists.
2) If anything does exist, it can't be known.
3) If anything does exist, and can be known, it can't be communicated.

For a thing to exist, Gorgias reasoned, it has to have had a beginning. But unless something has always existed, it would have had to emerge from a state of nonexistence at some prior point in time (which is impossible, since something can't come out of nothing). But if it had always existed, then it never began, which is also impossible. Therefore, Gorgias concluded, nothing exists. So much for proposition one. As for propositions two and three, we can never know a thing directly, in and of itself—we can only know our perceptions of it, which are in our minds. Since nobody can know what's in somebody else's mind, we can never communicate about what we see and experience. *Quod erat demonstrandum.*

Of course, solipsism is not a viable belief. It is deeply problematic—from a moral, a psychological, and an epistemological point of view. Only a philosopher could defend the proposition; only a psychopath could actually believe in it. If solipsism is a logical inevitability, the solipsistic position is unfalsifiable, and thus meaningless. Solipsism is a conundrum or a thought experiment, something to tie up your mind in knots; it is also a feeling, an intimation, and as such can be a harbinger of despair or nirvana. But it is not a fact.

Bishop George Berkeley's (1685–1753) solution to the problem of solipsism was a religious one: If we can never be certain that anything exists except as an idea, the ultimate mind isn't the human percipient's but God's, who is aware of all things at all times. Things exist as divine thoughts even when we're not thinking about them. A much-quoted passage in Boswell's *Life of Johnson* vividly illustrates how exasperating to a practical thinker the philosophical turn of mind can be. The great lexicographer Samuel Johnson (1709–84) had one of the sharpest minds of his age, but he was clearly no philosopher.

> After we came out of the church, we stood talking for some time together of Bishop Berkeley's ingenious sophistry to prove the nonexistence of matter, and that every thing in the universe is merely ideal. I observed, that though we are satisfied his doctrine is not true, it is impossible to refute it. I never shall forget the alacrity with which Johnson answered, striking his foot with mighty force against a large stone, till he rebounded from it—"I refute it thus."

SOPHISM

A manifestly false but plausible-sounding argument, like the ones the Sophists, the itinerant teachers of rhetoric and philosophy who appeared in Greece around the fifth century BCE (the Greek word *Sophistēs* literally means "one who does wisdom"), taught their students how to make. When a slick defense lawyer convinces a jury that black is white, the arguments he's using are sophistic.

Though the eminent classicist Bernard Knox has defended the Sophists as "the first professors of humanities," Plato and Aristotle detested them because of the generous fees they extracted from their students and, more important, for their skeptical, relativistic attitude toward the truth. Thus the famous statement of Protagoras (ca. 481–ca. 411 BCE): "Man is the measure of all things, of the things that are, that they are and of things that are not, that they are not." Gorgias famously defended Helen of Troy in front of a Greek jury in a moot court, to demonstrate how a skilled rhetorician should be able to argue any side of an argument. Aristotle accused the Sophists of teaching sham knowledge

for gain; in fact, they instructed the democratic and highly liti-
gious Athenians of the Age of Pericles how to argue like lawyers
and politicians—which is perhaps even more blameworthy.

STOICISM

A philosophical movement that originated in Athens around 300
BCE that took its name from the *stoa poikile,* or "painted porch,"
on the north side of the marketplace of Athens where Zeno of
Citium (333–264 BCE) held his classes. Zeno had been a student
of the Cynic Crates of Thebes (ca. 366–ca. 288 BCE); though he
was not as outrageously eccentric as the Cynics, the essence of
Zeno's wisdom was that one needed to look beyond social conventions and received opinion if one sought the truth, and also
that it behooves one to "steel your sensibilities, so that life shall
hurt you as little as possible."

Zeno's student Chrysippus (280–207 BCE) would develop
Stoicism into a full-fledged philosophy. One's highest aspiration,
he taught, should be to live in accordance with the Logos, or divine reason, that was manifest in all things. Like Buddhists, the
Stoics held that one can transcend the realm of suffering by con-
templating higher things. This freedom from suffering is attained
by disciplining one's desires and feelings, and cultivating a state
of detachment. As the Christian Stoic Epictetus (ca. 55–ca. 135
CE) would write, "Man is disturbed not by things, but by the
views he takes of them."

"The universe is either a confusion, and a mutual involution
of things, and a dispersion; or it is unity and order and providence," wrote the Stoic philosopher and Roman emperor Marcus
Aurelius (121–180 CE).

> If then it is the former, why do I desire to tarry in a fortuitous
> combination of things and such a disorder? And why do I care
> about anything else than how I shall at last become earth? And
> why am I disturbed, for the dispersion of my elements will hap-
> pen whatever I do. But if the other supposition is true, I vener-
> ate, and I am firm, and I trust in him who governs.

STRUCTURALISM

An intellectual movement, primarily derived from the linguistics theories of Ferdinand de Saussure (1857–1913), that examines social structures, mythology, works of art and even human psychology, mathematics, and science, as a set of underlying relationships among their irreducible parts.

The anthropologist Claude Lévi-Strauss (b. 1908) looked to kinship systems to find the basic underlying structures of societies; his many books include *Tristes tropiques* (1955) and *The Raw and the Cooked* (1964). A structuralist literary critic might analyze a poem in terms of the sounds of its words (its phonemes) rather than their dictionary meanings; a novel can be reduced to its basic narrative structure (James Joyce's *Ulysses*, for example, is based on *The Odyssey* and ultimately on Greek myths; *Huckleberry Finn* is the story of the moral growth of a young man, and as such is related to other bildungsromans like Dickens's *Great Expectations* and Thomas Mann's *The Magic Mountain*).

In his many books and essays, which include *Writing Degree Zero* (1953), *Mythologies* (1957), and *The Empire of Signs* (1970), the French semiotician Roland Barthes (1915–1980) extended the New Criticism's notion of an autonomous, autotelic text. Barthes explored not so much the "what" but the "how" of literature—the innumerable ways that language, myth, form, cultural context, and both readers' and writers' personal biographies interact with one another. The result is a text that is not, as Barthes wrote in his seminal essay "The Death of the Author,"

> . . . a line of words releasing a single "theological" meaning (the "message" of the Author-God) but a multi-dimensional space in which a variety of writings, none of them original, blend and clash. The text is a tissue of quotations drawn from the innumerable centres of culture . . . the birth of the reader must be at the cost of the death of the Author.

Poststructuralism was never a formal school; many of its practitioners, such as Barthes, Lévi-Strauss, the psychologist Jacques Lacan (1901–81) (see Lacanism), and the philosopher Michel

Foucault (1926–84), began their intellectual lives as structural-ists. To the extent that it's possible to generalize about poststruc-turalist thought, it does not seek an underlying framework as much as it revels in the process of analysis. Thus, it is both more contextual and less reductive than structuralism. Its insights, many of them acute, tend to be communicated in a dense, multi-layered, often maddeningly opaque prose style replete with neol-ogisms and scientific and philosophical jargon.

Poststructuralists are interested not only in the historical circumstances in which ideas are engendered, but in how those ideas are retrospectively interpreted and how the subjects that are doing the interpreting are themselves formed by a nexus of ideas and brute social forces. Poststructuralists deconstruct literature and in-tellectual systems to show how slippery, how illusory and unstable and relative the idea of any one, definitive "meaning" is. Power rela-tions play an important role: societies' winners not only get to write the histories, they get to interpret them too. In Foucault's words,

> the critical history of thought is neither a history of acquisi-tions nor a history of concealments of truth; it is the history of "veridictions," understood as the forms according to which dis-courses capable of being declared true or false are articulated concerning a domain of things.

Deconstructionism begins with the philosophical/linguistic stance that the meanings of texts are multifarious, indeterminate, and ceaselessly shifting; written language always subverts its au-thors' explicit intentions. Jacques Derrida (1930–2004) described this phenomenon as "the play of *différance*." He coined the word as a portmanteau of the words *differ,* which refers to a separation in space, and *defer,* which refers to a separation in time. It is in the nature of words and language to perpetually displace and de-fer their meanings, he declared; any text can thus be infinitely in-terpreted.

> It is the determination of Being as presence or as beingness that is interrogated by the thought of differance. Such a question

could not emerge and be understood unless the difference between Being and beings were somewhere to be broached. First consequence: differance is not. It is not a present being, however excellent, unique, principal, or transcendent. It governs nothing, reigns over nothing, and nowhere exercises any authority. It is not announced by any capital letter. Not only is there no kingdom of différance, but différance instigates the subversion of every kingdom. Which makes it obviously threatening and infallibly dreaded by everything within us that desires a kingdom, the past or future presence of a kingdom.

A favorite word of the deconstructionists is *aporia,* Greek for "impasse" or "difficulty"; they use it to describe the inevitable collapse of any closely analyzed specimen of language into self-contradiction.

One of Derrida's closest friends and colleagues was Paul de Man (1919–83), who was posthumously discovered to have lived a secret life as a pro-Nazi journalist in his native Belgium. This personal revelation sparked questions as to whether or not de Man had taken up deconstruction because its agnosticism about truth gave him an ethical and philosophical context in which he could reconstruct himself in good conscience. Other important deconstructionists are J. Hillis Miller (b. 1928), Jonathan Culler (b. 1944), and Barbara Johnson (b. 1947).

STURM UND DRANG

German for "storm and stress." A reader might declare that he prefers Jane Austen's quiet wit to the Brontës' Sturm und Drang. Writing about her famous stepbrother Paul's partnership with John Lennon, Ruth McCartney declared that the two "were meant to meet, meant to create and one was designed to play sturm and drang to the other's yin and yang."

The phrase comes from the title of the 1776 play *Der Wirrwarr, oder Sturm und Drang* ("Confusion, or Storm and Stress") by Friedrich Maximilian von Klinger (1752–1831) and was used to characterize the tempestuously emotional early writings of Goethe

(1749–1832), Friedrich Schiller (1759–1805), Johann Gottfried von Herder (1744–1803), and J. M. R. Lenz (1751–92).

SUPERNATURALISM   *See* **Naturalism.**

SUPREMATISM   *See* **Futurism.**

SURREALISM
Influential artistic movement that arose in the late teens and continued through the 1920s. The word literally means "superrealism"; it was coined in 1917 by the poet Guillaume Apollinaire (1880–1918) in his program notes for *Parade,* a ballet that Jean Cocteau (1889–1963), Pablo Picasso (1881–1973), Erik Satie (1866–1925), and Léonide Massine (1896–1979) collaborated on. Surrealistic paintings and poems dredged the subconscious for hallucinatory images that embodied naked truths, unmediated by reason or social conventions.

"Let us not mince words," André Breton (1896–1966) declared in his "Manifesto of Surrealism" (1924). "The marvelous is always beautiful, anything marvelous is beautiful, in fact only the marvelous is beautiful." Breton went on to provide formal definitions for the movement:

> SURREALISM, *n*. Psychic automatism in its pure state, by which one proposes to express—verbally, by means of the written word, or in any other manner—the actual functioning of thought. Dictated by the thought, in the absence of any control exercised by reason, exempt from any aesthetic or moral concern.

> ENCYCLOPEDIA. *Philosophy*. Surrealism is based on the belief in the superior reality of certain forms of previously neglected associations, in the omnipotence of dream, in the disinterested play of thought. It tends to ruin once and for all all other psychic mechanisms and to substitute itself for them in solving all the principal problems of life.

Inspired by the Freudian unconscious, the subversive spirit of Dada, and disgust with the supposed rationality of the "realistic attitude" ("I loathe it," the resolutely antibourgeois Breton, a committed Marxist, declared, "For it is made up of mediocrity, hate, and dull conceit"), surrealism relied on bizarre juxtapositions and naked eroticism for its startling, dreamlike effects. Salvador Dali (1904–89) and Luis Buñuel's (1900–83) film *Un chien andalou,* with its indelible image of a razor slicing across an eye; the genital imagery of Joan Miró (1893–1983); Giorgio de Chirico's (1888–1978) haunting scenes of deserted plazas; Paul Klee's (1879–1940) fabulous creatures; René Magritte's (1898–1967) paradoxical realism; Max Ernst's (1891–1976) grotesque birds all conspire, in Breton's words, to "bring about the state where the distinction between the subjective and the objective loses its necessity and its value."

SYMBOLISM

In its broadest sense, symbolism is something concrete and particular in a work of art standing in for something ideal and general: The albatross in Samuel Taylor Coleridge's (1772–1834) *Rime of the Ancient Mariner* is original sin; the eyes of Dr. T. J. Eckleberg in *The Great Gatsby* of F. Scott Fitzgerald (1896–1940) represent the inscrutable judgment of God.

Symbolism was a major movement in French poetry between the 1870s and 1890s. Its most prominent figures were Paul Verlaine (1844–96), Arthur Rimbaud (1854–91), and Stéphane Mallarmé (1842–98). Inspired by Charles Baudelaire's (1821–67) poem "Correspondences," in which a man crosses a "forest of symbols" in which "perfumes, colors, tones" chant "the ecstasies of spirit and senses," the Symbolists' poems revealed their oblique, often indecipherable images, "little by little," in Mallarmé's words, "so as to evoke a mood." Baudelaire, in turn, had been inspired by the Swedish mystic Emanuel Swedenborg (1688–1772), who believed "that natural things represent spiritual things, and that they correspond."

The German poet Rainer Maria Rilke (1875–1926) was

deeply influenced by the Symbolists, as was the Irish poet W. B. Yeats (1865–1939). Closely aligned to symbolism was aestheticism, which regarded beauty as an end in itself, and sought to purge the arts of every trace of didacticism and bourgeois prettiness. Many of the aesthetes cultivated intense sensations—they relished the gothic horrors of Edgar Allan Poe, experimented with sex and drugs, and obsessed about death. In France, Baudelaire, Gustave Flaubert (1821–80), and of course the Symbolists were aesthetes; in England there was Oscar Wilde (1854–1900), Walter Pater (1839–94), Algernon Charles Swinburne (1837–1909), and Ernest Dowson (1867–1900), among many others. A less flattering name for the aesthetes was the decadents.

In the visual arts, the symbolists (whose work overlaps with expressionism as well as aestheticism) painted dark, spooky, dreamlike images, often evocative of profound sexual anxiety, which anticipate surrealism's overt Freudianism. Some of the best-known aesthetes and Symbolists were Edward Burne-Jones (1833–98), Gustave Moreau (1826–98), James Whistler (1834–1903), Aubrey Beardsley (1872–98), Pierre-Cécile Puvis de Chavannes (1824–98), James Ensor (1860–1949), Edvard Munch (1863–1944), Odilon Redon (1840–1916), and Henri Rousseau (1844–1910).

The hallmark of art nouveau, a wide-ranging, international movement in the decorative arts, graphic design, and architecture as well as in painting, was serpentine vegetal imagery—lush vines grow along the margins of Beardsley's illustrations, often blending with women's long hair. Many art nouveau artists, such as Henri de Toulouse-Lautrec (1864–1901); the Catalan architect Antonio Gaudi (1852–1926), who, though traditionally religious, evolved a vast private symbolic vocabulary; and the Czech painter and graphic designer Alfons Mucha (1860–1939), are also considered to be Symbolists or aesthetes. The secessionists—artists who dropped out of the academies of fine arts in Berlin, Munich, and Vienna in the 1890s—are frequently classified under more than one of these categories. The best known of the secessionists were Gustav Klimt (1862–1918), Oskar Kokoschka (1886–1980), Egon Schiele (1890–1918), and Max Liebermann (1847–1935).

TRANSCENDENTALISM

A nineteenth-century American philosophical and literary movement that took its name from Kant's transcendental idealism; its chief exponents were Ralph Waldo Emerson (1803–82), Margaret Fuller (1810–50), Henry David Thoreau (1817–62), and Amos Bronson Alcott (1799–1888). Emerson wrote in 1842:

> The Transcendentalist adopts the whole connection of spiritual doctrine.
>
> He believes in miracle, in the perpetual openness of the human mind to new influx of light and power; he believes in inspiration, and in ecstasy . . . he resists all attempts to palm other rules and measures on the spirit than its own.

Though politically progressive and abolitionist, the transcendentalists tended to be more austere than the European Romantics. *Walden* (1854), Thoreau's classic account of the year he spent living in solitude and self-sufficiency in the woods outside of Concord, is as homely and practical as it is visionary; Emerson's essays, poetry and sermons (he began his career as a Unitarian minister) are hortatory and inspirational but unfailingly decorous. An exception is the ecstatically earthy, blatantly homoerotic poetry of Walt Whitman (1819–92).

UTILITARIANISM

Philosophical school, founded by Jeremy Bentham (1748–1832) and further developed by John Stuart Mill (1806–73), which holds that human beings apply a "hedonic calculus" to any activity they undertake, which weighs its potential for causing happiness against the unhappiness that might result. Although manual labor, for example, is inherently unpleasant, people choose to work as long as the pay they receive more than compensates for the misery it causes. Though education is an expensive and time-consuming investment, it promises generous returns—not just in income but in spiritual satisfaction, which is the highest form of happiness. Since happiness is intrinsically good, utilitarians believed, the state should provide a social system that guarantees, in Joseph

Priestly's (1733–1804) famous phrase, "the greatest happiness for the greatest number." The word *happiness* refers not just to sensual gratification and wealth but, especially in Mill's writings, to intellectual, aesthetic, spiritual, and moral fulfillment.

Utilitarianism is often characterized as reductive and heartless, especially in Herbert Spencer's (1820–1903) social Darwinist applications, in which the "happiness" of the greatest number is preserved by the extinction of their "unfit" neighbors. Nevertheless, Bentham was a consistent advocate of progressive judicial and penal reforms as well as an extension of voting rights, on the understanding that the certain benefits of good citizenship would be more attractive to the poor than the vagaries of the criminal life.

VORTICISM

Short-lived movement in British art originating around 1914 when the painter and novelist Wyndham Lewis (1882–1957) and the painter and critic Roger Fry (1866–1934) parted ways and Lewis formed the Rebel Art Centre. Deeply influenced by the cubists and the Italian futurists, with their hypermodern, machine-age geometries, Ezra Pound (1885–1972) coined the movement's name and edited the journal *Blast* (which only had two issues); Wyndham Lewis penned the *Vorticist Manifesto*. Though the Vorticists shared the futurists' fascination with speed and technology, instead of depicting motion through sequences of images as the futurists did, they captured it in a single, whirlpoollike image (the vortex, in Ezra Pound's words, being "the point of maximum energy").

Other artists associated with the movement include C. R. W. Nevinson (1889–1946), William Roberts (1895–1980), Edward Wadsworth (1889–1949), Jacob Epstein (1880–1959), Henri Gaudier-Brzeska (1891–1915), Jessica Dismorr (1885–1939), and Helen Saunders (1885–1963).

Science

⟨∞⟩

ALCHEMY

The quests to transmute base metal into gold, to discover a universal cure for disease (a panacea), and to concoct an elixir of immortality. Alchemy was practiced in pharaonic Egypt; there are ancient Chinese and Indian alchemical traditions as well. The holy grail of alchemy was the philosopher's stone, the catalyst that would make these transmutations possible. Like astrology, with which it is intimately associated, alchemy is an ancient esoteric study that has had a tremendous impact on the practice of modern science. Alchemists made many discoveries in metallurgy, medicine, chemistry, and other fields; their experimental protocols anticipated the scientific method.

The Emerald Tablet of Hermes Trismegistus (the mythical Egyptian god and sage who, the Greeks believed, was the founder of alchemy) expresses the underlying rationale of both alchemy and astrology: "Whatever is below is like that which is above, and whatever is above is like that which is below, to accomplish the miracles of one thing." Thus the motions of the stars affect the affairs of the world; the four elements that compose the world (earth, air, fire, and water) also make up the microcosm of the human body.

Roger Bacon (1214–94); Nicolas Flamel (1330–ca. 1417), who has a cameo role in the Harry Potter novels; and Theophrastus Bombastus von Hohenheim (1493–1541), or Paracelsus, were all major alchemists. Tycho Brahe (1546–1601), Robert Boyle (1627–91), and Isaac Newton (1642–1727) practiced alchemy as well.

ANTHROPIC COSMOLOGY

Seemingly a highly sophisticated brief for intelligent design, anthropic cosmology argues that the odds of the big bang producing carbon are vanishingly small. Thus, even if natural selection provides a sufficiently naturalistic explanation for the origin of life on earth, the structure of the universe itself—at a mathematical, quantum level—must have tilted the odds. Life is so unlikely, in other words, that it's hard to believe that it is accidental; the physical laws of the universe somehow conspired to make it inevitable.

The most sophisticated and influential exposition of this theory can be found in John Barrow and Frank Tipler's *The Anthropic Cosmological Principle* (1986), which, drawing on the most cutting-edge theories in cosmology and particle physics, argues that "intelligent information-processing must come into existence in the Universe, and once it comes into existence, it will never die out." Barrow and Tipler are brilliant physicists, and I can't claim to understand an awful lot of what they say. Anthropic cosmology comes out of a context that literally boggles the mind: Some advocates suggest there are multiple universes (not all of which contain life), or that big bangs are happening all the time. Others note that the big bang that produced our own cosmos may be different from other big bangs which produced non-life-sustaining universes. Nonetheless, as compelling—and to people with a religious turn of mind, as reassuring—as the idea that the universe was somehow primed for life on a fundamental level may be, it doesn't rise to the level of scientific theory.

The Nobel Prize–winning physicist Steven Weinberg is sometimes cited as a supporter of anthropic cosmology. Though he admits it has a certain fascination, he is hardly an advocate for it. "Reasoning like this is called 'anthropic,'" he said, in a talk he gave at the Conference on Cosmic Design of the American Association for the Advancement of Science in Washington, D.C. in 1999.

> Sometimes it just amounts to an assertion that the laws of nature are what they are so that we can exist, without further explanation. This seems to me to be little more than mystical

mumbo jumbo. On the other hand, if there really is a large number of worlds in which some constants take different values, then the anthropic explanation of why in our world they take values favorable for life is just common sense, like explaining why we live on the earth rather than Mercury or Pluto . . . One of the great achievements of science has been, if not to make it impossible for intelligent people to be religious, then at least to make it possible for them not to be religious. We should not retreat from this accomplishment.

BEHAVIORISM

A strictly experimental approach to psychology that examines the ways that human behavior is determined by the influences of physical environment rather than innate instincts and drives. Rejecting the subjectivity of the Freudian unconscious as philosophy and mysticism rather than empirical science, behaviorists examine (and manipulate) human behavior as a measurable, virtually physiological phenomenon.

John B. Watson (1878–1958), who taught at the University of Chicago and Johns Hopkins until his academic career was cut short by scandal (he divorced his wife and married one of his research assistants, whereupon he embarked on a successful second career in advertising), laid out the basic tenets of behaviorism in his books *Psychology from the Standpoint of a Behaviorist* (1919) and *Behaviorism* (1925).

B. F. Skinner (1904–90), who taught at the University of Minnesota, Indiana University, and Harvard, became enormously famous, both as an experimental scientist and as a media figure. He was notorious for the so-called "air crib," in which one of his daughters slept during her infancy (to give her the benefits of a thoroughly controlled environment) and for the countercultural ideas he espoused in his best-selling books *Walden II* (a fictional account of a utopian community based on behaviorist principles, published in 1948—ironically, the same year that George Orwell finished writing his dystopic novel *1984*) and *Beyond Freedom and*

Dignity (1971). The Skinner box, a cage in which animals are taught that certain actions (pulling a lever, say) will produce certain rewards and punishments under specific conditions (the scientific name for this is *operant conditioning*), has yielded many behavior-modification techniques, such as aversion therapy for sex offenders, which are still widely used today.

BROWNIAN MOTION

The random movements of minute particles in liquids. The phenomenon takes its name from the English botanist Robert Brown (1773–1858), who microscopically observed the zigzag motions of pollen grains and spores when they were suspended in water. When grains of inorganic dust moved in the same manner, he was able to rule out the explanation that the spores and grains were somehow "swimming," but the cause of the phenomenon remained an enigma until 1908 when Albert Einstein (1879–1955) hypothesized that it resulted from the random bombardment of the particles by the much-smaller molecules of the fluid. Jean Perrin (1870–1942) tested his supposition experimentally, proving Einstein correct and confirming, at long last, the main lineaments of John Dalton's (1766–1844) controversial atomic theory. Brownian motion can be modeled mathematically: the equations have been applied to such practical problems as predicting fluctuations in the stock market and charting the seepage of oil through porous rocks.

BUTTERFLY EFFECT   *See* Chaos Theory.

CATASTROPHISM

As opposed to gradualism or uniformitarianism, catastrophism is the notion in natural science that the earth was created spontaneously in the not terribly distant past and has since been subject to sudden violent changes—and that these catastrophic events account for both its geological features and the presence of fossils of extinct creatures. Bishop James Ussher (1581–1656), the Anglican primate of Ireland, had calculated, from the chronologies of the Bible and other sources, that the earth came into being on the evening before

October 23 in 4004 BCE. That time line is more or less what the young earth creationists believe in today. In their reckoning, Noah's flood carved out the Grand Canyon; fossils weren't laid down over millennia in neat layers but were violently stirred into the sediments by the floodwaters that engulfed the entire planet.

Thus the creationist Jonathan Sarfati, Ph.D., in his best-selling *Refuting Evolution* (1999):

> Because sedimentation usually occurs slowly today, it is *assumed* that it must have always occurred slowly . . . The philosophy that processes have always occurred at roughly constant rates . . . is often called *uniformitarianism* . . . A cataclysmic globe-covering (and fossil-forming) flood would have eroded huge quantities of sediment, and deposited them elsewhere. Many organisms would have been buried very quickly and fossilized . . . So when we start from the bias that the Bible is God's Word and is thus true, we can derive reasonable interpretations of the data . . . Ironically, NASA scientists accept that there have been "catastrophic floods" on Mars that carved out canyons although no liquid water is present today. But they deny that a global flood happened on earth, where there is enough water to cover the whole planet to a depth of 1.7 miles . . . If it weren't for the fact that the Bible teaches it, they probably wouldn't have any problem with a global flood on earth.

The theory of uniformitarianism that Sarfati summarily dismisses dates back to the eighteenth-century chemist and geologist James Hutton (1726–97), who argued in his many scientific papers and books (his unfinished *summa* was called *Theory of the Earth*) that the same processes that can be observed creating changes in the earth's surface today—the actions of winds, glaciers, tides, pressure, and volcanism—were also operative in the past. Darwin's friend Charles Lyell (1797–1875) would expand on Hutton's ideas in his seminal *Principles of Geology*, arguing not only that present geological processes could be extrapolated into the past, but that it was reasonable to assume that they had always occurred at the same rates and intensity. By insisting on a uniform application of observable laws, uniformity or gradualism made logical sense, since it allowed for a much older earth than Bishop Ussher's and the Bible's time line had; the theory gave erosion and evolution and tectonic shifts, among many other processes, enough time to work. But by categorically denying the possibility of catastrophe, it distorted the truth.

Scientists today allow for frequent catastrophic interruptions in the gradual processes that are shaping the planet. Meteor impacts, cosmic-ray bombardments, sudden changes in the composition of the earth's atmospheric gases, climate change (like the human-induced global warming we are living through today) might radically alter the direction of these processes, accounting for mass extinctions and geological anomalies. Ice ages carved out new features in the earth relatively quickly; ice dams held back vast seas. When they melted, the resulting deluges (more local than Noah's but in some cases even more devastating) changed the landscapes they flooded beyond recognition. The paleontologists Stephen Jay Gould and Niles Eldredge's notion of punctuated equilibrium injects catastrophism into the theory of natural selection. Most species, they argued, were relatively stable over time; changes occurred on the margins of their territories, where climatological or other environmental differences were significant enough to encourage natural selection. When catastrophes such as climate changes wiped out the bulk of a species in the central part of their habitat, their more evolved relatives on the edges of their niches were more likely to survive and move back into the center. Although they had evolved gradually, the extinctions and replacements were comparatively sudden. The fossil record thus seems to show long periods of stasis punctuated by bursts of activity.

CHAOS THEORY

A subdivision of dynamic systems theory, chaos theory uses mathematical algorithms to extract useful information from seemingly random events. The mathematics of chaos dates back to Henri Poincaré (1854–1912), who wrote:

It may happen that small differences in the initial conditions produce very great ones in the final phenomena. A small error in the former will produce an enormous error in the latter. Prediction becomes impossible, and we have the fortuitous phenomenon.

Modern chaos theory began in the early 1960s, when the meteorologist Edward Lorenz noted that minute changes in initial variables can result in massive changes as weather systems develop. His memorable name for this phenomenon is the butterfly effect, in which the fluttering of a butterfly's wings can set off a cascading series of atmospheric events that causes a tornado to develop halfway around the world. The Lorenz attractor uses a series of differential equations to graphically illustrate the ways dynamic systems can evolve; by studying these patterns, scientists can infer probabilities, if not hard-and-fast predictions. The mathematical physicist Mitchell Feigenbaum discovered in the 1970s the Feigenbaum constant, a ratio that allows one to calculate the rate at which dynamic systems approach a truly random state.

Fractals—complex patterns in which any one part looks like the whole (a crude example would be a twig, which looks like a branch, which looks like a tree)—are often discernible in dynamic systems. The mathematician Benoît Mandelbrot observed that the patterns of daily fluctuations of cotton prices often repeated themselves over larger periods of time. When applied to fractal geometry, the Mandelbrot set ($z \to z^2 + c$) allows scientists to discern underlying patterns in a great variety of phenomena, like the cellular structure of the human body, the spread of infectious diseases, and the flow of information in a computer system.

CHOMSKYAN LINGUISTICS

After Noam Chomsky, who has been on the faculty of MIT for more than fifty years. Chomsky gained notoriety in recent years for his radical politics (his book *Hegemony or Survival: America's Quest for Global Dominance* leaped onto best-seller lists when President

Hugo Chávez of Venezuela cited it in a speech at the United Nations in 2006), but his enormous academic reputation is based on his revolutionary work in linguistics. Chomsky's theory of transformational grammar, or as it is sometimes called, generative or transformational-generative grammar, posits deep structures that are common to all languages and correspond to innate capacities of the human brain. This notion clashes with the behaviorist model of the infant's mind as a blank slate. According to Chomsky, children come into the world knowing the basic rules of syntax and grammar. What they learn when they acquire language are the vocabulary and idiosyncratic features of the particular languages they are exposed to. Some of Chomsky's most influential publications on linguistics are *Syntactic Structures* (1957), *Language and Mind* (1972), and *Knowledge of Language* (1986).

COSMOLOGICAL CONSTANT
An equation Einstein introduced to his theory of general relativity to create a static model of the universe (without that adjustment, general relativity predicted that the universe should be expanding or contracting). Einstein called it "his biggest blunder" when the astronomer Edwin Hubble (1889–1953) proved that the universe was, in fact, expanding. The recent discovery that the universe's expansion seems to be accelerating has brought the problem of the cosmological constant back to the fore; the mystery is that the formula that best comports with observational evidence cannot be derived from particle physics. The solution may lie in the multiverses of string theory; some scientists attribute the anomaly to the anthropic principle, the universe's mysterious amenability to the creation of intelligent life.

DARWINISM
Though Darwinism is often used as shorthand for the theory of evolution, Charles Darwin (1809–82) was not the first naturalist to suggest that living things had gradually changed over time. Five hundred years before the birth of Christ, the Greek philosopher Anaximander theorized that life evolved from a primal ooze. In

1801 the Chevalier de Lamarck (see Lamarckism) had argued that
life possesses an innate tendency to become more complex. Darwin's grandfather Erasmus Darwin (1731–1802) published a book
called *Zoonomia,* which suggested that "all animals have a similar
origin, viz. from a single living filament" and that "if this gradual
production of the species and genera of animals be assented to, a
contrary circumstance may be supposed to have occurred,
namely, that some kinds by the great changes of the elements may
have been destroyed."

Darwin's great contribution to science is the theory of natural selection. He rightly shares credit for this epochal discovery
with Alfred Russel Wallace (1823–1913), who, though he formulated the idea decades after Darwin had, almost beat him to publication with it. Natural selection (which the philosopher Daniel
Dennett has called "the single best idea anyone has ever had") argues that when the small variations that naturally occur within a
species help an animal or plant survive and reproduce (or make
it more attractive to mates, with the same result), those variations
will eventually spread throughout the entire species. As the variations accumulate and less advantageously endowed kin die out,
new species are born.

As with all new scientific paradigms, the theory of natural selection unified a number of existing ideas. Once one considered
the possibility that all living things were descended from a common source, the taxonomic system of Carl Linnaeus (1707–78)
began to look like a family tree. James Hutton (1726–97) and
Charles Lyell's (1797–1875) theory of geological uniformitarianism vastly extended the time line of existence, giving natural selection the time it needed to work its gradual changes.

In contrast with Lamarck's teleological ideas, natural selection explains the physical mechanism of evolution. Darwin's
Origin of Species (1859) also presented a vast quantity of physical
evidence from his fieldwork on the *Beagle* and his subsequent
decades of research to back it up: the existence of vestigial organs,
the geographical distribution of species, paleontological evidence
for extinctions, etc. What's more, he reached his conclusions be-

fore the process of inheritance was fully understood (Gregor Mendel's studies of peas were published in a small way in 1866, but they weren't generally disseminated until a dozen years after Darwin's death; DNA wouldn't be discovered until 1953). The synthesis of genetics and Darwinism is known as neo-Darwinism.

Social Darwinism, the idea that natural selection acts as a principle of improvement in human societies, is associated with Herbert Spencer (1820–1903), who coined the phrase "survival of the fittest." Darwin's half cousin Francis Galton (1822–1911), a pioneer psychometrician as well as a geographer, anthropologist, meteorologist and inventor (he invented the weather map and the silent dog whistle), coined the word *eugenics* (from the Greek *eu,* "good," and *genos,* "birth") as well as the phrase "nature versus nurture." Galton thought it would be good policy to provide financial incentives to the members of gifted families to marry each other early and have lots of children. Eugenics, already dubious as science, took a sinister turn in the twentieth century when eugenicists advised the American Congress on quotas to apply to inferior racial stocks when they were drafting the Immigration Act of 1924. The Nazis' monstrous programs to improve "racial hygiene" would deal it a fatal blow.

In contrast to the eugenicists' barnyard vision of human progress, Pierre Teilhard de Chardin (1881–1955), a Jesuit priest and paleontologist who was silenced by the church for his attempts to reconcile science with his faith, believed that evolution was a natural process that led to mystical transcendence. In his posthumously published *The Phenomenon of Man,* he wrote:

> Is evolution a theory, a system or a hypothesis? It is much more: it is a general condition to which all theories, all hypotheses, as systems must bow and which they must satisfy henceforth if they are to be thinkable and true. Evolution is a light illuminating all facts, a curve that all lines must follow.

The ultimate goal of evolution, he said, is consciousness. This leads in turn to collective consciousness, then to superconsciousness on "a sidereal scale": the omega point, the all-in-all. "In one manner or the other," he wrote, "it still remains true that, even in the view of a mere biologist, the human epic resembles nothing so much as a way of the Cross."

Evolutionary psychology draws on neuroscience and anthropology for explanations of human behavior. Its underlying assumption is that many of our foibles—particularly in the realm of aggression and mating—are instinctual and serve an adaptive purpose. Since homo sapiens spent much more time living as wild animals than they have as civilized humans, most of these adaptations would have occurred in the distant past. As one evolutionary psychologist put it, we have had plenty of time to evolve instinctive responses to snakes and poisonous insects but only a century to adapt to automobiles.

Two pioneers of the field, Leda Cosmides and John Tooby, recently speculated about evolutionary psychology's future potential:

> Just as one can now flip open *Gray's Anatomy* to any page and find an intricately detailed depiction of some part of our evolved species-typical morphology, we anticipate that in 50 or 100 years one will be able to pick up an equivalent reference work for psychology and find in it detailed information-processing descriptions of the multitude of evolved species-typical adaptations of the human mind, including how they are mapped onto the corresponding neuroanatomy and how they are constructed by developmental programs.

EUGENICS *See* Darwinism.

FREUDIANISM

The psychological ideas and the therapeutic methods of the Austrian-born neurologist Sigmund Freud (1856–1939), the founder of psychoanalysis. "I am actually not a man of science at all," Freud is said to have remarked to his friend Wilhelm Fliess, "I am nothing but a conquistador by temperament, an adventurer." (Fliess, an otolaryngologist, had his own theories about the etiology and treatment of nervous diseases. Bizarrely enough,

Fliess believed that nose surgery could cure many of them; he also believed that there were physiological connections between the nose and the genitals.)

Freud's many critics today would second his self-characterization as a nonscientist. The literary critic Frederick Crews, for example, once an ardent Freudian, has disavowed the entire psychoanalytic enterprise in a number of polemical articles and books, dismissing Freud himself as an out-and-out mountebank. Here he is in a televised interview with Harry Kreisler in 1999:

> Freud portrayed himself as a person who reluctantly but courageously faced the twin demons of sex and aggression and, like Prometheus or like some other Greek god who goes into the underworld, he came back to Earth with these pieces of dangerous knowledge and he tamed them and made them accessible to us so that we can now be cured of our neurotic ailments, thanks to him. He turned himself into a god, a kind of man-god, and people fell for it, and at a certain point I fell for it.

There is no denying that some of Freud's key theories are unfalsifiable (as the philosopher of science Karl Popper defines a nonscientific statement), and that he encouraged a cult of personality among his acolytes, such as Carl Jung (1875–1961), Ernest Jones (1879–1958), Sándor Ferenczi (1873–1933), and Otto Rank (1884–1939), many of whom he later ostracized for straying from the reservation. Nonetheless, Freud's ideas about the structure of the human mind, the origins of mental illness, and the unconscious influence of sexuality on psychic development, remain enormously influential. If his reputation as a healer was exaggerated, his status as an original thinker is secure.

Freud first became interested in hysteria when he trained with the great French neurologist Jean-Martin Charcot (1825–93) in Paris. Hypnosis's power to induce physical effects, such as paralysis, through mere suggestion led him to the idea that some illnesses might originate in the mind. Since many of his female patients had told him about the incestuous sexual abuse they'd suffered as children, he at first assumed that their problems were caused by trauma. Then, in what was a seminal break-through in psychoanalysis (and for many advocates of the sexu-ally abused, an unforgivable betrayal), Freud decided that his patients were recalling long-repressed fantasies and desires rather than actual events. Children, he concluded, even infants, are filled with sexual feelings. Little boys lust for their mothers; little girls, for their fathers. Boys fear that their fathers would castrate them if they suspected their desire; girls, who are in ef-fect already castrated, envy their father's phalluses. The family drama of King Oedipus is universal, if unacknowledged.

Repressed desires are only displaced, they inevitably return in disguise, as Freud argued in his seminal *The Interpretation of Dreams* (1899) and *The Psychopathology of Everyday Life* (1904), which analyzed seemingly innocuous slips of the tongue and lapses of memory. Freud went on to articulate a new account of sexual development. An infant's orality, the desire for the breast, is succeeded by the toddler's anality, in which the natural plea-sures of defecation conflict with the repressions of potty training. Last, is the phallic phase. When an individual gets stuck in one of these early phases, dysfunction is the result.

Freud divided the psyche into three distinct, constantly con-tending parts: the id (or the "it"), the primal animal instinct for sense gratification and aggression; the superego, the seat of con-science and socialization; and last, the ego, the conscious self, a product of the ongoing dialectic between the psyche's uncon-scious constituents. Not all repression is bad—sublimated aggres-sion and guilt feelings can fuel creativity. In books like *Civiliza-tion and Its Discontents* and *Moses and Monotheism,* Freud applied his ideas about the individual psyche to human culture, which he feared (with good reason—already dying of jaw cancer, he would be forced to flee Vienna after the Nazi *Anschluss*) was teetering on the brink of barbarism.

In psychoanalysis, the therapist listens to the patient's free as-sociations and interprets them, gently leading him or her to talk about significant issues. If all goes well, the patient transfers child-hood feelings onto the therapist (literally falling in love). By recapitulating his or her formative experiences in a safe context, they come to terms with them. Freud recognized that the therapist often reciprocates the patient's romantic feelings; he called this countertransference. Though it presents dangerous temptations, it also offers opportunities for the therapist to gain a deeper understanding of the patient.

Classic Freudian psychoanalysis can be incredibly expensive because it's so open-ended—patients typically remain in analysis for years. In this era of penny-pinching HMOs, focused cognitive behavioral therapy, and highly effective medications like Prozac (not to mention more open-minded attitudes about sexuality), it is an experience that fewer and fewer people are likely to experience firsthand.

GAIAISM

Also known as earth systems science, Gaiaism is the controversial theory developed in the 1960s by the medical doctor, inventor, biologist, atmospheric scientist, and self-styled "geophysiologist" James E. Lovelock (b. 1919) and Lynn Margulis (b. 1938), a cell biologist and the originator of endosymbiotic theory.

In the mid-1960s, Lovelock was working at the Jet Propulsion Laboratory in Pasadena, California, designing life detection sensors for the Viking Mars probe. It occurred to him that life was unmistakably present on earth because its atmosphere contains so much free oxygen. What made earth's atmosphere so active, he speculated, was the presence of life; Mars had settled into a chemical equilibrium because it was lifeless. He recommended that NASA scrub the mission.

Lovelock's office mate Carl Sagan (1934–96) disagreed with Lovelock's theory, but Sagan's then-wife, Lynn Margulis, was intrigued. Together they developed the grand ecological theory that the Nobel Prize–winning novelist William Golding (1911–93) would dub Gaia, after the Greek god of the earth. In Lovelock's words, the earth is

A planet that has always, since its origins nearly four billion years ago, kept itself a fit home for the life that happened upon it and I thought that it did so by homeostasis, the wisdom of the body, just as you and I keep our temperature and chemistry constant . . . Evolution is a tightly coupled dance, with life and the material environment as partners. From the dance emerges the entity Gaia.

To the delight of New Agers and the exasperation of some scientists, who regard Gaia as the pathetic fallacy writ large, Lovelock has called the earth a superorganism. Margulis is less hyperbolic. Gaia is not a creature, she says, but "the series of interacting ecosystems that compose a single huge ecosystem at the Earth's surface. Period."

GRADUALISM *See* **Catastrophism.**

HOMEOPATHY

Medical practice that prescribes metals, herbs, minerals, and other substances in extremely diluted forms. If used at full strength, these remedies would exacerbate the symptoms; in microscopic doses, they are believed to effect cures.

The first homeopathic physician was a German doctor named Samuel Hahnemann (1755–1843), who observed, using himself as a guinea pig, that a healthy person will develop the symptoms of malaria when administered large doses of quinine, but when given to someone who already has the disease, quinine effects a cure. This led Hahnemann to formulate the law of similars, *similia similibus curantur* ("likes are cured by likes"). He published his first paper on the subject in 1796. A few years later, after extensive testing and documentation, which was probably the most scientific approach to pharmacology ever attempted, he concluded that medicines become more efficacious when they are given in very small doses and diluted—a process he called dynamization-potentiation. He published his magnum opus, *Organon der rationalen Heilkunst* (or *Organon of Rational Medicine*) in 1810.

Though homeopathy is still very popular among patients, especially in Great Britain, most modern scientists attribute its success to the placebo effect. Hahnemann himself noted that many of his cures didn't seem to stick; after their treatments were concluded, a good many of his patients' symptoms recurred. Still, it's worth remembering that Hahnemann's rejection of the notion of the four humors (blood, associated with the liver; black bile, associated with the gall bladder; yellow bile, associated with the spleen; and phlegm, associated with the brain and lungs), which dated back to Hippocrates and had been a staple of medieval medicine, was not only of scientific importance but of great benefit to his patients. Until Hahnemann's time, doctors assumed that most diseases resulted from an excess of one of the humors. This was treated by violent purges and bleedings, which often proved fatal. If some homeopathic remedies are so diluted that their active substance is chemically almost undetectable, that's not such a bad thing from a scientific point of view either. Many homeopathic cures would be quite dangerous taken at full strength.

Nineteenth-century homeopaths, working before the germ theory of disease, assumed that their tinctures effected spiritual forces active in the body; homeopaths today believe their treatments stimulate the body's immune system to heal itself.

JUNGIANISM

Psychological, religious, and literary ideas of Carl Jung (1875–1961), a Swiss psychiatrist who as a young man was considered the heir apparent to Freud, but formally broke with him in 1914. Jung's notion of the subconscious was markedly different from Freud's. He posited a deeper dimension that included archetypes belonging to the collective unconsciousness of humanity, an idea that had an enormous influence on Joseph Campbell's (1904–87) popular writings on myth. The goal of Jungian psychoanalysis is integration and individuation, the reconciliation of the conscious and the unconscious, the inner and the outer, the spiritual and the animal, the transcendent and the mundane aspects of the personality. The language of the Jungian unconscious is symbols, which can be found in dreams, world literature, myths, and religion. Jung's anima, or the feminine side of the psyche, is roughly akin to the Shekhinah in Kabbalah—it is the divine spirit, and as such can be a guide to the unconscious.

Complexes are nodes of unconscious associations that lie behind patterns of behavior. Someone who refuses to grow up, who clings to his or her youthful idealism, may have a *puer* complex; in other words, a dominant symbol in their unconscious is the *puer*, or the eternal youth. This complex only rises to the level of pathology if it interferes with the patient's ability to live a stable life. If it doesn't, it is simply noted as an aspect of the patient's personality.

In Jungian psychology, introversion and extroversion are characteristic modes of thinking and feeling. Introverts are intuitive; they are in closer touch with their inner life than the outer world; extroverts are the opposite. An integrated personality is equally comfortable in both realms. These categories provide the basis for the standardized Myers-Briggs personality assessment tests, which are widely administered in schools and corporate human resources departments today. Jung also wrote on such diverse subjects as synchronicity (meaningful coincidences), alchemy, Gnosticism, eastern religion, and flying saucers.

LAMARCKISM

The commonsensical (but completely mistaken) belief that acquired characteristics can be inherited. Giraffes' necks aren't long because generations of giraffes strained to reach high-growing leaves; it is rather because longer-necked giraffes can reach more leaves than their shorter-necked peers. Since such fortunately endowed giraffes are better nourished, they're more likely to reproduce and pass that attribute on to their progeny, who in turn pass the gene that controls neck length on to theirs.

Lamarckism is named after Jean-Baptiste-Pierre-Antoine de Monet, chevalier de Lamarck (1744–1829), a renowned botanist, zoologist, and early proponent of the theory of evolution. Unlike Darwin, Lamarck didn't believe that all life was descended from a single ancestor; rather, he posited that life possessed an innate teleological tendency to progress toward greater complexity. In combination with this general attribute, he theorized, environmental pressures propelled specific changes in species by causing them to either strengthen already existing capacities (for instance, the rodent that would evolve into a bat, already endowed with excellent hearing, would have its natural sonar evolve) or shed those attributes they no longer require (as the bat's ears developed, its eyesight atrophied).

LYSENKOISM

A wrong-headed approach to science that pays closer attention to ideology than evidence, Lysenkoism takes its name from the Soviet biologist and agronomist Trofim Denisovich Lysenko (1898–1976). While president of the Lenin All-Union Academy of Agricultural Sciences and head of the Institute of Genetics of the Soviet Academy of Sciences, Lysenko saw to it that his agricultural methods were widely applied and adopted, with disastrous consequences.

Wrongly assuming that acquired characteristics could be inherited, he created "new" strains of wheat and other crops by grafting, and insisted that his technique of "vernalizing" wheat would enable it to mature in the spring and thus increase yields, ignoring scientific evidence that suggested otherwise and ruthlessly purging his peers who practiced the "bourgeois pseudo-science" of genetics. Hundreds of them were imprisoned and died, including the renowned botanist Nikolai Ivanovich Vavilov (1887–1943).

Though contemporary biographers now believe that Lysenko was driven more by ego and stupidity than ideology, his Lamarckian ideas undoubtedly comported better with the deterministic theories of the Marxists than the politically neutral discoveries of the geneticists. Lysenkoism has thus become the byword for Marxist "science."

MESMERISM

After Friedrich Anton Mesmer (1734–1815), whose medical ideas were based on the theory of animal magnetism. Drawing heavily on the theories of the British doctor Richard Mead (1673–1754), Mesmer theorized that illness was caused by disruptions of the flow of an invisible magnetic fluid in the body. When a patient was

placed in a trance state induced by music and repetitive suggestions, a therapist could use his own magnetism to redirect the patients' fluid flow. Mesmer's claims were studied, and rejected, by a
panel of distinguished scientists appointed by Louis XVI, which
included Benjamin Franklin (1706–90) and the father of modern
chemistry, Antoine-Laurent Lavoisier (1743–94).

In 1843, in his book *Neurypnology,* the English physician
James Braid coined the word *hypnosis* (after Hypnos, the Greek
god of sleep) to describe the suggestible trance state that Mesmer
induced in his patients. Though Braid rejected the theory of animal magnetism, he saw many clinical applications for the technique, which could help patients endure the pain of surgery and
alleviate the symptoms of nervous diseases. Freud would use
hypnosis in some of his early cases. Though controversial and in-
completely understood, hypnosis is used to this day to prepare
patients for anesthesia, to help women through the rigors of
childbirth, and by the use of posthypnotic suggestions, to help
addicts overcome their cravings.

One dangerous feature of hypnosis is that some especially
suggestible patients will recall what they've talked or heard about
while in a trance state as a legitimate memory. A forgetful witness
to a crime who is hypnotized might "recall" a memory that was
actually suggested to them; some overeager therapists have inadvertently or irresponsibly planted recollections of childhood sexual abuse or abductions by aliens in the minds of their already
vulnerable and troubled patients.

MOORE'S LAW
After Gordon Moore, cofounder of Intel. In 1965, in a brief magazine article about the future of electronics, he noted that the
power of integrated circuits had roughly doubled every year since
their invention, while their cost had stayed roughly the same.
"Certainly over the short term, this rate can be expected to continue, if not to increase," he predicted. "Over the longer term, the
rate of increase is a bit more uncertain, although there is no reason to believe it will not remain nearly constant for at least 10

years." Ten years later, in 1975, he emended the rate of increase to every two years. In fact, over the past thirty years, the speed of doubling has averaged about eighteen months. In an interview in *Techworld* on the fortieth anniversary of his prediction, the now-retired Moore admitted that the "law" that bears his name won't hold true much longer. "It can't continue forever," he said. "The nature of exponentials is that you push them out and eventually disaster happens. In terms of size [of transistor] you can see that we're approaching the size of atoms . . . but . . . we have another ten to twenty years before we reach a fundamental limit."

OBJECT RELATIONS THEORY

School of psychology and psychotherapy that emphasizes relationships rather than frustrated instinctual drives as an explanation for neuroses. A child (the subject) who fails to form satisfying, balanced relationships with his parents or other caregivers (objects) is likely to project that failed relationship onto new objects—friends, lovers, spouses—and recapitulate it over and over again in the course of his or her adult life. Objects can be conceptualized as themselves or as a synecdoche (in which a significant part of the object stands in for the whole—a breast for the mother, say, or a phallus for the father). Objects are not only humans—stuffed animals, pets, toys, and other transitional objects play an important role in childhood individuation.

The goal of the Object Relations therapist is to help patients consciously resolve their childhood issues, rather than unconsciously reenact them. A boy who felt overprotected by his mother might have failed to develop a sense of independence; in adult life he might cling inappropriately to his spouse (or inappropriately resent her). A child who is neglected or abused by his or her caregivers may defensively interpret his pain as an expression of love; such a child is likely to form sadomasochistic attachments in later life.

Melanie Klein (1882–1960), D. W. Winnicott (1896–1971), and Otto Kernberg (b. 1928) are all important figures in Object Relations Theory.

OCCAM'S RAZOR

Also known as the principle of parsimony. Named after the English Scholastic William of Occam, also known as William of Ockham (1285–ca. 1349), who wrote, "Pluralitas non est ponenda sine neccesitate," or "Plurality should not be assumed unnecessarily." In other words, if you're trying to explain something, don't make your explanations more complicated than they have to be; similarly, if you must choose between alternative hypotheses, start out with the one that requires the fewest assumptions—if for no other reason than it will be the easiest to test.

Skeptics frequently use Occam's razor to slice paranormal claims down to size. For instance, when we see a photograph of a flying saucer on the cover of a supermarket tabloid, two possible explanations leap to mind: (1) It really is a picture of a space ship, or (2) The photograph is a fake. Both hypotheses offer possible explanations, but the first requires a plurality of supporting assumptions. We need to posit a point of origin for the space ship, a civilization to build it, a technology to power it, etc. For the second explanation, we need only assume the mendaciousness of the magazine's editors.

Occam's razor isn't a law—it's a heuristic tool, or as Carl Sagan put it, "a convenient rule of thumb." As the development of quantum physics in the twentieth century has amply demonstrated, the correct explanation for a phenomenon doesn't always turn out to be the most intuitive or the easiest to understand; sometimes the seemingly least likely explanation turns out to be true. If hostile aliens ever do train their laser beams on our cities, Occam's razor won't protect us from them.

PHLOGISTON THEORY

From the Greek word *phlogistos,* "inflammable." Phlogiston theory, formulated by Johann Joachim Becher (1635–82) and elaborated upon by George Ernst Stahl (1660–1734), proposed that all combustible materials contain a colorless, odorless, weightless substance called phlogiston, which is released when they are burned, or "dephlogistated." The chemist Antoine-Laurent

Lavoisier (1743–94) discovered the role that oxygen plays in combustion, disproving the existence of phlogiston.

PLATE TECTONICS

Frank B. Taylor (1860–1939) proposed the theory of continental drift as early as 1912; the German geophysicist Alfred Wegener (1880–1930) marshaled evidence for it in successive editions of his book *The Origin of Continents and Oceans* starting in 1915. Though geographers had long noted that Africa and South America seemed to fit together like pieces of a jigsaw puzzle, and paleontologists and biologists had observed that the distribution patterns of some fossils and living species suggested a prior connection between the continents, Taylor and Wegener's precocious theories were summarily rejected.

It wasn't until the 1960s that the wider theory of plate tectonics was proposed and confirmed, revolutionizing earth science and confirming Taylor and Wegener. Plate tectonics argues that the surface of the earth consists of more than a dozen large plates that are "floating" atop the earth's mantle. Convection currents within the mantle drive the plates to move at a speed of some one to ten centimeters per year. When the plates diverge, new oceanic crust is created (the sea floor literally spreads); when they collide, mountains may be pushed up or if one plate is thinner it may be subducted beneath the thicker one (which causes oceanic trenches and volcanos). When two plates slip against each other laterally, they "stick" at times; the pressure released when they jerk apart causes earthquakes.

PRINCIPLE OF INDETERMINACY   *See* Uncertainty Principle.

PUNCTUATED EQUILIBRIUM   *See* Catastrophism.

RED SHIFT

An optical phenomenon in astronomy. When an object is moving away from earth, its visible light shifts to the red end of the spectrum, where the wavelengths are longer (just as the sound an object makes as it moves away from you seems to drop in pitch as its wavelengths lengthen because of the Doppler effect). The red shift in distant objects was first noticed around the turn of the last century; in 1929, Edwin Hubble (1889–1953) hypothesized that it was because those objects were moving away from earth. Father Georges-Henri Lemaître (1894–1966) proposed that the universe was expanding from a "primeval atom," a notion that was elaborated on in 1948 when George Gamow (1904–68) hypothesized that that primeval atom had exploded and that the elements were forged in its heat. Arno Penzias and Robert Wilson would win the 1978 Nobel Prize for their discovery of cosmic microwave background radiation, which confirmed that primal explosion (or as it came to be known, the big bang).

STOCKHOLM SYNDROME
In psychology, the (by no means universal) tendency of hostages in life-threatening situations to identify with their captors. The term was coined by the Swedish psychologist and criminalist Nils Bejerot (1921–88) in connection with a 1973 hostage standoff in which he served as a police consultant. A bank robber had locked himself and four hostages in a vault; one of his demands, which the police acceded to, was that they allow an imprisoned friend to join him. Dynamite was strapped to the hostages' bodies; nooses were placed around their necks. When, after six days, police stormed the vault and freed the hostages, some of them resisted their rescuers and tried to protect the robbers; afterward, two of the hostages raised money for their captors' defense. Bejerot theorized that they had been so traumatized by fear and helplessness that they created a "false reality" for themselves, in which the very people who threatened them were perceived as their protectors.

Less than a year after the Stockholm incident, the heiresss Patricia Hearst was kidnapped by the Symbionese Liberation Army (SLA). Before she was rescued, she would change her name to Tanya, declare herself a convert to the SLA's cause, and participate in a bank robbery. Her unsuccessful defense would be the Stockholm syndrome. As she recounted it to Larry King when she received a pardon in 2001,

> Stockholm Syndrome is what it is called when you begin to identify with your captors. I mean, once they don't kill you, [you] start to think they're nice. They get nicer every day that they don't kill you.
>
> And, well that's why you hear people that have been, you know, kidnapped or abducted or held hostage even for a short time and they'll say, you know, well, how were they? And they go, well, you know, actually they were OK.

The Stockholm syndrome has been adduced to explain such diverse phenomena as the rarity of slave revolts and the reluctance of battered wives to separate from their spouses.

In the summer of 2006, Natascha Kampusch, an eighteen-year-old Austrian woman, slipped away from the kidnapper who'd confined her in a basement dungeon for the better part of eight years. Her reticence about her captor (a likely pederast, he commited suicide within hours of her escape), her reluctance to see her parents, and the possibility that she had passed up earlier opportunities to escape, were widely attributed to the Stockholm syndrome.

STRING THEORY

Field of physics that attempts to unify the discrepancies between general relativity and quantum mechanics by envisioning particles not as dimensionless points, but as tiny (about a billion billion times smaller than a proton) strings. As the well known physicist Brian Greene writes,

> Much as different vibrations of a violin string produce different musical notes, different vibrations of the theory's strings produce different kinds of particles. An electron is a tiny string vibrating in one pattern, a quark is a string vibrating in a different pattern. Particles like the photon that convey nature's forces in the quantum realm are strings vibrating in yet other patterns.

These strings not only vibrate in many different patterns but in many different dimensions—in some version of the theory, as many as ten or eleven of them. Later iterations of string theory envisage not just a multiplicity of dimensions but of universes. Though almost impossible to explain nonmathematically, string theory has swept the academy and captivated popular audiences in recent years (Brian Greene's book *The Elegant Universe* [2000] has sold more than one million copies); this is despite the fact that string theory has yet to make any predictions that have been successfully tested. Recently, the theory has come under sustained attack by such prominent figures as the mathematician Peter Woit and the physicist (and erstwhile string theorist) Lee Smolin.

THEORY OF RELATIVITY
The epochal theory proposed by Albert Einstein (1879–1955) in 1905, when he was a patent examiner in Bern, Switzerland. Central to twentieth-century science's new understanding of cosmology and quantum mechanics, and with real-world applications as far afield as nuclear weaponry and nanotechnology, relativity is as paradigm-shattering as Copernicus's heliocentrism and as fundamental as Newton's laws of motion, though despite many valiant attempts by popularizers, including Einstein himself, it is much harder to understand intuitively. Ideas at this level of sophistication and subtlety require the precision of mathematics to convey them; language and analogy are far too blunt a set of instruments.

That said, relativity acknowledges that it is impossible to measure "absolute motion"—measurements of motion made from within a moving system will be different from measurements of the same motion made from without it. Even so, both measurements will be correct. The only factor that remains constant is the speed of light.

Light emitted by a fast-moving object moves at the same velocity as light emitted by a slow-moving object. What is different are the space-times that the objects occupy. Absolute space and absolute time simply don't exist; they are always relative. The faster an object moves, the slower time moves relative to it, which keeps the speed of light constant. The mass of the object and the energy that it contains vary with its speed as well. This is where the famous equation $E=mc^2$ comes in: the energy of an object is equal to the square of its mass times the speed of light. This means that even a very tiny object can release an enormous amount of energy at a high speed, one of the reasons why nuclear bombs are so devastating.

In 1915, Einstein extended the theory to include the effects of gravity as well as motion. General relativity shows that gravity, like motion, produces curvatures in space-time, which accounts for the irregularities of orbiting bodies. The notions of black holes and the big bang follow from general relativity as well.

TROPISM

From the Greek word *tropos,* "to turn." Tropism is the directional response of a plant or organism to a stimulus. For example *phototropism* is the propensity of a plant to grow in the direction of light; *geotropism* is a response to gravity; it is what makes trees growing on steep hillsides point straight up at the sky.

The word is sometimes used in a derisive sense to describe reflexive or instinctual (i.e., unthinking) human behavior. Thus Maureen Dowd's deft and disingenuous evisceration of an ex-colleague in a *New York Times* op-ed piece: "The traits she has that drive many reporters at *The Times* crazy—her tropism toward powerful men, her frantic intensity and her peculiar mixture of hard work and hauteur—have never bothered me. I enjoy operatic types."

Michiko Kakutani, writing on a "floodlet" of political books in a *New York Times* "Critics Notebook," noted that they all reveal

A tropism, an instinctive reflex that informs the Bush White House's decision-making process, as well as its strategic and tactical thinking, a tropism that has played a major role in this increasingly embattled administration's approach to a host of issues from the war in Iraq to Social Security reform to the government's policy on torture.

UNCERTAINTY PRINCIPLE

Also called the principle of indeterminacy. First formulated in 1927 by the German physicist Werner Heisenberg (1901–76), the uncertainty principle states that when measuring subatomic particles, "The more precisely the position is determined, the less precisely the momentum is known . . . and vice versa." In other words, it is impossible to measure position and speed simultaneously—if we know one, we don't know the other; we can only calculate it within a certain range of probabilities. Before we know one aspect of the particle, it can be said to have all possible aspects or none of them. This phenomenon has nothing to do with the mechanical difficulties of measuring something so small—it is an intrinsic attribute of subatomic particles.

This feature of quantum mechanics has profound philosophical implications. Since science only acknowledges the existence of that which can be measured, the position or speed of the particle can't be said to exist until it is observed. Nor can we make confident predictions about the future. If we don't know the particle's speed and position in the present, we can't know what it will be in the future. As Heisenberg put it, "In the sharp formulation of the law of causality—'if we know the present exactly, we can calculate the future'—it is not the conclusion that is wrong but the premise."

The three laws of motion discovered by Isaac Newton (1642–1727)—that an object will stay at rest or continue its motion in a straight line and a constant speed unless acted upon by another force, that the rate of change of the momentum of a moving object is in direct proportion to the force acting upon it, and that every action has an opposite and equal reaction—provided the foundation for Newtonian mechanics, which allowed scientists to predict planetary movements and humble earthly phenomena with an equal degree of certainty. The clockwork universe of of the Deists ran according to those immutable laws. Quantum mechanics, with its implicit uncertainty, called all of that into question.

In recent years, many New Age writers have incorporated the

uncertainty principle into their writings as a "proof" of the power the mind exerts over reality. Since the nature of the subatomic particle depends upon its being observed, they say, our reality is whatever we choose to think it is. "Your body is simultaneously material (particlelike) and nonmaterial (wavelike)," writes Deepak Chopra. "You can choose to experience your body as physical or as a network of energy, transformation, and intelligence . . . Before you decide which biological age you choose to experience, you are all possible biological ages. It's up to you to decide what age you want to be." It's worth noting in this context that Heisenberg's discovery applies quite specifically to the subatomic world, and that the clearest exposition of his theory is mathematical. Though it provides a useful metaphor for some mystical ideas, in no way does it scientifically validate them.

UNIFORMITARIANISM   *See* Catastrophism.

Economics

BIMETALLISM *See* Metallism.

BULLIONISM *See* Mercantilism.

CAPITALISM

The word *capitalism* didn't come into use until long after the economic system, or more precisely, the *absence* of a centrally organized economic system, had already supplanted mercantilism, which itself had succeeded feudalism as the basis of European commercial life. The word was first used in its present sense—as a nonpejorative reference to the so-called free exchange of goods in a competitive marketplace, where prices are set strictly by laws of supply and demand—in the title of the book *Modern Capitalism,* by the German economist and sociologist Werner Sombart, which was published in 1902. Max Weber's classic *The Protestant Ethic and the Spirit of Capitalism* appeared two years later.

A century and a quarter earlier, in 1776, the *annus mirabilis* of Liberalism, the Scottish philosopher Adam Smith (1723–90) had written his classic treatise on the genius of the free market, *The Wealth of Nations.* In it he described the beginnings of the Industrial Revolution and the economies of scale that mass production makes possible. He also observed that in the absence of tariffs, taxes, and other mechanisms of centralized economic control, the laws of supply and demand created even more wealth for a society.

When entrepreneurs and workers were permitted to govern their own livelihoods, Smith observed, they gravitated toward the most productive—and the most remunerative—investments of their capital or labor.

Mercantilism had compelled colonies, which were ruinously expensive to protect and maintain, to consume their mother nations' manufactures, even when they could obtain them more cheaply elsewhere. It also taxed them dearly for the privilege. The overriding goal of mercantilism had been to acquire precious metals for the Crown. But if those precious metals were liquidated and turned into capital for private entrepreneurs—raw materials, factories, ships, warehouses—they could produce far more wealth; and then if those manufactures were bartered freely on the open market, even more wealth would be produced. When the government imposed its will on trade, Smith observed, more often than not it stifled it. Paradoxically, the more people pursued their own selfish ends, the more benefits accrued to society as a whole. This is an idea that the French physiocrats also believed, for somewhat different reasons.

Though the state is worse than useless when it comes to economic planning and control, Smith wrote, it still serves an essential function.

> According to the system of natural liberty, the sovereign has only three duties to attend to . . . first, the duty of protecting the society from the violence and invasion of other independent societies; secondly, the duty of protecting, so far as possible, every member of the society from the injustice or oppression of every other member of it, or the duty of establishing an exact administration of justice, and thirdly, the duty of erecting and maintaining certain public works and certain public institutions, which it can never be for the interest of any individual, or small number of individuals, to erect and maintain . . .

Most important, the authorities must scrupulously protect the marketplace from the rapacities of monopoly. "People of the same trade seldom meet together," Smith wrote, "even for merriment and diversion, but the conversation ends in a conspiracy against the public, or in some contrivance to raise prices." Apologists for laissez-faire capitalism (an abbreviation of the French phrase *laissez faire, laissez aller, laissez passer*—"let do, let go, let pass"—often forget that Smith saw a positive, indeed a necessary role for some governmental regulation. The same self-interest that guides the "invisible hand" of the economy toward prosperity can immiserate it when it goes too far.

Marxism recognized that the free market offered tremendous advantages for owners and entrepreneurs; it took issue with the idea that labor was as fungible or portable an asset as capital, regarding the lot of the wage laborer as no better than that of serfs in a feudal economy. Marxists assumed that capitalism was thus planting the seeds of its own destruction in an eventual but nonetheless inevitable revolution. They underestimated the power of trade unions to ameliorate the workers' conditions, the co-optive attractions of consumerism, and the adaptability of capitalism, which in modern first world economies has gradually taken on some of the aspects of socialism itself.

CHARTALISM   *See* Metallism.

DIALECTICAL MATERIALISM   *See* Marxism.

FOURIERISM

The utopian economic and social ideas of Charles Fourier (1772–1837), who memorably declared in his *Theory of the Four Movements* (1808) that "truth and commerce are as incompatible as Jesus and Satan."

Rather than attempting to repress human passions as traditional societies do, society itself should be reorganized into self-sufficient phalanxes consisting of about three hundred families each, or sixteen hundred to eighteen hundred people. "The personal and real estate of the Phalanx will be represented by stock divided into shares," Fourier wrote.

Each Phalanx will engage in both agriculture and industry.
Meals will be in common . . . The aim is to be self-sufficient in
both the agricultural and industrial spheres . . . We shall see
people engaged in attractive occupations, giving no thoughts to
material wants, free from all pecuniary cares and anxieties. As
women and children all work, there will be no idlers, all will
earn more than they consume. Universal happiness and gaiety
will reign. A unity of interests and views will arise, crime and
violence disappear.

Fourier's student Albert Brisbane (1809–90) carried his teacher's
ideas to America. The short-lived Brook Farm—satirized by
Nathaniel Hawthorne (1804–64) in *The Blithedale Romance*—was
founded in West Roxbury, Massachusetts, in 1841; a phalanx established near Red Bank, New Jersey, in 1844 lasted until the
mid-1850s.

GAME THEORY

"The Battle of Waterloo was won on the playing fields of Eton,"
is a saying that is often attributed to the Duke of Wellington.
Game theory, the mathematical study of strategies used to maximize one's advantage in conflicts that are fought according to
rules, or in situations where there are only a limited number of
choices and outcomes, takes his words to heart.

Prisoner's dilemma, the hypothetical scenario in which two
prisoners who can't communicate with each other are given the
choice to either cooperate with the police and receive a lesser sentence or not cooperate at all and take their chances, is a favorite
of logicians, mathematicians, and ethicists. If one prisoner be-
trays the other, he'll receive a lesser sentence, which makes him
a winner of sorts, though he still goes to jail. If they both betray
each other, they'll each receive lesser sentences. Neither the prisoners nor the police get as much as they could have, but they all
receive something. The only outcome with an unambiguous winner is if *neither* prisoner cooperates—then the police have to release both of them. That's the best outcome for the two prisoners

and a clear loss for the police, but since neither prisoner knows what the other will do, it's the least likely tactic for either of them to choose. All of these choices and strategies can be converted into equations, which can then be analyzed in terms of the best and worst and the likeliest and unlikeliest outcomes.

John von Neumann (1903–57) and Oskar Morgenstern's (1902–76) landmark book, *Theory of Games and Economic Behavior* (1944), was the first major application of mathematical game theory to economics, but they limited their study to "noncooperative" or zero-sum games, in which there are clear winners and losers. Poker, for example, is a zero-sum game—what one player wins, the other loses. The mathematician John Nash, of *A Beautiful Mind* fame, studied rivalries that held the possibility of mutual gain—non-zero-sum, or win-win situations, for instance, a labor negotiation from which both sides can emerge from the bargaining table feeling like they've accomplished something. The Nash equilibrium, the Nash bargaining solution, and the Nash program secured his fame before his tragic descent into schizophrenia. The 2005 Nobel Prize in economics was awarded to two game theorists, Thomas Schelling and Robert Aumann. Schelling's classic, *The Strategy of Conflict* (1960), applied game theory to the nuclear standoff of the cold war.

In addition to mathematics, logic, economics, and ethics, game theory has major applications in computer science, in biology (evolutionary biologists use it to understand how certain animal behaviors maximize evolutionary fitness), in military strategy (the Rand Corporation has long applied it to war games), in conflict resolution, and in business. In recent years win-win has become a favorite buzzword in management seminars.

GEORGEISM

Economic and social theories of Henry George (1839–97), a self-taught sailor and printer who went on to write the best selling *Progress and Poverty* (1879), ran for mayor of New York City, and was, for a time, one of the most famous men in America. At the heart of Henry George's economic philosophy was the idea that the vast majority of unearned wealth came from rents charged on land. If the government taxed only the unimproved value of land (a single tax), George argued, it would collect more than enough revenue to meet all its needs—without disincentivizing capital development, without depriving workers of the full fruits of their labors, and without causing scarcity in the marketplace. Since nobody makes or builds land and everybody needs it, George reasoned, the least that the landlords can do is to share a portion of their unjust windfall with the commons, or the state.

"It would require less than the fingers of the two hands to enumerate those who, from Plato down, rank with Henry George among the world's social philosophers," wrote John Dewey (1859–1952). Karl Marx (1818–83) dismissed George's single tax as "simply an attempt, decked out with socialism, to save capitalist domination and indeed to establish it afresh on an even wider basis than its present one." Capitalists, in turn, complained that it placed an unfair burden on landlords and that it discouraged improving any portion of one's property because it would drive up the taxes on the rest of it. However, Milton Friedman, the laissez-faire capitalist par excellence, noted, "In my opinion, the least bad tax is the property tax on the unimproved value of land, the Henry George argument of many, many years ago."

GRESHAM'S LAW   *See* Metallism.

KEYNESIANISM

The British economist John Maynard Keynes (1883–1946) argued in *The General Theory of Employment, Interest and Money* (1936) that governments can ameliorate the worst effects of periodic recessions and depressions by increasing their spending—and if necessary, running up deficits to do it. Though strenuously resisted by orthodox laissez-faire economists, Keynes' idea has been broadly accepted in its broad outlines, if not all of its particulars. Virtually all capitalist economies today are mixed, in that they rely on both the invisible hand of the market and timely government intervention to prime the pump when necessary. Another name for this is neomercantilism.

LAISSEZ-FAIRE   *See* **Capitalism.**

MALTHUSIANISM

The pessimistic demographic theories of the English economist Thomas R. Malthus (1766–1834). As elaborated in his study *An Essay on the Principle of Population* (first published in 1798, revised for the sixth and last time in 1826), Malthusianism proposes that since populations grow exponentially while resources increase arithmetically, a significant number of people are doomed to live in poverty until the imbalance is inevitably corrected by famine, war, or pestilence. Darwinism is deeply influenced by Malthusian population studies.

Malthus anticipated neither the green revolution in agriculture (the widespread use of pesticides, fertilizers, and hybrid plants), which has dramatically increased crop yields, nor the widespread availability of contraceptives, which has drastically curtailed the birth rate in the first world. But if well-to-do cultures have evaded the cycles of misery that he predicted, for much of the third world his ideas remain tragically cogent.

MARGINALISM

In economics, a theory of value derived from calculations of the utility or production cost of the *last* item sold or made rather than an average. A factory owner decides to cease production at a point where it costs more to produce an extra item than he could receive from selling it. It can be difficult to calculate where that equilibrium point falls because the cost of production includes so many factors—labor, machinery, maintenance, raw materials, distribution and marketing expenses—and a change in just one of them can cascade and affect them all. If fuel prices rise, for example, then the cost of electricity increases. If electricity goes up, then not only do the factories pay higher utility bills, but consumers do as well, possibly causing them to reduce their demand for a product if it's something that has to be plugged in.

The most accurate assessment of value on the supply side isn't in the cost of the first unit sold, which is astronomical, since it includes all the development and start-up costs. Nor is it in the dollar value of the excess inventory left over after demand for the product falls off, which will be liquidated for less than it cost to produce. It's not in the average between the two either (though that might be how its taxable value is determined). True value is found at the margin—in the return produced by the last unit produced that was actually sold at its intended price.

The most accurate assessment of value can also be found at the margins when you look at the demand side. To digress for a moment, Adam Smith famously compared the price of water (which is vital for life) to diamonds, which most of us can live without. Why do we pay so much more for the latter? Because water is naturally plentiful and people don't need more than they can consume, he concluded; diamonds, on the other hand, cost a lot to dig up and polish. (This is called the labor theory of value.) Diamonds are also fungible—they can be used like money. Water has high value only in arid places (where the law of supply and demand assures that it won't be cheap anyway).

But Adam Smith (1723–90) lived before people started buying designer bottled water. If you're an entrepreneur looking to make money in that market today, you need to be able to sell your product at a price that more than covers your costs (digging a well, buying empty bottles, paying an artist to design your labels, and a printer to print them, paying a bottler to fill up the bottles and a distributor to send them to stores, hiring a copywriter to devise a name for the product and a sports figure to drink it, contracting with an advertising agency to devise a campaign that shows the sports figure drinking it and with TV and magazines and billboard companies to run those ads, etc.). But if your surveys and focus groups and test-marketing campaigns suggest that a consumer from the right demographic group will spend a dollar for an eight-ounce bottle of thirst-quenching, status-enhancing water, can you quadruple your profits by selling him a quart bottle for four dollars? Maybe. A gallon bottle for sixteen dollars? A hundred-gallon tank for sixteen hundred dollars? Somewhere between one dollar and sixteen hundred dollars, the law of diminishing marginal utility kicks in. Once the consumer's thirst is slaked, each additional ounce of water is less useful and hence less valuable.

Another way of looking at marginal utility is by asking at what point the consumer will substitute a different product. If he is down to his last dollar when he goes to the store, will he spend it on a small bottle of water when he can use it instead to buy two packs of gum and still get a free drink from the public water fountain? Real-world decisions about spending and earning are often made at the margins. For instance, do I want to take a part-time job that will add an extra hundred dollars of income per week to the three hundred dollars a week that I already earn? Maybe. Do I still want to take the job when I find out that that extra hundred will put me in a different tax bracket, causing my taxes to rise from 30 percent to 40 percent, and shrinking my extra hundred dollars per week to sixty? Whatever I ultimately decide affects my aggregate income, but the decision was made at the margin.

Marginalism is the hallmark of neoclassical economics, in which producers and consumers are assumed to be rational actors, making myriads of complex decisions to maximize value. Alfred Marshall (1842–1924), William Stanley Jevons (1835–82), and Léon Walras (1834–1910) are a few of the important economists who pioneered the field.

MARXISM

The economic and political ideology of Karl Marx (1818–83) as it is applied in the political and economic sphere and also in aesthetic and cultural theory. Though Marxism has faced some major practical challenges in recent years—namely, the fall of the Soviet Union and the economic reforms of China—it continues to thrive in academia.

At the heart of Marxism is the theory of dialectical materialism. The philosopher G. W. F. Hegel (1770–1831) wrote that history is "the idea clothing itself with the form of events." To Hegel, human progress was the action of ideas, each contending with their opposite until they fused into a more complex synthesis.

Karl Marx perceived the same dialectic at work in "the history of the class struggle," but his philosophy remained determinedly earthbound. If Hegel believed that the culmination of history would be the realization of the Absolute Spirit, Marx anticipated a violent revolution followed by the establishment of a workers' paradise—a just and equitable society whose members owned the means of production.

If feudalism was the historical thesis, Marx theorized, capitalism was its antithesis. And as Marx saw things in the mid-nineteenth century, capitalism was about to collapse under the weight of its own contradictions. Communism would be the synthesis that brought history to an end. Capitalism was created by the bourgeoisie, but the sweat of its workers, the proletariat, was what made it possible. According to the labor theory of value, it was their toil that gave the commodities they produced their value, but the wages they earned didn't enable them to purchase anywhere near as much as they created. Surplus value, the difference between the value of what the proletariat produced and the value of what they earned, was the source of the ruling class's profits. Though the bourgeoisie had performed an important function in supplanting feudal with industrial societies, they had outlived their usefulness. Inevitably, Marx predicted, the workers would rise up and overthrow them.

Once the dust of the revolution settled, the proletariat would establish a dictatorship so they could exercise the power they needed to expropriate the capitalists' property, crush whatever resistance to the new order remained, and rapidly develop the economy. But this dictatorship was merely a transitional phase: Marx promised that as soon as the means of production were firmly in the people's hands, the state—along with its attendant coercive institutions that the bourgeoisie had used to keep the workers in thrall, like religion and the traditional family—would swiftly disappear.

V. I. Lenin (1870–1924), the leader of Russia's Marxist revolution, described this process in his book *State and Revolution:*

The exploiters are naturally unable to suppress *the people* without a highly complex machine for performing this task, but the people can suppress the exploiters even with a very simple "machine," almost without a "machine," without a special apparatus, by the simple *organization of the armed masses* . . . only Communism makes the state absolutely unnecessary, for there is *nobody* to be suppressed—"nobody" in the sense of a *class*, in the sense of a systematic struggle against a definite section of the population. We are not utopians, and do not in the least deny the possibility and inevitability of excesses on the part of *individual persons,* or the need to suppress *such* excesses. But . . . this will be done by the armed people itself, as simply and as readily as any crowd of civilized people, even in modern society, interferes to put a stop to a scuffle or to prevent a woman from being assaulted. And, secondly, we know that the fundamental social cause of excesses, which consist in the violation of the rules of social intercourse, is the exploitation of the masses, their want and their poverty. With the removal of this chief cause, excesses will inevitably begin to "*wither away.*"

Though there were a number of Communist revolutions in the last century, none of them took place in economically developed countries. The mature capitalist economies that Marx had assumed would be the first to fall instead co-opted their workers' loyalties with such halfway measures as political liberalism, Democratic socialism, labor unionism, rising wages, subsidized health care, and easy credit. The poor, mostly rural countries that did have Communist revolutions—Russia and China, Cambodia and Cuba—had to crush internal resistance and defend themselves from external enemies, while simultaneously building industrial infrastructures from scratch, not to mention reeducating their citizenry—especially their land-owning peasantry, who were ill-disposed to the prospect of surrendering their property to a people's state. It's perhaps no wonder that their dictatorships turned out to be permanent affairs. Even under the best of circumstances, people are remarkably difficult to reengineer. It's much more efficient to kill them, and that's what Stalin, Mao, and Pol Pot did, by the millions. Of course Marxist Leninism, Stalinism, and Maoism are by no means the same thing as orthodox Marxism; many ardent Marxists deplored the policies of the Soviet Union and the People's Republic of China from the beginning. Ironically, the devoutest Marxists were among the first to die in Stalin and Mao's purges.

Philosophers and social critics of the Frankfurt school, such as Walter Benjamin (1892–1940), Theodore Adorno (1903–69), Max Horkheimer (1895–1973), Herbert Marcuse (1898–1979), and Jürgen Habermas continue to be widely studied and read, as are Marxist or Marxist-influenced historians, literary critics, and theorists such as Terry Eagleton, Fredric Jameson, Georg Lukács (1885–1971), Antonio Gramsci (1891–1937), Jean Baudrillard (1929–2007), Hélène Cixous, Eric Hobsbawm, E. P. Thompson (1924–93), Gilles Deleuze (1925–95), Frantz Fanon (1925–61), Mikhail Bakhtin (1895–1975), and Raymond Williams (1921–88), to name a very few.

MERCANTILISM

The dominant economic philosophy in Europe in the sixteenth, seventeenth, and eighteenth centuries, mercantilism coincided with the rise of the great nation states and the age of exploration. The presiding idea of mercantilism is that the strength of a nation depends upon its wealth—specifically, its supply of precious metals. This belief is sometimes called bullionism. The best way to secure gold, the economic thinkers of this era believed, is to maintain a favorable balance of trade, in which more goods are exported than imported. This they accomplished by governmental regulation of every aspect of trade: by setting high tariffs on imports, by licensing monopolies and joint-stock ventures to encourage investment in expensive but potentially profitable enterprises like exploration, by establishing colonies and forcing them to trade with the mother country exclusively, by licensing pirates to attack rival nations' shipping, by judicious diplomacy and alliances, and by all-out wars.

Adam Smith's (1723–90) *The Wealth of Nations* excoriated many of the basic tenets of mercantilism. On the inefficiencies of colonialism he said:

> A great empire has been established for the sole purpose of raising up a nation of customers who should be obliged to buy from the shops or our different producers all the goods which these could supply them. For the sake of that little enhancement of price which this monopoly might afford our producers, the home-consumers have been burdened with the whole expense of maintaining and defending that empire.

As to the follies of central planning, he maintained:

> The statesman who should attempt to direct private people in what manner they ought to employ their capitals, would not only load himself with a most unnecessary attention, but assume an authority which could safely be trusted, not only to no single person, but to no council or senate whatever, and which would nowhere be so dangerous as in the hands of a man who had folly and presumption enough to fancy himself fit to exercise it.

Keynesianism is sometimes called neomercantilism for its advocacy of governmental intervention in a nation's economy. Indeed, Keynes defended the historical mercantilists' obsessions with the balance of trade and the supply of bullion, noting that a positive trade balance and the ability to control the money supply are both important determinants of a nation's economic health.

METALLISM
The belief that money must have an intrinsic value in order to maintain its stability; it either has to be coined from a precious metal or backed by precious metal held in reserve by the issuing bank or the state. Chartalism, from the Latin *charta,* or "ticket,"

is the idea that money is merely a token or a coupon, with no intrinsic value of its own, and it is the monetary system that virtually all modern economies have adopted.

The failure of metallism can be explained by Gresham's law, which states that "bad" money drives out "good." People will use coins that have been shaved or clipped or adulterated with baser metals for their purchases and keep the best coins in reserve—either to melt them down (if the metal they are made of is worth more than their face value) or to use in foreign exchange. Some credit the astronomer Copernicus with this discovery, but the law took its name from the English merchant and statesman Sir Thomas Gresham, who warned Queen Elizabeth that because of the "unexampled state of badness" of England's coins, "all your ffine goold was convayd ought of this your realm."

Bimetallism is the theory that money can be backed by or minted from two different metals with different intrinsic values— say, silver and gold—as long as the ratio between them, set by law, remains constant. Gresham's law explains why this inevitably leads to inflation. As long as the cheaper silver coins will be accepted at face value, people will spend them and keep the gold coins for their investment value. As more and more gold coins disappear from circulation, the pressure of demand drives their value up even more. When new mines flooded the market with silver in nineteenth-century America, creditors demanded that the government revert to a gold standard to prevent debtors from retiring their loans with cheaper coins. Agrarian populists like William Jennings Bryan advocated that the silver standard be retained, lest farmers, wage laborers, and small business men be crucified "upon a cross of gold." Bryan came within twenty thousand votes of an electoral college victory in the presidential election of 1896.

MONETARISM
Economic theory that the supply of money is what chiefly determines the short-term behavior of a national economy. The Nobel Prize–winning economist Milton Friedman (in 1963 he co-authored *A Monetary History of the United States, 1867–1960* with

Anna J. Schwartz) is most closely associated with monetarism, which he believed amounted to a wholesale repudiation of Keynesianism's constant fine-tuning of fiscal policies—i.e., taxes and spending—to stimulate or calm troubled economies.

Key to monetarism is the equation of exchange: MV=PQ, in which M is money, V is velocity or the rate of turnover (the number of times an average dollar is spent on a good or service), P is the average price level of a good or service, and Q is the quantity of goods and services produced. As long as M is adjusted to keep pace with Q, Friedman theorized, market forces should balance the other two factors in the equation. Friedman is said to have told G. William Miller, former US President Jimmy Carter's appointee as chairman of the Federal Reserve, that with the use of this formula he could set the Fed on automatic pilot. Miller's successor Paul Volcker applied monetarist principles to the stagflation crisis of the 1970s (when persistent inflation accompanied stagnant economic growth and high unemployment), sharply curtailing the money supply. Inflation was drastically reduced, but at the cost of even higher unemployment.

Though Volcker's successors Alan Greenspan and Ben Bernanke were also sympathetic to monetarism in theory, most economists, including Friedman himself (before his death at the age of 94 in 2006), now admit that M and Q are much harder to quantify than was once believed and that pure monetarism has yielded disappointing results in practice.

MONOPOLISM

A business, or an illegally collusive consortium of businesses, is said to enjoy a monopoly when it dominates the market for a product or controls its sources to the extent that it can set its prices artificially high (or artificially low for long enough to eliminate its potential competitors). The software company Microsoft was accused of monopolistic practices when it deliberately designed the Windows operating system to be incompatible with its competitor's applications, taking advantage of its dominance in one sector of the market to squeeze out competition in another.

Patents and copyrights are legal monopolies in which an inventor or a creator of intellectual property is granted a limited period of exclusivity to recoup development costs and earn a profit. Historically, public utilities were granted monopolies as an incentive for them to make the required massive investments in infrastructure (dams, pipelines, power plants, cables), but they were closely regulated to ensure that they didn't take undue advantage of their captive market. The recent vogue for deregulation has been changing this practice.

Adam Smith recognized that the same invisible hand of self-interest that manages an ideally competitive marketplace inevitably nudges its most successful participants toward monopolism. "When I want to buy up any politician I always find the antimonopolists the most purchasable," the robber baron William Henry Vanderbilt cynically quipped. "They don't come so high."

PHYSIOCRATISM

The Greek word literally means "rule of nature." The physiocrats (also called *économistes* or the sect—and they were widely criticized in their day for their cultishness) were followers of François Quesnay (1694–1774), a self-taught French country surgeon who rose to become the personal physician to Madame de Pompadour, the mistress of Louis XV. Quesnay developed his economic theories when he was asked to contribute to Alembert and Diderot's *Encyclopédie* in 1756; his book *Tableau Économique* appeared in 1758.

Quesnay attacked the mercantilistic ideas that had long governed French economic life, arguing that they underemphasized agriculture, which he claimed was the only economic activity that produced net product (more economic output than input), and was thus the true source of a nation's wealth. Comparing the flow of income from one economic sector to another to the flow of blood in the human body, Quesnay argued that an economy was healthiest when it was allowed to remain in its natural state—the less a government interfered with it, the better. Quesnay and the physiocrats would influence the writings of the Scottish philosopher Adam Smith.

Quesnay's disciple the Marquis de Mirabeau (1715–89), who was the father of the revolutionary Comte de Mirabeau (1749–91), elaborated the physiocratic single-tax theory that would influence the American economist Henry George (1839–97) a century later. Since land was the only source of real wealth, he argued, only land should be taxed.

PROTECTIONISM

Government intervention to protect a domestic industry or resource from foreign competition. Protectionism can take many forms: the imposition of tariffs on cheaper foreign imports, which obviates their competitive advantage, and the enforcement of quotas (which can backfire—if there is sufficient demand for a product, scarcity will not only raise its price but its exporter's profits). Or the government can subsidize a whole industry, as the United States does with agriculture, by reimbursing domestic producers when they are forced to sell their product at a loss.

Conventional capitalist wisdom argues that protectionism is rarely good for a country in the long run. If an industry is uncompetitive, the argument goes, it makes more sense to liquidate it and invest the money in a different business that can prevail in the open market, and which would presumably absorb the unemployed workers in due course. For better or worse, these free marketeers say, we live in a global economy. Sure, Iceland could grow pineapples in hothouses and force its citizens to buy them for fifty dollars each by imposing punitive tariffs on cheaper pineapples from tropical climes, but neither the Icelanders, who would be forced to bear the artificially high cost of pineapples (or more likely, do without them) nor the Icelandic economy would realize much benefit from the arrangement. The money squandered on hothouses could have yielded ten times the return had it been invested in, say, a new technology that converts molten lava, a resource that Iceland is rich in, into fertilizer, a product that pineapple-growing countries might pay a premium to buy.

Protectionists offer the counter argument that when a rival country enjoys a monopoly on a valuable resource, or dumps its

manufactured products at a loss to undermine its competitors, re-
taliatory tariffs might be the only defensive weapon that works.
Furthermore, economic efficiency isn't the sole measure of a
country's weal. Though investors and corporations might not
have an immediate interest in resuscitating anemic industries or
keeping domestic workers employed, a case can be made that society as a whole enjoys compensatory benefits from full employment and economic and industrial self-sufficiency.

SUPPLY-SIDE ECONOMICS

Economic theory popularized by Jude Wanniski (1936–2005)
while he was an editorial writer at the *Wall Street Journal* in the
1970s. Supply-side economics draws on the economic thinking of
Arthur Laffer (b. 1940, the inventor of the eponymous bell curve
that graphically shows how tax cuts can increase federal revenue)
and the Nobel Prize winner Robert Mundell (b. 1932). It also
reaches back to the writings of the French economist Jean-
Baptiste Say (1767–1832) and the medieval Moslem thinker Ibn
Khaldûn (1332–1406), who wrote: "At the beginning of a dynasty, taxation yields a large revenue from small assessments.
At the end of the dynasty, taxation yields a small revenue from
large assessments."

At the heart of supply-side thinking is Say's notion that supply creates demand. Thus, the secret of rousing a slow economy
is to stimulate the supply side by making sure entrepreneurs have
lots of money to invest in production, rather than the demand
side, by, say, raising the minimum wage, which will only compel
factory owners to reduce their payrolls by downsizing. High
taxes, the argument goes, discourage productive investment. If
someone earns enough money to live on already, and they're being taxed at a rate of 80 percent, they're not going to go to the
trouble of earning an extra hundred dollars if they can only keep
a fraction of it. Lower the tax rate and they'll invest their savings,
which will create more jobs and more goods—which, in turn, according to Say's law, will stimulate demand. Everybody makes
more money. Some of it trickles down to the workers, because

there are more and better-paying jobs, and some of it flows into the government's coffers, because, even if it's getting a smaller slice, it's cut from a bigger pie.

Although supply-side thinking dominated the administrations of Ronald Reagan and George W. Bush, there are many skeptics. George H. W. Bush famously disparaged the theory as "voodoo economics" before he adopted it. Liberal economists like Paul Krugman regard it as out-and-out charlatanry. Biologist Richard Dawkins has argued famously that ideas spread from mind to mind much as viruses spread from host to host. Writing in *Slate* magazine, Krugman compared supply-side economics to a thought contagion.

> An idea need not be true or even useful, as long as it has what it takes to propagate itself . . . Supply-side economics, then, is like one of those African viruses that, however often it may be eradicated from the settled areas, is always out there in the bush, waiting for new victims.

TAYLORISM

After Frederick Winslow Taylor (1865–1915), author of *The Principles of Scientific Management* (1911). As a manager at the Simonds Roller Bearing Company and Bethlehem Iron, Taylor used time-motion studies to analyze the ways that workers performed repetitive tasks. By changing both their procedures and their pay incentives, and better matching the men to their jobs, he increased productivity while cutting payrolls. He also modernized machinery, reorganized management structures to allow for better supervision, instituted modern purchasing and bookkeeping systems, streamlined bureaucracies, and generally improved profitability. Unfortunately, all this activity alienated both workers and management—Bethlehem ultimately fired Taylor, despite the fact that he had virtually doubled its production while halving its costs. Like so many displaced executives today, Taylor became a management consultant.

Stalin imported Taylor's scientific management to the Soviet

Union; Stakhanovism was one of the results. Anyone who visits the kitchen of a fast-food establishment or the phone banks of a telemarketing concern—or any other business facility where workers are programmed to perform quickly, efficiently, and with all the independence, initiative, and creativity of robots— will see Taylorism in action.

Advocates of Total Quality Management (TQM) fault Taylorism, or neo-Taylorism, as it is called today, for its strict division between management and labor. TQM adopts a holistic approach, in which workers are acknowledged to be people, rather than biological machines, and management and workers alike are understood to share the goal of serving the customer.

WIN-WIN   *See* **Game Theory.**

ZERO SUM   *See* **Game Theory.**

Religion

ADOPTIONISM   *See* Nestorianism.

AGNOSTICISM
A principled doubt or skepticism as to the existence of God. The
literal Greek translation is "theory of the absence of knowledge."
The word was coined by T. H. Huxley (1825–95), who defined it
as follows:

> Agnosticism, in fact, is not a creed, but a method, the
> essence of which lies in the rigorous application of a single
> principle . . . Positively the principle may be expressed: In
> matters of the intellect, follow your reason as far as it will
> take you, without regard to any other consideration. And
> negatively: In matters of the intellect do not pretend that con-
> clusions are certain which are not demonstrated or demon-
> strable. That I take to be the agnostic faith, which if a man
> keep whole and undefiled, he shall not be ashamed to look
> the universe in the face, whatever the future may have in store
> for him.

Clarence Darrow's (1857–1938) famous essay "Why I Am an Ag-
nostic" ends with the observation, "The fear of God is not the beginning of wisdom. The fear of God is the death of wisdom. Skepticism
and doubt lead to study and investigation, and investigation is the
beginning of wisdom."

ALBIGENSIANISM

Also known as Catharism, from the Greek word for "puritanism." Albigensianism was Gnostic heresy that traveled from the Balkans and the Middle East to Toulouse, France, some time in the early 1000s and eventually spread throughout Provence and parts of Italy. By the mid-twelfth century, the Cathari had their own liturgy and church hierarchy. Albigensianism takes its name from the city of Albi, where one of its bishoprics was located.

Most of what we know about the heresy today comes from its enemies, so much of what follows should be taken with a grain of salt. By most accounts, the Albigensians believed that Satan, who masqueraded as the God of the Old Testament, was the actual creator of the world; Jesus was not the Son of God but an angel. By renouncing all sensual pleasures, and especially the Roman Catholic Church, which they regarded as irrevocably corrupt, the Albigensians hoped to reunite their souls with the true God. The Cathari's abhorrence of sex followed from their belief in the transmigration of souls, or reincarnation, which they regarded as one of Satan's cruelest tricks—it was his way of making sure that souls remained trapped in the lower world. Pope Innocent III began the exceptionally bloody Albigensian crusade in 1209; by the end of the thirteenth century the Cathari had gone underground; by the early 1400s the Inquisition had eliminated them entirely.

AMILLENNIALISM   *See* Millenarianism.

ANABAPTISM

From the Greek *ana,* or "again," the belief that infant baptism is inefficacious and that adult Christians need to be rebaptized. In the sixteenth century, several Anabaptist movements arose in Germany, Switzerland, Moravia, and the Netherlands, most notably the Swiss Brethren, who separated from Ulrich Zwingli's (1484–1531) church in Zurich and lived in small communities modeled on the early Christians; the Hutterian or Moravian Brethren, followers of Jacob Hutter, who was burned at the stake in 1536; and the Mennonites, followers of the Dutch reformer Menno Simons (1496–1561).

Though never formally unified, these movements agreed on a number of principles. They were pacifists, they refused to take oaths, and they disassociated themselves from the political world. They also shared a belief in the necessity of repentance, conversion, and adult baptism and rejected predestination (the notion that some souls were born saved and others damned). Anabaptists vested authority in scripture rather than theological doctrine, held to a strict morality that put religious obligations first when they conflicted with the law, and attempted to emulate Christ in the conduct of their lives. Many of these groups immigrated to the United States, particularly Pennsylvania. The Amish—who speak German with one another, wear homespun clothes in an eighteenth-century style, and reject modern conveniences such as automobiles, electricity, and telephones (except when necessary for their livelihoods)—are the most conservative and strictly separatist of the Mennonite denominations today.

ANIMATISM   *See* Syncretism.

ANIMISM

Animism is the belief that the world is inhabited by invisible, noncorporeal beings—spirits—who often reside in animals, plants, and inanimate objects, such as rocks, rivers, and mountains. The term was first used in connection with primitive religion by the influential English anthropologist Edward Tylor (1832–1917) in his landmark book *Primitive Culture*. Tylor regarded animism as a first step in the evolution of religion. The idea that people and things have souls led to the idea of shamanism (the belief that special individuals have the power—often aided by psychedelic mushrooms and herbs—to leave their bodies and have direct commerce with the spirit world); fetishism (the belief that physical objects can have occult power—the bones of an ancestor might be venerated; an enemy's skull might be fashioned into a cup, etc.); and totemism (the identification of a social group with the spirit of a plant or animal). As the religious consciousness evolves, Tylor suggested, spirits take on identities of their own; they become gods and demons and lesser supernatural creatures. As these gods become increasingly associated with great moral and metaphysical questions, polytheism gives way to monotheism. Most contemporary anthropologists reject Tylor's ethnocentric perspective—few would share his Victorian certainty that European Christianity is any "higher" or more evolved a manifestation of the religious impulse than Yoruban animism or Japanese Shintoism.

Similar but not identical to animism is animatism, the belief that powerful but impersonal and nonpersonified forces exist in the natural world, occasionally erupting in spectacular displays of power like volcanos and thunderstorms and sometimes vesting themselves in powerful personages, like tribal chiefs or great hunters.

ANTHROPOSOPHISM   *See* Syncretism.

ANTINOMIANISM
The belief in Christianity that the bestowal of divine grace relieves the believer of the obligation to obey the moral law—once saved, always saved. Martin Luther (1483–1546) coined the term, which literally means "against the law," in a rejoinder to his fellow Protestant John Agricola (ca. 1492–1566), who had declared, "Art thou steeped in sin—an adulterer or thief? If thou believest, thou art in salvation. All who follow Moses must go to the devil." Anne Hutchinson (1591–1643) was expelled from Massachusetts for the heresy of antinomianism, but she hadn't proposed to break any laws. Though she denied the covenant of works, more likely her real crime was that she had had the temerity to criticize the established clergy. Though the word *antinomianism* might date to the Reformation, the idea goes back to the very beginnings of Christianity, indeed to the New Testament itself. Taken out of context, some of Paul's statements in the Epistles about salvation by faith without "deeds of righteousness" seem to support it.

The Carpocratians, a Gnostic sect of the second century that was accused of every imaginable depravity by the orthodox church, held that the world was the creation of inferior angels and inherently corrupt. They regarded Jesus as an enlightened mortal who had discovered the way to transcendence. The secret, they believed, was to allow the soul to experience everything that life in the material world could offer, no matter how base or sinful. Once its thirst for worldly experience was satisfied, the soul would break out of the cycle of reincarnation and return to the higher realm where it had been born.

The Marcionites, a quasi-Gnostic group who thrived in the same era, believed that the Jewish God was an evil demiurge; they rejected not only the Old Testament in its entirety—including the Ten Commandments—but anything in the Gospels that seemed to be tainted by it. The Ranters of the Puritan era in England were notorious for their supposed embrace of free love.

In a jeremiad that appeared in *The American Christian* in 1997, the evangelical Ben Williams declared that:

> Antinomianism is epidemic today because man has become obsessed with self . . . Idioms of our culture are obvious. "Self-assertiveness," "self-awareness," "self-adjustment," "self-actualization," "self, self, self"! . . . Thus, the spirit of man is the spirit of lawlessness. It is true anarchy, and is the natural result of self-worship. Anarchy (rejection of God) starts in childhood and develops through church and public school teachings. It finds its home environment in modern society's commerce and entertainment. Its ultimate pinnacle is reached in Washington D.C., where anarchy is officially established as *the Beast who disguises itself as a lamb, but speaks as a dragon* (Revelation 13:11).

ARIANISM

A major heresy of early Christianity, propounded by Arius of Alexandria (250–336 CE). Influenced by Gnosticism and Neoplatonism, Arianism threatened the integrity of the Trinity with its teaching that Jesus was one of God's creations. Though still divine, Jesus was thus thought to be a lesser divinity, made of a different substance than his father's, and not eternal, since he had not always existed. Emperor Constantine I called the Council of

Nicaea in 325, the first ecumenical council in the history of the church, to settle the controversy once and for all. At its conclusion, Arius was exiled to Ilyria and the first version of the Nicene Creed was promulgated (it would be expanded after a second council in 381), which firmly avowed that God and Jesus were consubstantial (*houmoousis* in Greek), or made of the same substance. A similar Trinitarian controversy would lead to the schism that separated the Roman from the Eastern Orthodox Church.

ARMINIANISM

After Jacobus Arminius (1560–1609), a Dutch Reformed theologian, who debated Franciscus Gomarus (1563–1641), his colleague at the University of Leiden, about the Calvinist doctrine of predestination, or the belief that some souls were born already damned, others were born saved. Arminius held that Christ died for all men, not just for a special elect of saints who were fortunate from birth, and that salvation is available for anyone who chooses it. Arminianism is bedrock tenet of Wesleyan Methodism and the Disciples of Christ; many Baptists are Arminians as well.

ATHEISM

The active, principled denial of the existence of God, as opposed to skepticism, indifference, or ignorance on the subject. As the philosopher Thomas Nagel wrote in his book *The Last Word* (1997),

> I want atheism to be true and am made uneasy by the fact that some of the most intelligent and well-informed people I know are religious believers . . . It isn't just that I don't believe in God . . . It's that I hope there is no God! I don't want there to be a God; I don't want the universe to be like that.

C. S. Lewis, in *The Problem of Pain,* noted the irony that "atheists express their rage against God although in their view He does not exist."

ATHLICANISM   *See* Rastafarianism.

AUGUSTINIANISM

The beliefs and doctrines of the church father St. Augustine of Hippo (354–430 CE), the author of the *Confessions, The City of God,* and many other treatises, and by most accounts the most influential Christian after Jesus and Paul. Raised a Christian, he converted to Manichaeanism as a young man and fathered a child out of wedlock (his ambivalence about sex and other carnal pleasures is captured in his oft-quoted prayer, "O Lord, help me to be pure, but not yet"). His discovery of Neoplatonism would lead him back to Christianity, a journey he recounts in his *Confessions. The City of God,* written as the Roman Empire was crumbling under the onslaught of pagans, offers a view of history in which the sacred and secular spheres of life are constantly in conflict, but in which the sacred ultimately triumphs.

More a polemicist than a systematic philosopher, Augustine fought against the Pelagian (which denies original sin) and the Donatist (which holds that a sinful priest can't perform the Eucharist) heresies, insisting on mankind's essential corruption and the ultimate authority of the institutional church.

BABISM See Syncretism.

BAHAISM See Syncretism.

BAPTISM

The Greek word for "dipping." A sacrament in most Christian churches (though not the Quakers), Baptism is a rite of purification by water, which cleanses a person from sin and confers membership in the church. Some churches baptize infants; others, only adults. Some insist on complete immersion; others merely drip water onto the initiate. Most Christians baptize in the name of the Father, Son, and Holy Spirit, but antitrinitarians, like the Oneness Pentecostals, baptize in Jesus' name only.

The Baptist movement began in the seventeenth-century when a group of separatist English Christians living in exile in Holland came under the influence of the Anabaptist Mennonites. Some of them returned to London and founded a church known as the General Baptists, since they subscribed to the Arminian doctrine that Christ had atoned for everyone, not just those predestined for salvation. In 1633, the Particular Baptists, Calvinists who believed that atonement was an individual act, were founded. The General and Particular Baptists would be united in 1891 as the Baptist Union of Great Britain and Ireland.

Particular Baptists established a church in Rhode Island in 1639; in 1684 a group of Baptists immigrated to Charleston, South Carolina, to escape Puritan persecution. General Baptists were accepted in the Southeast; in the Appalachians, the settlers preferred the Calvinist Particular Baptists, who came to be called Primitive or Hard Shell Baptists. The Southern Baptist Convention was established in 1845 when slavery became an issue; it is the largest denomination of Baptists in America today. There are two major organizations of black Baptists; the National Baptist Convention and the National Baptist Convention of America. Though there are tremendous variations within the Baptist movement, Baptists are distinguished by their communitarian outlook—they regard their churches as a fellowship of believers, much as they believe the early Christians did. Adult baptism underscores their deliberate, conscious commitment to living a Christian life.

Ritual immersion is not just a Christian rite. Jesus was baptized, which shows that at least some Jews of his day followed the custom; to this day when observant Jews adopt a gentile baby, it is formally converted and "dipped" in a *mikvah*, or a ritual bath. Mithraism, the mystery religion popular among Roman soldiers, held baptism ceremonies; Japanese Shintoists ritually cleanse themselves before they enter their shrines.

BLACK MUSLIMISM   *See* **Nation of Islam.**

BOGOMILISM
Heretical cult that arose in Bulgaria in the tenth century and was dispersed throughout Europe in the next four hundred years. It

was a likely influence on the Albigensian heresy, also known as Catharism. The word *Bogomil* is reputed to be the name of the cult's founder; it means "favored by God" in Slavic.

Like the Cathars and many Gnostics from the early Christian era, the Bogomils were dualists in that they believed the world was the creation of a demiurge, a lesser divine being, rather than God himself. According to the Bogomils' origin myth, God had two sons. The elder a rebellious one, was named Satanail. He created the earth and mankind, though he had to appeal to God to give men their souls. Adam and his descendants were formally bound to him until his younger brother, Michael, came to earth as a man—Jesus—and voided Satanail's contract with humanity. The Bogomils held that everything material—including the Crucifixion and Resurrection, the virgin birth, and in fact virtually all of orthodox Christianity— was Satanic. The only way to achieve redemption, they believed, was to reject all of the things of the world.

Interestingly, the Latin name for the movement was Bulgaris, or Bulgarian. In French, Bulgaris became *bougre,* which spawned the Italian word *buggero,* the Spanish word *bujarrón,* and the English word *bugger,* all pejoratives for people who perform a sex act that was considered to be as unnatural, disreputable, and contemptible as this heresy.

BRITISH ISRAELITISM   *See* Christian Identity.

BUDDHISM

Born a prince in Nepal, Siddhārtha Gautama (581–501 BCE) gave up his possessions and set out to search for a solution to human suffering when he was twenty-nine years old. After six years, he achieved enlightenment and spent the remaining forty-five years of his life teaching and organizing a formal religion. The four "noble truths" of Buddhism (from the Sanskrit *bodhati,* "he awakes") are:

1) *dukkha,* existence is suffering
2) *trishna,* the cause of suffering is attachment and desire
3) *nirvana,* suffering desists

4) the eightfold path to the end of suffering is:
    right views
    right resolve
    right speech
    right action
    right livelihood
    right effort
    right mindfulness
    right concentration

Experience is broken down into five categories: *rupa,* or material existence; *vedana,* or sensations; *samjna,* or perceptions; *samskara,* or psychic constructs; and *vijnana,* or psychological processes. In none of them can an immutable, transcendent self be found. All physical phenomena are dependent on contingent causes; all are transitory. Life is a cycle of birth and death and rebirth; the only way to escape it is by dint of saintly discipline, by right living and the austerity and focus of monastic life, which leads to nirvana, the bliss that results from the elimination of desire and the dissolution of individual consciousness. Notably absent from Buddhism is the notion of a personal God.

The Buddha's teachings were transmitted orally until about the first century BCE. The earliest surviving texts are from the Theravada (literally, doctrine of the Elders) Buddhism of Sri Lanka and Southeast Asia. The Theravada texts are called the Tripitaka, or the Three Baskets, and include the Vinaya Pitaka, rules for monastic life; the Sutra Pitaka, dialogues of the Buddha; and the Abhidhamma Pitaka, or treatises. Mahayana (literally, the great Vehicle) Buddhism traveled to Tibet, Mongolia, China, Korea, and Japan. Most of its doctrines agree with Theravada Buddhism, but Mahayana does contain a transcendent element: Tathata, or suchness: the truth that governs the universe. To the enlightened mind, everything is a manifestation of Tathata; it is present within the self as Buddha Nature. Mahayana Buddhism also introduces the notion of the Bodhisattva, an enlightened being, who postpones his entry into nirvana until everybody else is saved. Bodhisattva is both a goal for practicing Buddhists and a divine being who is worshipped.

The Saddharmapundarika Sutra, the Lotus Sutra, teaches that all beings will attain Buddhahood by the grace of the eternal, cosmic Buddha. Buddhists of the Pure Land schools rely on the Buddha Amitābha, the Buddha of Infinite Light, to bring them into Sukhavati, or the Western Paradise. Amitābha was once a monk named Dharmakāra; when he achieved nirvana he created a Buddhaksetra, or Buddha field, a place where souls who are not able to achieve nirvana on their own can be reborn into.

One of the Prajnaparamita, or the Sutras on the Perfection of Wisdom, is the Vajracchedika Prajnaparamita, or the Diamond Sutra. Its paradoxical utterances led to the formation of Zen (in Japanese) schools of Buddhism. Zen koans (literally, public propositions) short-circuit logic; they startle the mind into using its intuition. The following koan dates from the late thirteenth century; it was written by the Japanese teacher Muju.

> Hakuin used to tell his pupils about an old woman who had a teashop, praising her understanding of Zen. The pupils refused to believe what he told them and would go to the teashop to find out for themselves.
>
> Whenever the woman saw them coming she could tell at once whether they had come for tea or to look into her grasp of Zen. In the former case, she would serve them graciously. In the latter, she would beckon to the pupils to come behind her screen. The instant they obeyed, she would strike them with a fire-poker.
>
> Nine out of ten of them could not escape her beating.

Tibetan Buddhism adds elements of Tantrism and Yoga to Mahayana doctrine as well as some vestiges of its native Bon tradition, which preceded the arrival of Buddhism in Tibet.

CALVINISM *See* Protestantism.

CAMPBELLISM

From Thomas Campbell (1763–1854) and his son Alexander (1788–1866), Irish-born Presbyterian ministers who emigrated to America and abandoned their denominations for a creedless, antiauthoritarian, antisectarian, purely Biblical Protestantism. Alexander joined forces with Barton W. Stone (1772–1844), and their Restoration movement (so called because it was modeled on the primitive church) eventually culminated in the formation of the Disciples of Christ, which has since spawned the Churches of Christ and the Christian Church, organizations of autonomously controlled, creedless churches led by lay preachers, which emphasize Bible study and forbid instrumental music in their services. Though religiously conservative, many Restoration churches are socially liberal, especially on gay issues.

CARPOCRATIANISM   *See* Gnosticism.

CATHARISM   *See* Albigensianism.

CHILIASM   *See* Millenarianism.

CHRISTIANITY

With more than 2 billion adherents, Christianity is the largest religion in the world today (Islam, with 1.2 billion followers, comes in second; Hinduism, with just over .75 billion, comes in third; Buddhism runs a distant fourth at 360 million).

In its broadest outlines, Christianity is the belief that Jesus of Nazareth, a radical Jewish rabbi who preached in Palestine some two thousand years ago, was the son of God, born of an unmarried mother (the Virgin Mary), and sent into the world by his father to redeem mankind from Adam's sin. He was crucified by the Romans in his thirty-third year and miraculously resurrected; those who believe in him today will be granted eternal life.

Even as general an account of Christianity as this one is contentious—for every assertion one might make, there are sects, denominations, and movements that would argue with it. Many

Unitarians, though they consider themselves Christian, would deny that Jesus was the son of God or his mother a virgin; a Roman Catholic would argue that belief is not sufficient for redemption without the sacraments of the church; a strict Calvinist might argue that along with faith you need to be predestined for salvation. Those who believe that Jesus is divine are not necessarily in accord on whether he is consubstantial with his father or created by him. The mystery of the Trinity, the idea that the Father, Son, and the Holy Spirit are separate aspects of the One God, has been a cause of contention since it was first articulated. Some believe that Jesus' teachings supersede those of the Jews; others, that they cannot be fulfilled without the existence of a Jewish state. Doctrine is not the only thing that Christians argue about. Though the Jesus of the Gospels did not seem to have a high regard for wealth, many contemporary Christians believe that he rewards his followers with riches; though Jesus famously preached that one should turn the other cheek when struck, many wars have been fought in his name. Capitalists and communalists, anarchists and monarchs, pacifists and militarists have all styled themselves as true Christians.

It is tempting to simply quote Nietzsche (no friend of Christianity) and leave it at that: "In reality there has only been one true Christian, and he died on the cross." Instead, I have tried, in dozens of separate entries on Christian heresies, denominations, and doctrines, to do justice to its complexity.

CHRISTIAN IDENTITY

Millenarian, racist, and anti-Semitic theology followed by a number of small churches and organizations in the United States and South Africa, including the Aryan Nations; the Church of Jesus Christ Christian, Kingdom Identity Ministries; the White Aryan Resistance (WAR) and White Separatist Banner.

Most of these churches are influenced by the undoubtedly crackpot but relatively innocuous tenets of British Israelitism—the belief that the Anglo-Saxon and Celtic peoples are descended from the lost tribes of Israel. British Israelitism sprang from the preaching of Richard Brothers (1757–1824), a former sailor who, upon the instructions of an angel, attempted to gather up England's Jews—many of them, he believed, unaware of their origins—and return them to Israel. While confined to a mental hospital, he prophesied that he would be revealed as the Messiah on November 19, 1795; his movement lost steam when this event failed to transpire.

In 1840, John Wilson published a best-selling book called *Our Israelitish Origin*. M. M. Eshelman, the author of *Two Sticks or the Lost Tribes of Israel Discovered* (1887); W. H. Poole, who wrote *Anglo-Israel or the Saxon Race Proved to be the Lost Tribes of the Bible* (1889), and especially Charles Fox Parham (1873–1927), one of the founders of modern Pentecostalism; and John Allen, the author of *Judah's Sceptre and Joseph's Birthright* (1902) all helped spread British Israelitism to the United States, where it was adopted by the Adventist Church of God.

The Christian Identity movement adds a strong racist and anti-Semitic component to this origins theory. In 1947, Gerald L. K. Smith (1898–1976), a former associate of Louisiana's populist governor Huey Long and the founder of the America First party, launched the Christian Nationalist Crusade, which called for the deportation of Zionists and blacks, and the dismantling of the United Nations. Around the same time, Dr. Wesley Swift, a former KKK kleagle and the editor of Smith's magazine *The Cross and the Flag,* founded the White Identity Church of Jesus Christ-Christian (which changed its name in 1957 to the Church of Jesus Christ-Christian). Throughout the 1950s and 1960s, Swift's daily radio broadcasts reached a large audience. After Swift died in 1970, Richard Butler, one of his pastors, opened up a branch of the church in Idaho; in 1982, Butler would organize the International Congress of Aryan Nations. The Church of Israel is a splinter group of the schismatic Mormon Church of Christ (Temple Lot); when its leader Daniel Gayman espoused white supremacist ideas, he sparked a court battle with its former members for control of the church; when he lost that battle, he would organize a new church in 1974 called the Church of Christian Heritage.

Though there are subtle doctrinal differences among the

various Identity churches, most of them believe that the true Israelites and the authentic people of the Covenant are the so-called Aryan descendants of the lost tribes of Israel, who in the guise of Celts and Anglo-Saxons invaded and civilized Europe (some believe that the Danes are descended from the tribe of Dan). According to Identity orthodoxy, the "impostors" who call themselves Jews today are not Israelites at all but the descendants of Edomites (the Semitic nation founded by Esau), or in some accounts, of the Khazars, a Turkic tribe that converted to Judaism in the Middle Ages. The most fanciful Christian Identity origin myths claim that the dark races are the mongrel progeny of Cain, whose father was not Adam but Satan. Cain supposedly married a nonhuman woman who was a relic from a pre-Adamic creation, so the nonwhite races are only one quarter human.

Many Christian Identity churches believe that the United States is an illegitimate state that's secretly controlled by Zionists (they call it ZOG, or the Zionist Occupation Government); some (postmillennialist dominionists) believe that Jesus will return as soon as they overthrow the state, expel or destroy the lesser races, and establish a theocratic government. More quietist Identity Christians cultivate a strict separatism. Still others are stockpiling weapons and food supplies in isolated compounds in expectation of the End Times, which they believe will take the form of an all-out race war.

CHRISTIAN RECONSTRUCTIONISM
See Millenarianism.

CHRISTIAN RESTORATIONISM   See Campbellism.

CHRISTIAN SCIENCE
Religious movement founded in 1879 by Mary Baker Eddy (1821–1910), a former patient of Phineas Parkhurst Quimby (1802–66), the creator of New Thought. Eddy's book *Science and Health with Key to the Scriptures* (1875) lays out her philosophy in detail. To Eddy, the essence of reality is spiritual, and Jesus Christ is the "Way-shower"—his crucifixion and resurrection

"served to uplift faith to understand eternal life, even the allness of soul, Spirit, and the nothingness of matter." Since matter is illusory, she wrote, illness and even death are matters of false belief: "Sickness, as well as sin, is an error that Christ, Truth, alone can destroy." "Of all the strange and frantic and incomprehensible and uninterpretable books which the imagination of man has created," Mark Twain memorably wrote, "surely this one is the prize sample."

Rather than treating illnesses with medicine, Christian Scientists purify their minds through prayer. When a patient's own prayers fail to effect a cure, Christian Science practitioners offer counsel. While the church does not officially forbid its members to avail themselves of conventional medicine in extreme cases, there is considerable social pressure in many of its self-governed congregations not to.

CONFUCIANISM

Deeply conservative political and ethical school of philosophy founded by Confucius (551–479 BCE) in China. Other transliterations of his name are K'ung Ch'iu and K'ung Chung'ni; he was also known as K'ung Fu-tzu or Master K'ung. A scholar, a ritualist, an itinerant teacher, and a one-time minor government official, Confucius strove to return the tumultuous China of his day to the ethical and religious perfection of its Golden Age.

Confucius was only the first contributor to the school that bears his name. Other important Confucians are Mencius (ca. 372–ca. 289 BCE), Hsün-tzu (ca. 298–ca. 230 BCE), and Tung Chung-shu (ca. 179–ca. 104 BCE). Neo-Confucianists in the Middle Ages include Han Yü (768–824), Shao Yung (1011–1077), Chou Tun-i (1017–1073), Chang Tsai (1020–1077), Ch'eng Hao (1032–1085), and Ch'eng I (1033–1107). Still later Confucian thinkers include Wang Fu-chih (1619–1692), Yen Yüan (1635–1704), and Tai Chen (1724–27). The school of Confucius, which encompasses many diverse traditions, is known collectively as Ju-chia, or the school of Ju; Ju, which means weak, implicitly contrasts the aristocratic gentleness and introspection of the Confucian scholars with the unthinking violence of the warrior class.

At the heart of Confucianism is what Westerners call the Golden Rule: the injunction not to do to others as you would not wish done to yourself. Central concepts are *tao*, the way, the ideal way of life, and *te,* virtue, especially a ruler's. The ideal ruler is humble, self-sacrificing, pious, and mild. Thus we read in the *Analects:* "When a prince's personal conduct is correct, his government is effective without the issuing of orders. If his personal conduct is not correct, he may issue orders, but they will not be followed." Also, "Good government obtains when those who are near are made happy, and those who are far off are attracted."

Jen is the quality of benevolence; *li* originally referred to the correct performance of sacrificial rites but came to encompass the norms of decency: "When rulers love to observe the rules of propriety, the people respond readily to the calls on them for service." *Yi* is the courage to do right, regardless of the consequences. Different Confucian schools disagreed as to the nature of *hsing*, or nature: Some maintained that, like the Freudian id, it is intrinsically selfish and needs to be disciplined and restrained; others, that it is essentially good and needs to be cultivated. Some Confucianists absorbed aspects of Buddhism, others didn't. All agreed that respect for ancestors and tradition were essential attributes, as was self knowledge.

Confucius says:

> The superior man has nine things which are subjects with him of thoughtful consideration. In regard to the use of his eyes, he is anxious to see clearly. In regard to the use of his ears, he is anxious to hear distinctly. In regard to his countenance, he is anxious that it should be benign. In regard to his demeanor, he is anxious that it should be respectful. In regard to his speech, he is anxious that it should be sincere. In regard to his doing of business, he is anxious that it should be reverently careful. In regard to what he doubts about, he is anxious to question others. When

he is angry, he thinks of the difficulties his anger may involve him in. When he sees gain to be got, he thinks of righteousness.

CONGREGATIONALISM   *See* Puritanism.

CREATIONISM

A continuum of religious beliefs about the origins of life on earth, all of which differ sharply from the naturalistic Darwinian theory of evolution. At one end are the so-called young earth creationists, who subscribe to the literal account of Genesis: God made the world, mankind, and all of the plants and animals that are in it in six days, less than ten thousand years ago. Geological features that scientists claim took millions of years to form—such as the Grand Canyon, slowly carved into the earth by the actions of erosion, or the White Cliffs of Dover, which science claims are an accumulation of millions of years of calciferous deposits from tiny marine creatures—are really the result of the upheavals caused by the worldwide deluge. Radio carbon dating and other high-tech dating methods that seem to contradict their beliefs are simply mistaken. To the young earth creationists, the Bible is a seamless whole. If you question whether or not Eve was formed from Adam's rib, then what's to prevent you from questioning whether or not she ate of the forbidden fruit? And if you don't believe in the fall, why would you believe that Jesus lived and died in order to redeem mankind?

Old earth creationists and advocates of intelligent design take a different approach. They allow that the six Biblical "days" might have actually been epochs; they even entertain the possibility that a naturalistic process of evolution could have played a limited role in improving and diversifying some already existing life-forms. But natural selection, they say, fails to explain the process of speciation. How does an insect turn into a mammal? Or a land mammal turn into a whale? How could intermediate species—a land animal, say, with fins instead of feet—ever have survived in its state of inbetweenness? Where is the fossil evidence? Why is it that the most important links always seem to be missing? How could a body part as complex as the brain, or for that matter, an amino acid, have evolved by dumb chance? The odds of that happening are about the same as a tornado blowing through a junkyard and leaving a trailer park in its place. At best, natural selection is blind faith, and as such, its adversaries claim, it has no more business being taught exclusively in schools than the Bible does. Not only basic fairness and freedom of religion and expression, but scientific skepticism and healthy open-mindedness would seem to demand that students be exposed to both points of view.

This of course is creationism's ultimate agenda: to bring a religious point of view back into America's schools, to undercut the secular bias in public education that, according to every Supreme Court decision thus far, the nonestablishment clause of the First Amendment of the Constitution requires.

DARBYISM   *See* **Millenarianism.**

DEISM

The belief that God exists as a supreme intelligence and the Creator of the universe, that his existence is manifest in the laws of nature, but that he has long since disassociated himself from human affairs. This was the view of many of the important philosophers of the eighteenth-century Enlightenment. Although he was personally opposed to Deism, John Locke's (1632–1704) books *An Essay Concerning Human Understanding* and *The Reasonableness of Christianity* nevertheless provide Deism with its philosophical underpinning.

Voltaire (1694–1778), Jean-Jacques Rousseau (1712–78), and Benjamin Franklin (1706–90) were Deists, as was Thomas Jefferson (1743–1826), who referred to "Nature's God" in the Declaration of Independence, and who, in writing of the "life, character & doctrines of Jesus," noted that he sought to reform the "degraded" theism and ethics of the Old Testament, by bringing to them:

> The principles of a pure deism, and juster notions of the attributes
> of God, to reform their moral doctrines to the standard of reason,

justice & philanthropy, and to inculcate the belief of a future state. This view would purposely omit the question of his divinity, & even his inspiration. To do him justice, it would be necessary to remark . . . that his system of morality was the most benevolent & sublime probably that has been ever taught, and consequently more perfect than those of any of the antient philosophers.

Deism is most often mentioned today in the context of the battle between Darwinism and creationism. So-called Deistic creationists believe that God created the world and the major classes of life ex nihilo (from nothing), but then left them to develop and diversify on their own, as if he were a clockmaker who, once he'd wound up his creation, abandoned it to run on its own.

DISPENSATIONALISM   *See* Millennialism.

DOMINIONISM   *See* Millenarianism.

DONATISM
The schismatic movement that arose among the Christians of North Africa in the fourth century CE. In 303, the Roman emperor Diocletian had issued an edict that outlawed Christianity. Church buildings were razed, sacred books were burned, and Christians were ordered to offer incense to Roman gods or die. In the aftermath of the great persecution, the church venerated its martyrs. Those who were condemned but survived were honored as "confessors," which gave them the power to forgive sins and celebrate the sacraments. Collaborators—those who handed over holy books or cooperated in other ways with the Roman authorities—were branded as *traditores*, which literally means "the ones who handed over."

After Diocletian died in 305, the church set about rebuilding itself. One of the problems it faced was what to do with its *traditores*. The church's decision was to forgive those who were penitent, an idea that did not sit well with many of the confessors. In 311, Caecilian was consecrated bishop of Carthage. One of the Bishops who consecrated him, however, Felix of Aptunga, had been a *traditore*. A renegade group of North Africans was so outraged by Aptunga's participation that they refused to acknowledge the blameless Caecilian. In 313, they consecrated a rival bishop named Donatus (whose name was thereafter attached to the movement). The treachery of the *traditores,* the Donatists declared, put them beyond any possible hope of forgiveness. Thus compromised, a priest could not perform the Eucharist or any other sacerdotal functions efficaciously, they believed. The church strenuously disagreed. The moral character of the priest administering the sacraments was irrelevant, since the miraculous power of such rites came directly from God.

Condemned by the Synod of Arles in 314, the Donatists seceded from the Roman church (and the Roman Empire—they refused to acknowledge the emperor's religious authority either) and set up their own ecclesiastical hierarchy. They also demanded that anyone baptized under Roman authority be rebaptized by them. The Circumcellions, a peasant army that supported the Donatists, terrorized orthodox Catholics, tax collectors, and anyone representing papal or imperial authority. By 350, there were more Donatists than Roman Catholics in North Africa. It wasn't until 411, when the immensely influential bishop Augustine of Hippo (354–430 CE) debated Donatist bishops in Carthage, that the tide finally began to turn.

As with so many other heresies, the primary issue was power; the Donatist challenge to papal and imperial authority could not go unanswered. But this time the Roman church had a compelling moral argument to make as well. The Donatists called their purified church a "sealed fountain" or an "enclosed garden." The Roman church's rejoinder—that no one is free of the shadow of sin, that all who truly repent can hope for forgiveness—is very much in the spirit of the Gospels. "Why have you so improperly separated yourselves from the seed of Abraham?" Saint Augustine challenged the Donatists. "You do not enter into communion with all the earthly nations, the holy seed of Abraham, and that is a very serious crime not only for some of you, but for all of you."

The Donatist challenge has reasserted itself in recent years over such issues as the Catholic Church's reluctance to defrock priests accused of pederasty or to turn them over to the civil authorities. Some defenders of the Vatican's policy found a theological justification in the *ex opere operato* (literally "from the work itself") benefits of the sacraments—the doctrine that no matter how corrupt the priest who performs the rites may be, the sacraments still retain their sacred power. Though this argument might provide some comfort to parishioners who are compelled to receive the host from wicked priests, it offers scant comfort to their past and future victims.

EASTERN ORTHODOX CHRISTIANITY

With the Great Schism of 1054, the separation between the Latin- and Greek-speaking churches, long festering, became a formal divorce. The immediate cause of the schism was a question of papal power: The pope believed that he had formal authority over four Eastern patriarchs; the Eastern church insisted that his primacy was merely honorary. There was a Trinitarian issue too: Without consulting with the Easterners, the Western church had amended the Nicene Creed to say "And I believe in the Holy Ghost, the Lord, and Giver of Life, who proceedeth from the Father *and the Son*." This is known as the *filioque* (literally "and the son") clause, which Eastern Orthodoxy rejects to this day.

There were other doctrinal and jurisdictional issues as well. The patriarch of Constantinople regarded himself as the first of equals among his bishops and regarded the pope in the same way. Papal decisions could not be considered binding, according to the Orthodox, without the concordance of a church council. Because the patriarch was less disposed to interfere with the affairs of the various national churches that he oversaw, the Eastern church has enjoyed considerably less fraught relations with secular powers than Catholicism has. Other differences between Eastern and Roman churches are that priests, but not bishops, can marry; the Communion bread is dipped in the wine before it is served.

The autocephalous (self-governing) churches of the East are the Orthodox Church of Constantinople, the Orthodox Church of

Alexandria, the Orthodox Church of Antioch, the Orthodox Church of Jerusalem, the Russian Orthodox Church, the Georgian Orthodox and Apostolic Church, the Romanian Orthodox Church, the Bulgarian Orthodox Church, the Orthodox Church of Cyprus, the Church of Greece, the Polish Orthodox Church, the Albanian Orthodox Church, the Czech and Slovak Orthodox Church, and the Orthodox Church in America. Autonomous churches—their bishops are appointed by a patriarch—include the Orthodox Church of Mt. Sinai, the Finnish Orthodox Church, the Estonian Orthodox Church, the Latvian Orthodox Church, the Japanese Orthodox Church, the Chinese Orthodox Church, the Ukranian Orthodox Church, the Metropolis of Western Europe, the Metropolitan Church of Bessarabia, the Moldovan Metropolitan Church, and the Orthodox Ohrid Archbishopric.

EBIONITISM

The beliefs of a Middle Eastern Jewish cult that existed in the first centuries of the Christian era and venerated Jesus of Nazareth. Few Ebionite writings have survived, but from Christian heresiologists, such as Irenaeus (130–202 CE), we know that they believed that Jesus, though mortal and the natural son of Joseph and Mary, was the Messiah. Paradoxically (especially in the light of Paul's teachings about the validity of Old Testament commandments), the Ebionites believed that Jesus was able to perform miracles *because* of his fealty to Mosaic law. The Ebionites' name is derived from the Hebrew word *ebionim,* which means "the poor" and refers to their asceticism; they practiced vegetarianism and were opposed to animal sacrifice.

A modern movement that calls itself Ebionite has arisen in recent years. Though small in membership, it is large enough to have already endured several schisms. Modern-day Ebionites, most of them fallen Christians, believe that Jesus was a radical Jew who sought to bring about a messianic age of social justice. Orthodox Christianity, according to these neo-Ebionites, was a mystery cult that essentially hijacked Jesus' teachings and distorted them to serve their own ends.

EPISCOPALIANISM   *See* Protestantism.

ESSENISM

Beliefs and practices of the Essenes, a Jewish monastic sect that existed in Palestine between the second century BCE and the destruction of the Second Temple in 70 CE. The Essenes were celibate men who held their possessions in common, forbade animal sacrifice, and ate only uncooked vegetables and fruits. They also forswore violence (except in self-defense), trade, and oath taking (except the oaths new members took to remain loyal to the order and keep its secrets). Their belief in the immortality of the soul and multiple messiahs, and their practice of ritual immersion almost certainly influenced Christianity.

The Dead Sea scrolls, a repository of parchment and papyrus scrolls found in caves near Qumran in Jordan, where the Essenes were believed to have lived, have shed additional light on their beliefs, which had previously been documented only in the writings of Josephus (37–100 CE), Philo of Alexandria (ca. 13–ca. 50 CE), and Pliny the Elder (23–79 CE). *The Manual of Discipline* describes the rules of the community; the eschatological *War of the Sons of Light with the Sons of Darkness* exhibits fascinating parallels with the beliefs of Zoroastrianism. Some scholars believe that traces of the later Essene writings that are gathered in the Temple Scrolls can be found in the Gospel of Mark.

ETHICAL CULTURE MOVEMENT

Founded in 1876 by Felix Adler (1851–1933), a professor of Hebrew and Oriental literature at Cornell University and the son of a prominent rabbi, the Ethical Culture movement asserts that "If God and good, and good and God be one, there is no God save what dawns upon us in the experience of doing good." Ethical Culture substitutes an impassioned belief in social reform and intellectual, moral, and spiritual uplift for the rituals and creeds of conventional religions. In its founder's words:

Spiritual evolution is the progressive advance of mankind toward a state of things in which the light of ethical perfection shall be reflected from the face of human society; that is, in which all men shall live and move and have their being in mutually promoting the highest life of each and all. It means that the object of social reformation shall not be a mere change in the conditions under which men live, but a change in human nature itself. It means that we shall look forward consciously to the breaking forth of new powers in ourselves, to the release, through our own efforts, of capacities dimly latent in us.

Unlike secular humanism, which Ethical Culture is often mistaken for, Ethical Culturists consider their movement to be a true religion, albeit one that is purged of anachronisms like supernaturalism and dogmatism, and that is exclusively geared toward building community, raising consciousness, and inculcating moral values. To that end, they hold services, conduct weddings and funerals, name babies, and teach Sunday school.

EUTYCHEANISM   *See* **Monophysitism.**

EVANGELICALISM
Not to be confused with evangelism, which means proselytizing for Christianity (the word is derived from the Greek *euangelos,* which means, roughly, "bringing good news"). Evangelicalism refers to a number of tendencies—some of them specifically doctrinal, some of them relating to a style of preaching and the subjective experience of faith—shared by a variety of Protestant sects. Contemporary evangelicalism differs in some ways from its historical antecedents; though it is often associated with a complex of conservative cultural and political beliefs, not all evangelicals share them.

 Evangelische Kirche, or Evangelical Church, is synonymous with Protestantism in Germany. Evangelicalism in its narrower sense emerged from Pietism, a reform movement within Lutheranism that was founded by Philipp Jakob Spener (1635–1705); August Hermann Francke (1663–1727) would propound Pietist teachings from the University of Halle. Pietism called for a return to Bible reading (it regarded the Bible as the literal word of God), increased lay participation in churches, a heightened emphasis on the emotional experience of faith, and a strengthened commitment to integrating religion into every aspect of daily life. By the early 1700s, some Pietists, such as Alexander Mack (1679–1735), had become involved with Anabaptist brethren. Many members of these groups would emigrate to the United States.

By the beginning of the nineteenth century, the seeds for the Second Great Awakening had been planted in America. Methodists, Mennonites and the Moravian Brethren, Pietistic Lutherans, Baptists, and the Presbyterians who would follow Thomas and Alexander Campbell and Barton W. Stone into the nondenominational Christian Church and the Disciples of Christ, brought a new fervor and emotionalism to the experience of religion. Preachers from different evangelical denominations shared the pulpit at camp meetings; the boundaries of sectarianism began to dissolve as the emphasis of sermons shifted from doctrine and damnation to the miraculous power of saving grace. Preachers like Dwight L. Moody (1837–99) and Charles Grandison Finney (1792–1875) emphasized the importance of an intimate, personal relationship with Jesus. Here is Finney on the experience of justification by grace:

> Dear hearer, are you now in a state of wrath? Now believe in Christ. All your waiting and groaning will not bring you any nearer. Do you say you want more conviction? I tell you to come now to Christ. Do you say you must wait till you prayed more? What is the use of praying in unbelief? Will the prayers of a condemned rebel avail? Do you say you are so unworthy? But Christ died for just such as you. He comes right to you now, on your seat. Where do you sit? Where is that individual I am speaking to? Sinner, you need not wait. You need not go home in your sins, with that heavy load on your heart. Now is the day of salvation. Hear the word of God: "If thou believe in thine

heart in the Lord Jesus Christ, and if thou confess with thy mouth that God raised him from the dead, thou shalt be saved."

Nineteenth-century evangelicals spearheaded the temperance movement; they were also at the vanguard of a number of progressive social causes. Evangelicalism lent its moral fervor to abolitionism; the egalitarian ethos of many of the churches offered women leadership roles. Missionary and benevolent societies sprung up under their auspices; the YMCA and the Salvation Army, both founded in England, also took root in the United States.

Inspired by Darbyism (see Millenarianism), many evangelicals began to take a special interest in eschatology, or the study of the end of the world. James Inglis (1813–72), James H. Brookes (1830–97), and Dwight Moody did much to spread Darby's notion of dispensationalism (a complex theory of history that discerns the beginnings of the End Times predicted in the Book of Revelation in contemporary world affairs); the annotated *Scofield Reference Bible* popularized it even more.

But for all of evangelicalism's successes in America, by the beginning of the twentieth century, the rise of Darwinism and higher criticism (an approach to the Bible that questioned its literal truth) and especially liberal theology had put many of them on the defensive. With the publication in the teens of the multivolume work *The Fundamentals* (see Fundamentalism), the ecumenicism and social involvement that had characterized so much of evangelicalism in the first half of the nineteenth century began to fade. After the Scopes trial in 1925, many fundamentalist evangelicals adopted a policy of separatism, avoiding contact with liberal Christians, withdrawing from the political sphere, and sending their children to Bible schools.

This began to change in the 1940s as neoevangelicals like Billy Graham began to conduct crusades and meetings. Harold Ockenga (1905–85), the pastor of the Park Street Congregational Church in Boston, the founder of the National Association of Evangelicals, cofounder and president of Fuller Theological Seminary, and chairman of the board and editor of *Christianity Today*, described the New Evangelicalism's philosophy:

> Neo-evangelicalism was born in 1948 in connection with a convocation address which I gave in the Civic Auditorium in Pasadena. While reaffirming the theological view of fundamentalism, this address repudiated its ecclesiology and its social theory. The ringing call for a repudiation of separatism and the summons to social involvement received a hearty response from many Evangelicals . . . It differed from fundamentalism in its repudiation of separatism and its determination to engage itself in the theological dialogue of the day. It had a new emphasis upon the application of the gospel to the sociological, political, and economic areas of life.

Many fundamentalists, in turn, deplored the willingness of Ockenga, Graham, and their fellow preachers to engage with Catholics, Jews, and representatives of Christian denominations who didn't believe that the Bible was God's inerrant word, and to interject themselves into secular affairs. Others—Pat Robertson, Jerry Falwell, and James Dobson leap to mind—have been less diffident. Touchstone issues for conservative evangelicals today are ending the movement toward tolerance for homosexuality, taking sex education and the theory of evolution out of classrooms and putting prayer back in, and promoting uncritical support for the state of Israel (which plays a key role in the End Time scenario they believe in). Not all evangelicals are socially conservative, however. It's worth remembering that the divisions between fundamentalists and evangelicals, evangelicals and evangelicals, and fundamentalists and fundamentalists are just as wide as those between evangelicals and nonevangelicals. If evangelical Protestant Christianity is an increasingly powerful and outspoken force in public life, it is far from a monolithic or even a universally conservative one.

EVANGELISM   *See* **Evangelicalism.**

FETISHISM   *See* **Animism.**

FINITE GODISM   *See* Meliorism.

FREEMASONRY

Popular tradition has it that the fraternal order of the Free and Accepted Masons, better known as the Freemasons, dates back to the construction of King Solomon's temple (the organization's initiation rites reenact the supposed martyrdom of Hiram Abiff, the temple's architect, who died protecting the order's secrets) and the mystery cults of ancient Egypt and Greece. Long before *The Da Vinci Code* was ever thought of, conspiratorially minded writers averred that the Masons were the heirs to the Knights Templar — and that its highest-ranking members were privy to their secrets.

Freemasonry does, in fact, date back to the craft guilds that the stonemasons who built the great cathedrals of the Middle Ages belonged to. They were called "free" masons because, as skilled laborers, they were permitted to travel across national borders; "accepted" members were nonstoneworkers who were patrons of the fraternity. The fraternal order that exists today—its worldwide membership is estimated to be about five million—began in England in the early 1700s. The first lodge in America was founded in Philadelphia in 1730 (Benjamin Franklin was one of its members). Today Masonic lodges can be found in almost every country of the world. Though Masonic rites and symbolism are mystical (some of them vestiges of Masonry's medieval origins; some of them borrowed from alchemy, astrology, Rosicrucianism, Christian Qabalah, and other occult interests of the seventeenth and eighteenth centuries), Masonry is not a religion. Beyond the requirement that its members believe in a Supreme Being, the bylaws of most of Masonry's autonomous national organizations, called Grand Lodges, are liberal and nonsectarian. Masonry's stated values are the cultivation of brotherly love, tolerance, and philanthropy.

Because it was both an esoteric and, in its early days, an elite society (notable European members included Voltaire, Goethe, and the Marquis de Lafayette; George Washington joined the Masons in 1752; Paul Revere, John Hancock, James Madison, Andrew Jackson, and James Monroe were all members), the Masons have often been viewed with suspicion. The Supreme Being of the eighteenth-century Masons was the Divine Architect of the Deists—a God who, having designed and created the world, left it to run according to the laws of nature.

The Catholic Church has forbidden its members to become Masons since 1738. John Robison's *Proofs of a Conspiracy Against All the Religions and Governments of Europe Carried on in the Secret Meetings of Freemasons, Illuminati and Reading Societies* was a best seller in Great Britain in 1798. When a bricklayer named William Morgan disappeared from upstate New York in 1826, and was rumored to have been murdered for planning to publish the organization's secrets, widespread outrage led to the formation of the Anti-Masonic Party, which put a presidential candidate on the ballot in 1832. It's worth noting in this context that the disquieting eye in the pyramid that appears on the Great Seal of the United States was not a Masonic emblem (though some Masonic lodges later adapted it to their own purposes). The all-seeing eye had long been a symbol of God's providence; the pyramid, though an occult symbol, plays no role in Masonic iconography. The designers of the seal explained that the pyramid was a representation of strength and durability.

Membership in the Masons is no longer the exclusive prerogative of the rich, powerful, and brilliant; Masonic temples play the same homely role in most American communities as the Lions Club, the Knights of Columbus, and the Veterans of Foreign Wars (VFW). While one can still rise through its ranks and petition for admittance to the Ancient Arabic Order of the Nobles of the Mystic Shrine (better known as the fez-wearing Shriners), and though the Masons still raise millions of dollars for charities, their membership is much smaller than it once was and is aging rapidly.

FUNDAMENTALISM

In general usage, fundamentalism means a strictly literal, unbending adherence to religious or ideological orthodoxy. Thus, such mutually hostile religious/political movements as the Wahhabism of Saudi Arabian Sunnis and the theocratic Shiite regime in Iran are bundled together as "fundamentalist Islam" because they both claim to be Koranic. The *haridim,* or ultra-observant Orthodox Jews, are sometimes styled fundamentalists, as are militant Zionists or even die-hard Marxist Leninists.

Fundamentalism has a more specific provenance, however, in the history of twentieth-century American Protestantism. In 1909, Lyman and Milton Stewart, the cofounders of the Union Oil Company of California and of the Bible Institute of Los Angeles, underwrote the publication of ninety essays (ultimately titled *The Fundamentals*) by leading conservative Protestant theologians and mailed them gratis to some three hundred thousand ministers, missionaries, and lay teachers. The essays, edited by R. A. Torrey (1856–1928), purported to defend Protestantism against the rising tide of Darwinism, secularism, and higher and lower Biblical criticism. Higher and lower criticism is the use of philological methods to reconstruct the editorial history of Biblical texts and discern their original authorship. It is from the efforts of these scholars that the Q strand in the New Testament (aphorisms and phrases that are believed to be the historical Jesus' genuine words) and the Book of J in the Old Testament (an embedded Ur text that predates the later, highly redacted canonical Torah, and that is attributed to an unknown ancient writer called J after his or her use of the name Jahweh for God) have been isolated. Obviously, this is a troubling practice for people who believe that whatever translation of the Bible their church prefers is a transcription of God's literal words.

Conservative Protestants felt especially threatened by liberal theology, the effort to reconcile scriptures with modern ideas, and to explain away accounts of miracles as folklore or symbolism. To the authors of *The Fundamentals,* all of these efforts seemed to be undermining Christianity's foundation in divine revelation. In the words of one of its contributors, the distinguished Scottish theologian James Orr (1844–1913),

> I am quite well aware that many of our friends who accept these newer critical theories claim to be just as firm believers in

Divine revelation as I am myself, and in Jesus Christ and all
that concerns Him. I rejoice in the fact . . . But what I maintain
is that this theory of the religion of the Bible which has been
evolved, which has peculiarly come to be known as the critical
view, had a very different origin—in men who did not believe
in the supernatural revelation of God in the Bible.

In 1918, the essays were gathered into a multivolume set called *The
Fundamentals* and published by the Bible Institute of Los Angeles at
"the cheapest price possible." In 1919, the Baptist minister William
Bell Riley (1861–1947) founded the World Christian Fundamentals Association. In 1920, Curtis Lee Laws (1868–1946), editor of
the *Watchman-Examiner,* a Baptist journal, used the word *fundamentalist* as a rallying call for those "who still cling to the great fundamentals and who mean to do battle royal" for their religion.

By the mid-1920s, there was broad agreement among a number of conservative, mostly millennialist, churches (who take
Revelation 20:1–3 in the literal sense, that the saints will rule for
a thousand years before time comes to an end) as to the five fundamentals of the Christian faith:

1) The literal inerrancy of Scripture
2) The virgin birth of Jesus
3) The substitutionary atonement
4) The bodily Resurrection of Jesus
5) The authenticity of Jesus' miracles (or alternatively,
     in millennialist churches, in the Second Coming
     of Christ)

In addition, many of these churches adopted a stance of separatism
from both the secular and the nonfundamentalist world, withdrawing their children from public schools and refusing to participate in
ecumenical activities with liberal churches. The neoevangelicalism
of preachers like Billy Graham, who rose to prominence in the
1950s, was in part a reaction against this separatism.

GALLICANISM   *See* Ultramontanism.

GNOSTICISM

The religious beliefs of any of a number of syncretic sects (*syncretic* means that their tenets were derived from more than one religious tradition) that arose in the Greco-Roman world in the centuries before and after the time of Jesus. The word *gnosticism* is derived from the Greek *gnosis* or "knowledge"; the term was coined by scholars in the nineteenth century to describe these groups. Though it is difficult to generalize about these very different schools of belief, almost all of them believe that salvation is attained through secret knowledge (rather than through ritual, faith, divine grace, or works).

Though scholars are still arguing about Gnosticism's origins (was it Jewish? Persian? Hellenic? Egyptian? Hermetic? Christian?), most agree that it borrowed from all of these sources. Most Gnostics were dualists in that they believed that this world was created and ruled by less-than-perfect beings (in some Gnostic cosmologies, the God of the Old Testament was a Satanic impostor), which suggests some affinities with Zoroastrianism and Manichaeanism. Aspects of Greek mystery cults, of Egyptian Hermeticism, of Pythagoreanism, of Platonism, and especially of Neoplatonism can be discerned in the beliefs of the Christian Gnostics as well. Many of the tenets of Christian orthodoxy were formulated as specific responses to Gnostic heresies; as the sects were declared apostate, their writings were systematically suppressed and destroyed. Until quite recently, the principal source of information about the Gnostics was the polemics against them by the church fathers, who not only attacked their ideas, but in many cases, their characters.

In 1945, a vast trove of scrolls that had been hidden in a cave near the town of Nag Hammadi, probably since the fourth century, was discovered by three Egyptian youths. After a complicated journey through the black market, most of them came into the hands of scholars and were translated and redacted (unfortunately, the boys' mother had used some of them to kindle her cooking fires). Among the fifty texts that were ultimately recovered were Gnostic creation stories, such as *The Hypostasis of the Archons* and *The Apocalypse of Adam;* treatises on Gnostic beliefs, such as *The Teachings of Silvanus* and *The Gospel of Truth;* and texts about the Divine Sophia (in some Gnostic cosmologies, Sophia, the spirit of Wisdom, created the world without God's approval—and seriously botched the job), such as *The Thunder, Perfect Mind.* There were a number of alternative, noncanonical versions of Gospels as well, such as the Gospel of Thomas and the Gospel of Philip. Other Gnostic texts have since come to light—some of them had been moldering uncataloged in museum collections since the nineteenth century. In the spring of 2006, a recently discovered gnostic Gospel of Judas made headlines around the world.

So what did the Gnostics believe? Most of them believed that the physical world and their bodies were created by a lesser divine artisan spirit (a demiurge); these beings (and the real world of Spirit) were both parts of an infinite Pleroma (plenitude), which was the source of the Aeons, the divine powers who ruled the universe. Just as in the movie *The Matrix,* the everyday world was believed to be a hallucination. But unlike *The Matrix,* gunfights and martial arts were not the means of restoring Truth; Gnostics used their minds instead. They analyzed biblical texts for esoteric meanings and constructed complex philosophic systems. Some Antinomian sects believed that the way to break their ties with the illusory physical world was to experience it to the full—the church fathers accused these cults of libertinism and even cannibalism. Some sects had baptism rites, some of them spoke in tongues, some of them used magic spells and incantations to influence angels and demons. The end goal of these diverse efforts was the subordination of the body (the *hylic* self) and the soul (*psyche*) and the liberation of the spirit (*pneuma*)—the divine spark that resides deep within, and that is *houmoousios* (of the same substance) as God.

The Sethian Gnostics traced their descent from Seth, the third son of Adam, who they believed carried the key to escaping from the world that was created by Yaltabaoth, a monster who was in turn the creation of Sophia. The Valentinian Gnostics believed that a wayward Aeon, the Mother, created a Shadow and a Savior. When the Savior returned to the Pleroma, the Mother created the demiurge who made the world and pretended to be God. The Savior, as Jesus, then came back from the Pleroma to save the world. The Carpocratians, one of the Antinomian sects, were believed to have a secret Gospel of Mark in their possession, which, among other shocking things, depicted Jesus spending the night with a naked young male disciple.

Mandaeanism, an esoteric, dualist religion still practiced by a small number of worshippers in southern Iraq and in Khuzestan, a province of Iran, appears to be a Gnostic survival from the early Christian era. Though the Mandaeans don't hold Jesus in particular regard, one of the major figures in their theology is John the Baptist. Interestingly, while they believe that their souls are imprisoned in a world that was created by an evil demiurge, they are not ascetics—they deplore fasting and celibacy.

HASIDISM

From the Hebrew word *hasid,* or "pious one." Hasidism began in Eastern Europe in the eighteenth century (the Hasidei Ashkenaz of eleventh- and twelfth-century Germany were an entirely unrelated movement), led by Israel ben Eliezer (1698–1760), better known as the Baal Shem Tov (Master of the Divine Name). Born in the village of Okup, in the Carpathian Mountains in western Ukraine, the Besht, as he was often called (an acronym from his initials), was orphaned at age five—his father's last words to him were reputed to have been, "Fear nothing other than God"—and eked out a living as a lowly synagogue custodian until he married the sister of a renowned Talmudist. After seven years of solitary study, he at last made a name for himself as an itinerant healer, preacher, and miracle worker.

The Baal Shems were practical Kabbalists who used prayers, invocations, amulets, herbal concoctions, and the names of angels, demons, and God (which was why they were called Baal Shems) to exorcise demons and cure illnesses. The Baal Shem Tov, however, was much more than a sorcerer. A genuine visionary, he transformed his uniquely personal vision into a far-reaching popular movement. By the 1730s, the Baal Shem had a circle of disciples. He taught them that God was present in all things and in all people—that one should cleave to God not just in study and formal prayer but in ecstatic devotion and meditation. Since sparks of God were present in all things, the Besht taught, everything could be redeemed (this was essentially Lurianic Kabbalism, absent its daunting theological apparatus).

Hasids prayed in the vernacular, drank liquor, sang and danced wildly, and cheerfully acknowledged the erotic side of life—even as they strove to maintain the highest ethical standards. "Even after one has achieved the spirituality of an angel, one must still abide by the commandments like a simple Jew," the Besht declared. A mass movement almost from its inception, Hasidism acknowledged that not everybody could be a saint or a scholar. The wonder-working *tzaddiks* (or "righteous ones"), the rabbis, or rebbes, served their adoring followers as intermediaries between the secular and the sacred worlds. As Hasidism spread and matured, its rebbes took on more and more power, providing their communities with the last word not just on moral and religious issues but on marital, financial, and legal matters as well. Some of the early great *tzaddiks* include Schneur Zalman (1745–1812), the author of the great mystical text *The Tanya;* his son Dov Baer (1773–1827), and Nachman of Breslov (1772–1810), the great grandson of the Besht. By the nineteenth century, as Hasidism continued to spread throughout Eastern Europe, many rebbes created dynasties, often with lamentable results—some of the Hasidic "courts" were as fractious, materialistic, and self-aggrandizing as their secular counterparts.

Hasidism survived the early attempts of conventional rabbis (*mitnagdim,* or "opponents") to discredit it. The legendary Gaon of Vilna, Lithuania, Rabbi Eliyahu ben Shlomo Zalman Kremer (1720–97), issued several edicts of excommunication; the Yiddish writer I. L. Peretz wrote about the Brisker *rov,* a bitter opponent of Hasidism who was as vengeful as a snake. If anyone was found with a Zohar or a Pardes, the *rov* would curse, and threaten the miscreant with excommunication. Once, when a student was caught with a book of kabbalah, the *rov* allowed Gentiles to shave off his beard. What do you think happened? The man lost his mind.

In the nineteenth century, Hasidism faced a graver peril as the attitudes of the Enlightenment spread through Jewish communities, as well as Reform Judaism, emigration, Zionism (which most Hasids opposed), and Marxism. The increasingly murderous anti-Semitism that had been endemic in Europe since medieval times would climax in the Shoah in the twentieth century. Ironically, in just a few generations, what had begun as a revolutionary movement had become the most conservative form of Judaism.

Though virtually all of the great Hasidic communities of Eastern Europe were destroyed in the holocaust, some of them managed to replant themselves in New York City and Israel. In the 1950s, the Sorbonne-educated Rabbi Menachem Mendel Schneerson (1902–94) assumed the leadership of the Chabad-Lubavitch movement in Brooklyn; many of his followers still believe that he is the Messiah. With its outreach to secular Jews and its high birth rates, Chabad has become one of the fastest-growing denominations in Judaism today, with centers in forty-five states and more than sixty countries. The Satmar, the Bobov, and the Belzer Hasids (most communities are named after the Eastern European town they originated in; the garments their members wear reflect the styles favored by the Jews of those towns in the eighteenth century) are a few of the other communities in New York that have substantial memberships.

HENOTHEISM *See* **Polytheism.**

HERMETICISM
Ancient metaphysical writings putatively authored by Hermes Trismegistus (Greek for Thoth the Thrice Great, the Egyptian god of

wisdom). The Hermetic communities of the early Christian era were intellectually and spiritually omnivorous; they left numerous texts on philosophy, theology, science, anthropology, astrology, alchemy, and magic. Though they were not Gnostics per se, a strong strain of Gnosticism ran through their writings, in that they believed their knowledge would bring them into the presence of God.

In 1462, Marsilio Ficino (1433–99) translated a Hermetic treatise that Cosimo de'Medici had obtained from the Byzantine East, which struck a sympathetic chord among the intellectuals of the Italian Renaissance. Hermeticism gave them their first taste of a theological system that was free of Catholic dogma. Later generations of alchemists seized on the occult arcana of the Hermeticists, as did Freemasons, Rosicrucians, Theosophists, and Aleister Crowley. Through these intermediaries, it continues to exercise an influence on many of the writings on astrology, witchcraft, divining, and sympathetic magic that can be found in the New Age sections of book stores today.

HINDUISM

The traditional view of Hinduism, developed by nineteenth-century Orientalists, was that it came out of a synthesis of the myths of the indigenous occupants of the Indian Subcontinent with the Vedantic legends brought from Europe by invading Indo-Aryans in 1500 BCE. Current scholarship questions whether an Indo-Aryan invasion ever took place; it also extends the time line for Hinduism considerably further back into the past.

Hinduism's principal texts are the Vedas: the Rig Veda, Sama Veda, Yajur Veda, and Atharva Veda, which collect hymns, incantations and descriptions of sacrificial rituals. Their estimated date of composition falls somewhere between 1500 BCE and 4000 BCE; transmitted orally for generations, they weren't written down until as late as 500 BC. The Upanishads are speculative works that develop the doctrine of Brahma, the absolute reality that the individual soul, Atman, seeks to be united with. They also establish the idea of Karma, through which the consequences of the good and bad things that one does in one lifetime are played out in successive incarnations.

The two great Sanskrit epics are the Ramayana and the Mahabharata. The Ramayana, attributed to the poet Valmiki, is the story of Prince Rama, an incarnation of the god Vishnu, who rescues his wife Sita from a demon king. The seventy-four thousand verses of the Mahabharata recount the legends of the kings, princes, sages, and warriors of the divine Bharata dynasty; it culminates in the Bhagavad Gita, which recounts a philosophical conversation between the god Krishna and a warrior. Of the more than thirty gods mentioned in the Vedas, the most important are the fire god Agni; Indra the warrior god; Varuna, the god of justice and guardian of *rita,* the cosmic order; and Brahma, the creator.

Vaishnavism is a movement in Hinduism that worships Vishnu, the preserver of Dharma (law, duty, righteousness), as the ultimate diety; Shivaism gives precedence to Shiva, the force of eros who is compassionate but destructive. Many rural Hindis worship a local god or an earth goddess.

Hinduism's doctrine of the fourfold aims of life lists four goals that one should strive for: *dharma,* or righteousness; *artha,* or prosperity; *kama,* or sensual and intellectual pleasure. For the spiritual, the chief goal is *moksha,* liberation from the cycle of birth and death.

HISTORICISM *See* Millennialism.

HUMANISM
Any philosophical, moral, political, artistic, or scientific system with a human, rather than a supernatural, frame of reference. Also the belief that the highest ideals of human existence can be fulfilled without regard to revealed religion.

Renaissance humanism refers to the revival of interest in classical literature and philosophy that began at the end of the Middle Ages, around the middle of the fourteenth century. Some of its most important intellectual figures were Francesco Petrarch

(1304–74), a lawyer and churchman as well as a poet and classical scholar, who is often called the father of Renaissance humanism; Giovanni Boccaccio (1313–75), author of *The Decameron,* notable for the worldliness of its characters; Desiderius Erasmus, of Rotterdam (ca. 1466–1536), a Latinist and church reformer; the prodigy Giovanni Pico della Mirandola (1463–94), whose interests ranged from Plato and Aristotle to Egyptian Hermeticism and the Kabbalah, and who was the author of the "Oration on the Dignity of Man" (1486), which argued that the intellect alone gives mankind the power to ascend the chain of being. Other important figures include Niccolò Machiavelli (1469–1527), whose notorious *The Prince* laid out the principles (some would argue the lack of principles) of political realism, and Nicolaus Copernicus (1473–1543), the Polish physician, lawyer, economist, and astronomer who declared that the earth orbited the sun. Leonardo da Vinci (1452–1519) was the Renaissance man par excellence—not only a painter and sculptor of genius but an architect, inventor, engineer, anatomist, geometer, composer, and musician. His famous drawing *Vitruvian Man,* two superimposed views of a naked man in a circle, illustrate the supposed mathematical proportions of the human body as they were described by the Roman architect Vitruvius; it also exemplifies, in the art historian Kenneth Clark's (1903–83) words, the idea that "through proportion we can reconcile the two parts of our being, the physical and the intellectual."

The Humanist Manifesto of 1933, largely written by the Unitarian Universalist minister Raymond Bragg (1902–79), took the position that the universe was "self-created" and that mankind was a part of nature. Denying that there were any "supernatural or cosmic guarantees of human values," and rejecting Deism and Theism as anachronisms, it insisted "that the way to determine the existence and value of any and all realities is by means of intelligent inquiry and by the assessment of their relations to human needs. Religion must formulate its hopes and plans in the light of the scientific spirit and method." The Humanist Manifesto of 1973 added codicils about the importance of sexual tolerance, political liberty, economic equity, the rights of the disabled, and the importance of the separation of religion and state.

Secular humanism is the bugaboo of many fundamentalist Christian groups in the United States. Dr. David Noebel, the founder of Summit Ministries and the author of many books, including *Thinking Like a Christian, The Homosexual Revolution,* and *Communism, Hypnotism and the Beatles,* argues that secular

> humanists preach a faith every bit as dogmatic as Christianity. Moral relativism is foundational for Secular Humanist ethics; spontaneous generation and evolution are basis to their biology; naturalism is foundational to their philosophy; and atheism is their theological perspective.

Though humanists do indeed provisionally accept the theory of evolution and in general prefer naturalistic explanations for natural phenomena, these biases are not at all analogous to faith. What differentiates the humanist and the religious mind are their very different understandings of what constitutes the "truth." The religious mind identifies it with God—a static, unchanging absolute that can reveal itself whole through revelation. In contrast, the humanist regards the truth as something emergent and evolving. The secular humanist's characteristic attitude of skepticism and open-mindedness is naturally immune to religious dogmatism.

ICONOCLASM
Literally, the tendency to smash idols (from the Greek *eikono,* "image" and *klan,* "break"). The Taliban's destruction of the massive Buddhas of Bamiyan in Afghanistan, fifteen-hundred-year-old statues carved into cliff faces, is one of the most notable acts of iconoclasm of our own day.

In general use, the word applies to anyone who scorns society's sacred cows. A society lady who wears pants to a formal luncheon might be called an iconoclast; so would a conservative Republican who suddenly begins citing Marx as an economic authority. The Biblical patriarch Abraham was literally an iconoclast when, as legend tells us, he destroyed the idols his father had carved. The Protestant Reformation unleashed some notable acts of icon smashing throughout Europe (Calvinists in particular regarded religious statues as idolatrous), as did the French and Russian revolutions.

The literal sense of iconoclasm figures in an important way in the history of the Byzantine Empire. Around 726 CE, Emperor Leo III ordered that an image of Jesus be removed from the gates of Constantinople; later he issued an imperial edict forbidding all religious images. Leo's son Constantine convened the Iconoclast Council in Hiera in 754 CE, which upheld the ban (neither the pope nor any of the church's patriarchs were present); over the vehement protests of iconodules (icon plus the Greek word *doulos,* or "slave," hence "slaves to icons") and iconophiles (lovers of icons), monasteries were attacked, monks persecuted, and statues destroyed. The Seventh Council of Nicaea, in 787, overturned the ban, but the controversy erupted again twenty-five years later during the reign of Leo V and continued until 843, when Theodora, the regent for Michael III, restored orthodoxy. Though the controversy generated a wealth of learned theological arguments—iconoclasts argued that icons not only violated the commandment against idolotry but that paintings and statues of Jesus, which could only depict his human nature, were therefore instances of the Nestorian heresy. Iconodules countered by insisting that once God had been incarnated as a human, there was no possible reason not to represent his form; that images were only idolatrous when they were of false gods, and that (perhaps the most important argument) religious and ritual decisions were properly made by the pope and not the emperor.

IDIOTISM

The charismatic Greek-Armenian mystic G. I. Gurdjieff (ca. 1872–1949)—his gaze was said to be so powerful that he could induce an orgasm in a woman simply by looking at her from across a room—taught his followers a variety of ways to rouse themselves from the sleep of daily life and access their innermost spiritual selves: through dance, ascetism, music, work, sex, and even eating. One of his rituals sounds almost like a parlor game. Beginning in 1922, he held a nightly Toast to the Idiots, when each member of his circle would intuitively guess which category of idiot they belonged to. Gurdjieff used the word *idiot* in its original Greek sense of "one's own" to refer to one's unique inner self; undoubtedly he was using it in its Russian sense too, of a holy fool. His Science of Idiotism classified twenty-one distinct types of idiots hierarchically, with Normal Idiot at the bottom and Unique Idiot at the top—this last one was God. Intermediate stages included Swaggering Idiot, Zigzag Idiot, and Polyhedral Idiot.

INTELLIGENT DESIGN   *See* Creationism.

ISLAM

The youngest of the Abrahamic religions, Islam was founded by Muhammad (570–632 CE). In Arabic, *islam* means "submission to God." Islam proclaims the oneness of Allah, the only all-powerful God, who called on the prophets Adam, Noah, Abraham, Ishmael, Moses, and Jesus to proclaim his message. The angel Gabriel dictated the 114 *suras,* or chapters, of the Koran to the unlettered Muhammad, who in turn recited them to his followers. Since the Koran, Allah's final revelation, is written in Arabic, Arabic remains the language of Islamic devotion. Muslims believe in reward and punishment after death and the unity of the *Umma,* or the nation of Islam. The five pillars of Islamic life are

1) *Shahadah*, the affirmation that there is no God but God, and Muhammad is the messenger of God
2) *Salah*, the five daily prayers
3) *Zakat*, the giving of alms
4) *Sawm*, the obligation to fast during the month of Ramadan
5) *Hajj*, the pilgrimage to Mecca

Other Islamic obligations are to eschew pork and alcohol, avoid gambling or lending money for profit, and eat only animals that are slaughtered according to ritual. *Jihad*, the duty to strive for God, is both a communal and a personal obligation—it doesn't necessarily mean the obligation to wage holy war; it can be as basic as fighting temptation, as general as in the words of the Koran "commanding the right and forbidding the wrong."

The first great schism in Islam came over the succession of the movement's leader. Sunni Muslims, the vast majority of Islam today, accepted the legitimacy of the first four caliphs (from *khalifa*, or "successor") after Muhammad. The Shiites (the word means sect) preferred Muhammad's son-in-law Ali, who they insist the dying Muhammad had specifically chosen as his heir. Ali's youngest son, Husayn, who inherited Ali's right of succession, was martyred in 680 CE in Karbalā, Iraq, an event Shiites commemorate annually to this day.

Like some Protestants, many Shiites are preoccupied with the end of the world. Shiite eschatology revolves around the belief that there have only been twelve legitimate imams, or direct descendants of Muhammad, since his death (thus the name Twelvers, or Twelfth Imam Shiites). Legend has it that Muhammad al Mahdi, the Twelfth Imam, was born in 868 CE to a Byzantine princess who had disguised herself as a slave to travel to Arabia; his father was the Eleventh Imam. Because the Sunni caliph was persecuting the Shiites at the time, Muhammad was kept hidden until it was time for him to assert his claim to the imamate. Shortly afterward, he hid again, this time in a well, but he maintained communication with his four assistants, or Babs (Gates), for seventy years. This is known as the Lesser Occultation.

When the Twelfth Imam was on his deathbed, his last surviving Bab produced a letter from him, declaring his intention to disappear until shortly before Judgment Day, when he would return as the Mahdi (the Guided One) to establish perfect justice. This was the beginning of the Greater Occultation, which has continued until this day. While they await his return, senior Shiite clerics, known as mullahs, act as the Twelfth Imam's deputies.

Sufism is another minority movement in Islam. The word is derived from *suf,* or "wool," which refers to their rough garments and by implication to their asceticism. The earliest Sufis were pietists, but by the time of Junayd ibn Muhammad Abu al-Qasim al-Khazzaz al-Baghdadi (830–910 CE), they were beginning to articulate a coherent mysticism. Bayazid Bastami (804–874) wrote of "drunkenness" and "annihilation of the self in God"; the towering scholar Muhammad al-Ghazali (1058–1111) would articulate a full-fledged intellectual system that assimilated mystical Sufism with doctrinal Islam. Over the next two hundred years, Sufism spread as far afield as India, North Africa, Spain, and Kazakhstan. Rumi (1207–73) wrote his great poetry and founded the Mevlevi in Turkey (the whirling dervishes, who achieve ecstatic union with God through music and dance); Khawaja Moinuddin Chishti (1141–1230) brought Sufism to India.

An unknown Sufi scholar offered a memorable metaphor for the Sufi passion for transcendent experience: "There are three ways of knowing a thing. Take for instance a flame. One can be told of the flame, one can see the flame with his own eyes, and finally one can reach out and be burned by it. In this way, we Sufis seek to be burned by God."

JAINISM

Religious system founded in India as early as the ninth century BCE that has absorbed elements of Hinduism, and to a lesser degree the younger religions Buddhism and Islam.

According to Jain tradition, it was founded by twenty-four *tirthankaras* ("crossing makers," or saints), the most recent of them Lord Parshva (877–777 BCE) and Lord Mahavira (599–527 BCE). Lord Mahavira (in Sanskrit, his name means the great hero; he is also known as Jina, or the conqueror—the word *Jain* comes from the same Sanskrit root, *ji,* or "follower of the conqueror") reformed and codified the religion's beliefs and practices.

At the heart of Jainism is the belief that the universe is uncreated and eternal, that history moves in vast cycles, and that individual souls are reincarnated over and over again until they are purified. The universe, which operates according to unchange-able laws, is composed of five elements: *jiva,* or soul; *pugdala,* or matter or atoms; *akasha,* or space; *adharma,* or rest; and *dharma,* or motion. Some Jains consider time a sixth element. Soul is im-material, infinite, and perfect; every animate being contains some aspect of soul in itself. Karma is the matter that sticks to the soul and keeps it from attaining its pure essence, or Moksha. Jains as-pire to "conquer" karma by living a life that follows five spiritual and ethical principles: Ahimsa, or nonviolence—which means that one does no harm to any creature, and constantly asks for Kshamapana, or forgiveness for any inadvertent harm one might have done; Satya, or truth; Asteya, not stealing; Brahmacharya, or continence; and Aparigraha, or nonmaterialism.

Monks and nuns take *mahavrat,* or "great vows" and carry these principles out to an extreme—they live as mendicants, eat a sparse vegetarian diet, and fast frequently; are celibate; and even brush the ground they walk on to avoid killing insects. Histori-cally some ascetics would literally starve themselves to death. Monks in the Digambar sect go naked and don't believe that women can achieve Moksha unless they are reincarnated as men. The Sve-tambar monks, who wear white garments, believe that women are capable of transcendence; they also maintain that Lord Mahavira was married and had a daughter. Jain laymen take *anuvrat,* or "small vows," and strive to live according to the same principles as the monks and nuns, though they are permitted to marry and conduct business. Perhaps because of their reputation for truthfulness, Jains have thrived in finance—they are among the most literate and wealthy of Indians, and they are also noted for their scholarship. A major Jain value is *anekantavada,* or "nonsingular conclusivity." Another way of putting this is the willingness to look at things from more than one point of view, to keep an open mind, and to recog-nize that truth is multifaceted and deeply complex.

JANSENISM
Heretical movement in Catholicism, inspired by the writings of Cornelius Jansen (1585–1638), the bishop of Ypres. Jansen re-

turned to the writings of Saint Augustine to fashion a doctrine that emphasized original sin, and insisted that salvation was impossible without divine assistance. Jansen urged believers to take Communion less often than was customary and prepare for it more rigorously with prayer and confession. Jansenism also accepted the notion of predestination, declaring that only a small portion of humanity, the "elect," would be saved, and that not even they know who they are. The resemblance to Calvinism was unmistakable. Jansenism was condemned by popes Innocent X, Alexander VII, Clement XI, and Pius X.

JEHOVAH'S WITNESSES

Offshoot of the Millenarian Seventh-Day Adventists, founded in the 1870s by Charles Taze Russell (1852–1916). Though Russell never formerly disassociated his church from the Seventh-Day Adventists (it didn't become known by its present name until 1931), he differed with them on important points. In his magazine, *Zion's Watch Tower and Herald of Christ's Presence*, which he began publishing in 1879 (the Zion's Watch Tower Tract Society would be incorporated in 1884), and in his *Studies in the Scriptures*, he argued that Jesus' reign over the earth had already begun, albeit "invisibly," in 1874; he predicted that Armageddon, or the final battle between the forces of God and Satan, would occur in 1914. These dates would be revised in the 1920s and 1930s.

The Witnesses do not believe in the Trinity. Jehovah is the Old Testament God, and Jesus, his first and most perfect creation, was originally the archangel Michael. Born of a virgin as a man, he was resurrected as spirit after he was executed—on a vertical pole, not a cross. The Holy Spirit is not God, but the means by which he acts on earth. Neither do the Witnesses believe in Hell. They teach that only 144,000 Christians will be admitted to heaven; the rest of the saved will live eternally on earth after the Millennium. Nonrepentant people will be destroyed, along with Satan and his minions. Since Jehovah's Witnesses do not acknowledge earthly nations, they refuse to salute the flag or perform military service. Blood transfusions are forbidden in accordance with Leviticus 17:10 ("He must not eat the blood, because the life is in the blood.")

JUDAISM

The oldest of the Abrahamic faiths, Judaism is at once a revealed religion—the first monotheistic faith—and an ethnicity, a body of doctrine and laws, a promise of national destiny, and a deeply humanistic system of values. The Tanakh, the Hebrew acronym (Torah; Nevi'im, or prophets; Ketuvim, or writings) for what Christians refer to as the Old Testament, tells the story of the Hebrew people's fraught relationship and special covenant with God, from when he first revealed himself to the patriarch Abraham to the Exodus from Egypt, from the conquest of Canaan to the rise of King David, from the destruction of Solomon's Temple to the return from the Babylonian exile. Ironically, it was only after the destruction of the Second Temple in 70 CE and the second Diaspora (dispersion) that Judaism would become the religion that we know it as today.

Although the Tanakh is filled with profound ethical teachings, inspirational stories, and divine mysteries, the great temple in Jerusalem that was the literal center of Jewish nationality and ritual life for so many centuries was also a slaughterhouse, and its hereditary priests were butchers—animal sacrifice, rather than prayer, was the chief means of honoring and appeasing God. The synagogues and study halls of Rabbinic Judaism that sprang up after the destruction, where Jews gathered to pore over the Talmud and other learned commentaries, to split legalistic and exegetical hairs, and to *daven*, or pray, were very different sorts of places. In the absence of Jewish kings and sacred altars, daily life was sanctified by nonsanguinary rituals and blessings, and by keeping the dietary laws; the Sabbath, the most important of all the Jewish holidays, sanctified the week. The major life-cycle rituals—circumcision of newborn males after eight days, a visible sign of the covenant; a bar mitzvah after thirteen years, when a boy reads the Torah for the first time and becomes a full-fledged member of the tribe; and for both genders, marriages and funerals—assured the continuity of the community. In addition to the Torah, the written law, Jews studied the vast body of commentary on the Torah, the Talmud or the oral law, which began to be compiled in the centuries after the destruction of the Second Temple.

Maimonides' (1135–1204) Thirteen Principles of Faith are the closest thing to a Jewish creed; they epitomize mainstream Jewish beliefs in the Middle Ages—and for many Orthodox Jews—to this day. They state that the one God is the first and the last and the sole creator of the universe, that he is incorporeal and that he is the only being that Jews pray to. They aver that the words of the prophets, and especially Moses, are all true, and that the Torah has not changed since the time of Moses and that it never will change. They declare that God knows all things and will punish those who transgress the Commandments and reward those who keep them; that at the end of time he will send a Messiah to redeem the world and that he will raise the dead.

Kabbalah would bring a strain of esotericism and mysticism into the forefront of European Judaism, starting around the 1200s. The centuries of persecution and expulsions that began in medieval times with the Crusades and continued through the wars of the Reformation took a horrendous moral and physical toll on the Jewish people (see anti-Semitism), as did their disappointment in the false messiah Sabbatai Zevi (1626–76). By the 1700s, two separate tendencies were beginning to make themselves felt in Judaism: In Eastern Europe Hasidism (covered separately) was taking hold; in Europe's urban centers, it was the spirit of the Enlightenment. In Holland, Baruch Spinoza (1632–77), an ethicist, mathematician, philosopher, and an excommunicated Jew, anticipated by centuries the succession of secular Jewish thinkers who would emerge in the nineteenth century, such as: Karl Marx (1818–83), Sigmund Freud (1856–1939), and Albert Einstein (1879–1959). Although Diaspora Jews have always thought of themselves as a people in exile, Zionism, the belief that Jews should make an active effort to reoccupy the lands they ruled in biblical times, rather than wait for the Messiah to come and restore them, didn't become a political movement until the end of the nineteenth century. The devastation of European Jewry in

World War II, along with the creation of the state of Israel in 1948, lent a new urgency to the Zionist project.

Today there are four main movements in religious Judaism. The adherents of Orthodoxy continue to obey all of the oral and written laws (except those pertaining to sacrifice and other rituals specific to the temple), and they follow the traditional liturgy. There is a continuum within Orthodoxy, however—modern, or centrist, Orthodox allow a certain degree of engagement with the secular and scientific world; the Haredi, or ultra-Orthodox, do not. Orthodox men keep their heads covered at all times and sit separately from women in synagogue; many of them grow beards and wear tzitzis, the fringed garment mandated in Leviticus. Conservative Jews stake out a middle ground: They keep kosher, for example, but they wear modern clothes and are more relaxed than the Orthodox in their observance of the Sabbath. Reform Jews ignore the vast majority of biblical laws and conduct much of their religious services in English—they value Judaism primarily as a tradition and a source of ethics and ethnicity. Jewish reconstructionists have a humanistic orientation when it comes to doctrine—they reject the notion of "chosenness," for example, and deny the reality of miracles and a personal God—but they conduct their services in a traditional manner. The fifth and largest "movement" among contemporary Jews is no movement at all—it's secularism. But after thousands of years of cognitive dissonance (what does it mean to be "chosen" if everybody hates us so much?), most secular Jews remain deeply aware of their Jewishness if for no other reason than, as Bernard Malamud (1914–86) famously remarked, "If you ever forget you're a Jew, a Gentile will remind you."

KABBALISM

A Jewish mystical tradition that began in Provence and the Rhine Valley in the twelfth century and continued to develop in Spain and Palestine in subsequent centuries. The literal meaning of the word is "receiving," which underlines both its antiquity and its esotericism—for centuries the teachings of Kabbalah were orally transmitted to only a chosen few. A theosophy (a religious teaching based on revelation as opposed to reason) rather than a philosophy, Kabbalah nonetheless developed a cosmology and metaphysics, which are reminiscent in significant ways of Gnosticism and Neoplatonism.

According to the Kabbalists, the ultimate constituents of creation are a compound of Hebrew letters, numbers, and the Sefirot—the latter a series of ten emanations from the Godhead, which in its purest, most absolute form is known as Ein Sof (the changeless infinite) and in its most materialized, the Shekhinah (the presence of God and the personification of the spirit of the Jewish people). Through meditation, Kabbalists ascend the Sefirot and merge with God; by manipulating letters and numbers (gematria, one of their modes of scriptural interpretation, takes advantage of the fact that Hebrew letters also serve as numbers), Kabbalists interpret the Torah on an esoteric level. Legend has it that they can also perform astonishing feats of magic, including the creation of life. The first Frankenstein monster was a clay golem (an artificial being), animated when a Hebrew letter was inscribed on its forehead. Most Kabbalists believed in reincarnation as well.

The great Rabbi Isaac Luria (1534–72) developed a creation myth in which the world came into being when God withdrew a part of himself (this is called *tzimtzum,* or contraction) to make room for Creation. The emptiness took the form of a giant man, Adam Kadmon, into whom God poured a part of himself. Light streamed out of the man's eyes, nose, and mouth and took the shapes of the ten Sefirot, but the vessels that held them weren't strong enough—the highest vessels (the Sefirot, which are closest to the undivided, infinite essence of God) cracked, and the lowest seven shattered, dividing the emptiness into an upper world and a lower world. The result of this shattering (*shevirah*) is our universe—a mixture of *kelipot* (shards of the lower Sefirot) and remnant sparks of the divine light. The sparks long to be reunited with their source, but the *kelipot* hold on to them greedily, for this unholy mixture of divine light and corrupt matter is the source of evil.

God created Adam, the myth continues, to repair the world (*tikkun olam*) by liberating the sparks. God originally intended that Adam would be the only person he created and so equipped him with the souls of every person who ever was or will be. But when Adam fell, the shattering that created our world was recapitulated on a human scale—Adam's innumerable souls were scattered, and now each of them is required to perform the work of cosmic redemption individually. Whenever a person performs a mitzvah (obeys a biblical commandment or does a good deed), a spark is liberated; when, after any number of incarnations, a soul has liberated its quota of sparks, it is reunited with its fellows in Adam. When the last spark is raised, the Messiah will come.

Kabbalah's greatest text is the Zohar, or the Book of Splendor, a massive compilation of midrash (biblical commentary), sermons, homilies, visions, dialogues, treatises, and more. Most scholars believe it was written in the late 1200s by the Spanish Kabbalist Moses ben Shem Tov de León, though observant Jews credit it to Shimon bar Yochai, a sage who lived in Palestine in the second century CE.

Hasidism incorporates many elements of Kabbalah in its teachings and practices; starting as early as the 1200s, there have been Christian and occult variants of Kabbalah too, which in turn have influenced Freemasonry, Theosophy, and Rosicrucianism. Today the international Kabbalah Centre, which has succeeded in attracting a number of celebrities into its fold, aggressively markets its own cultic (and highly commercialized) variation of the tradition, promising its followers that they can be enlightened by "scanning" the Aramaic text of the Zohar, even if they don't know the language, redeemed by drinking specially blessed bottles of water, and protected from the evil eye by wearing a bracelet fashioned out of red string. The pop singer Madonna and the actress Demi Moore are among their most visible converts.

KARAISM
The beliefs of the Jewish sect originally known as the Ananites, who rejected the oral law of Rabbinic Judaism (the teachings of

the Talmud) and interpreted the Bible literally. The movement was founded in the eighth century BCE in Persia and declined after the twelfth century, though a few adherents can still be found in Israel and in the Crimea. These latter, however, may not be ethnically Jewish.

LATITUDINARIANISM

Term used to characterize those seventeenth-century Anglicans who opposed narrow dogmatism and depended upon reason rather than tradition. The latitudinarians anticipated the nineteenth-century Broad Church movement in the Church of England, which staked out a middle ground between High Church Anglo-Catholicism (an Episcopalianism that hewed as close to Roman Catholicism as it could in its outward forms) and Low Church (whose rituals were more like those of the dissenting Protestants, such as the Methodists or Baptists). In general use, latitudinarianism means broad-mindedness, an easygoing tolerance—a quality that not all religious people admire. Thus John Wesley (1703–91) declared: "A catholic spirit is not speculative latitudinarianism. It is not an indifference to all opinions: This is the spawn of hell, not the offspring of heaven."

LAUDIANISM

Vehement anti-Puritanism. After William Laud (1573–1645), chancellor of Oxford, bishop of London, and archbishop of Canterbury. A staunch supporter of Charles I and the divine right of kings, he used the Star Chamber to persecute Puritans, torturing and mutilating many of his critics, and attempted to restore Catholic rituals to the Church of England. He was condemned to death by the House of Commons and beheaded.

LUTHERANISM   *See* Protestantism.

MAGIANISM   *See* Zoroastrianism.

MANDAEANISM   *See* Gnosticism.

MANICHAEANISM

A dualistic religious movement founded by Mani (ca. 216–276 CE). Mani, a Persian, was raised as a Zoroastrian; he joined the Elkasites (a Jewish/Christian offshoot of the Essenes), but was expelled in 240, after which he spent several years in India, where he was exposed to Buddhism. Upon his return to Persia, he called himself Mani, apostle of Jesus Christ, declaring himself to be the Paraclete (holy spirit) promised in the Gospel of John (16:7–8): "It is to your advantage that I go away, for if I do not go away, the Paraclete will not come to you; but if I go, I will send him to you. And when he comes, he will convince the world of sin and of righteousness and of judgment."

Combining elements of Zoroastrianism, Christianity, Buddhism, and Gnosticism, Manichaeanism divided the cosmos into two separate realms: a world of light and a world of darkness. The material world that we live in commingles elements of both, according to Mani. Physical matter is controlled by Satan; the light that's trapped within it belongs to God. Thus sin was not a weakness of the spirit or the will but an intrinsic attribute of the flesh. Saint Augustine, who formulated the orthodox doctrine of original sin, was a Manichaean in his youth. The Manichaeans nonetheless believed that through asceticism, vegetarianism, celibacy, and faith in Christ, believers can liberate the light that's trapped within their bodies and return it to its divine source.

Manichaeanism spread into France and the Balkans, throughout Persia, Egypt, and Syria, and as far East as central China. It died out in the West by the sixth century, but continued in China for another five hundred years.

MARCIONITISM   *See* Antinomianism.

MARONISM

The beliefs of the Maronite Christians of Lebanon. Founded by the fourth-century mystic Saint Maroun, the Maronites split from Roman Catholicism in the seventh century over the monotheletism controversy; they returned to communion with the pope in the 1100s. Their ecclesiastical leader is called the patriarch of Antioch; their priests are married.

MARRANOISM

Also known as Marranism. The ritual practices of Crypto-Jews, especially the descendants of Conversos, or New Christians— Jews from the Iberian peninsula who were coerced into converting to Catholicism between the pogroms of 1391 and the expulsion of 1492, but who secretly held on to some Jewish customs and rituals. These included soaking and salting meat and avoiding pork and shellfish, lighting candles and putting bread on the table on Friday nights, eating unleavened bread during Passover, venerating saints with Jewish names, burying their dead within twenty-four hours, etc. Marrano practices have been reported in contemporary South and Central America, the Caribbean and New Mexico, and even Spain itself. Of course, many converted Jews did assimilate into Catholic society over the generations. The Spanish archbishop Paul de Burgos was a convert; Saint Teresa of Ávila had a Jewish grandfather.

The origins of the word *marrano* are unclear. In contemporary Spanish it means "pig" or "pork," and it was certainly used as a term of contempt for converted Jews. But there is reason to believe that the word's origins lie in the Jewish and Muslim communities. In Arabic, *muh arran* means "something forbidden," which Christian Baptism certainly was to Jews and Muslims. The word was only extended to real swine after it had already found its way into the Spanish language. The Hebrew term anusim, or "coerced ones," distinguishes those who converted unwillingly (and who were thus, according to rabbinic law, still Jews in good standing) from *mumarim*, or "genuine apostates."

MESSIANIC JUDAISM

The beliefs of "completed" Jews, Hebrew Christians, Jewish Christians, or Christian Jews—ethnically Jewish converts to Christianity who believe that Jesus was/is the Messiah and

Christianity the natural fulfillment of biblical Judaism. Rather than abandoning the rituals and practices of Judaism when they convert, Messianic Jews continue to embrace them, while also embracing the theological apparatus of evangelical Protestantism (more particularly, Dispensationalist and Restorationist Protestantism, whose End Times require the conversion and redemption of large numbers of Jews). Many of these Jews evangelize to Protestants as well as their fellow Jews, and a significant number of Protestants have joined their congregations, donning yarmulkes, learning Hebrew, keeping kosher, and otherwise worshipping as they believe the earliest Christians did.

Jesus and his apostles were Jewish, of course. It wasn't until after the Crucifixion and Resurrection that his followers began to evangelize among the Gentiles and distinguish themselves from Jews. We know from the Book of Acts that Peter and James, who kept kosher, circumcised their children, and obeyed the Mosaic law, thought of themselves as Nazarenes rather than Christians as the word would come to be understood in later generations. Early Christian sects such as the Ebionites and the Elkasites considered themselves Jewish as well.

The Messianic Jewish Alliance of America was founded in 1915 as the Hebrew Christian Alliance of America; the Union of Messianic Jewish Congregations was founded in 1979 "as a movement of Jewish congregations and groups committed to Yeshua the Messiah that embrace the covenantal responsibility of Jewish life and identity rooted in Torah, expressed in tradition, and renewed and applied in the context of the New Covenant." Another well-known movement of Messianic Christians is the Jews for Jesus, who are perhaps the most aggressively evangelistic.

METHODISM
The doctrines and denominations of the churches that formed out of the Christian revival movement begun in England in 1738 by the brothers John (1703–91) and Charles Wesley (1707–88).

George Whitefield (1714–70), the third founder of the movement, broke away in 1741.

Vowing to conduct their lives according to "rule and method," the Wesleys and Whitefield began a worship group at Oxford in the 1720s. The Wesley brothers spent time in the American colony of Georgia; when they returned to England, they both had conversion experiences while worshipping with Moravians. Shortly afterward, they began evangelizing to impoverished coal miners in the city of Bristol. The theology of the Wesleys was almost identical to Arminianism, which denies predestination. It was Whitefield's belief in predestination that prompted his parting from the Wesleys. He would become the leader of the Calvinist Methodists. The Wesleys never officially left the Church of England (Methodism didn't officially break away until after their deaths); they hoped to infuse Anglicanism with their missionary spirit, their emphasis on repentance, their passion for social reform and their insistence that, by the power of prevenient grace, the privilege of salvation is available to anyone who chooses it. The Methodist Book of Discipline defines prevenient grace as

> The divine love that surrounds all humanity and precedes any and all of our conscious impulses. This grace prompts our first wish to please God, our first glimmer of understanding concerning God's will, and our "first slight transient conviction" of having sinned against God. God's grace also awakens in us an earnest longing for deliverance from sin and death and moves us toward repentance and faith.

Methodists baptize infants and believe that God is present in the Eucharist.

There have been many schisms and reconciliations in Methodism. In Great Britain, the Methodist New Connection, the Primitive Methodists, the Bible Christians, the Protestant Methodists, and the Wesleyan Reformers all broke away from the principal movement; in America the proslavery Independent Methodist

Episcopal Church, South, began in 1845 (in 1939 they merged with the Methodist Episcopal Church, North, and the Methodist Protestant Church). Among the African American denominations are the African Methodist Episcopal Church, the African Methodist Episcopal Zion Church, and the Christian Methodist Episcopal Church.

MILLENARIANISM

In general usage, millenarianism can refer to any apocalyptic religious, political, or social movement—from the Amerindian Ghost Dance movement of the 1890s, in which a Paiute shaman named Wovoka (ca. 1856–1932) prophesied that the destruction of the civilization of the white man would occur in the spring of 1891 (the U.S. Cavalry's efforts to quell the movement would set in motion the events that led to the massacre at Wounded Knee), to white-supremacist anticipation of the coming racial holy war; from the false messiah Sabbatai Zevi's (1626–76) announcement to the Jews that his reign would begin in 1666, and the Great Disappointment of 1844 of the Millerites, to communism's anticipation of the eventual "withering away of the state." Y2K hysteria (the not unjustified fear that computers would break down en masse when their calendars switched to the year 2000—billions of dollars were invested to adjust those computers), the mass suicide of the Heaven's Gate UFO cult when the comet Hale-Bopp appeared in 1997, even stock market investors' fears of the coming peak oil crisis (the economic tipping point when worldwide demand for oil outpaces production by several orders of magnitude) share many of the hallmarks of millenarianism.

In Christian eschatology, millenarianism is synonymous with millennialism and chiliasm (the root of the first two words is the Latin *millennial,* or "one thousand years"; the second comes from the Greek *chilias,* which means "one thousand"). All three terms refer to the prophetic vision recounted in Revelation 20:1–3:

> And I saw an angel come down from heaven, having the key of
> the bottomless pit and a great chain in his hand.

And he laid hold on the dragon, that old serpent, which is
the Devil, and Satan, and bound him a thousand years,

And cast him into the bottomless pit, and shut him up, and
set a seal upon him, that he should deceive the nations no
more, till the thousand years should be fulfilled: and after that
he must be loosed a little season.

The Book of Revelation is notoriously opaque, and its translations
differ widely; even when it's read literally, as fundamentalist
Protestants prefer, there is wide latitude for interpretation. Saint
Augustine, in *The City of God*, wrote of this passage

The evangelist John has spoken of these two resurrections in
the book which is called the Apocalypse, but in such a way that
some Christians do not understand the first of the two, and so
construe the passage into ridiculous fancies . . . They who do
believe them are called by the spiritual Chiliasts, which we may
literally reproduce by the name Millenarians. It were a tedious
process to refute these opinions point by point.

Augustine's impatience notwithstanding, for every possible interpretation of this and every other apocalyptic passage in Christian
scripture, one or more isms has sprung up. Symbolists assume that
the evangelist was speaking figuratively, that, as Augustine did,
John's prophecies should be interpreted hermeneutically. Preterism (from the Latin *preter,* or "the past") is the belief that the
Evangelist's and Jesus' own prophecies have already been fulfilled.
Scriptural exegetes, the belief goes, should look to events that happened shortly after the life of Jesus, specifically, to the destruction
of the Second Temple in 70 CE. Moderate preterists allow that Jesus will return in the flesh at some unspecified time in the future;
radical preterists deny that there will be a Second Coming and an
Apocalypse at all, hence they are also called amillennialists.

Premillennialists believe that Jesus will return to the world
before the millennial kingdom begins and will reign over it for a
thousand years, after which Satan will emerge "for a time" before
some last judgments are enacted and the earthly kingdom merges

with God's eternal kingdom. Premillennial dispensationalists believe that vast numbers of Jews will convert in the End Times, bringing about Israel's restoration (a belief that is also fittingly called restorationism). This is the fulfillment of God's covenant with David in 2 Samuel 7:16, "And thine house and thy kingdom shall be established for ever before thee: thy throne shall be established for ever." The father of premillennial dispensationalism was the Irish-born John Nelson Darby (1800–82), the enormously influential founder of the evangelical movement called the Plymouth Brethren. Darby rejected supersessionism, arguing that rather than *replacing* Judaism, Christianity redeems it. Darbyism divides history into a series of Biblical Dispensations, in which God has used different methods to bring about salvation:

1) The dispensation of innocence (prelapsarian)
2) Of conscience (Adam to Noah)
3) Of government (Noah to Abraham)
4) Of patriarchal rule (Abraham to Moses)
5) Of the Mosaic law (Moses to Jesus)
6) Of grace (the present)
7) Of the thousand-year millennial kingdom

Just before the coming of the thousand-year kingdom, premillennial dispensationalists believe, there will be a seven-year period of tribulations, but Christians won't be there to see it; they will be swept up to heaven in the rapture. This was depicted in the *Left Behind* series of novels, cowritten by Jerry B. Jenkins and the influential preacher Dr. Tim LeHaye. The books have all been phenomenal best sellers and have even spawned movies and computer games.

As the tribulations continue, according to the premillennial dispensationalist narrative, the Anti-christ will become the ruler of the world and proscribe Jewish worship in Jerusalem. Then, as bloody judgment after bloody judgment is visited on earth, a "remnant" of Israel will convert to Christianity and save a multitude of Gentiles. Only then will the Battle of Armageddon begin. Christ and the raptured church will return in Glory, ensuring victory, the vast majority of Jews will be converted, and Satan will be bound and imprisoned for one thousand years.

There are innumerable sectarian variations on this scenario, especially on the timing of the rapture. Pretribulationists believe the rapture will occur before the tribulation; midtribulationists, in the midst of the tribulation; and posttribulationists, just after. Neither do all premillennial dispensationalists agree on the timing of the various dispensations. But this brief description at least makes clear why a certain segment of the evangelical right has been so steadfast in its support for Israel.

Postmillennialists believe that Christ will return only *after* the world has been converted and the millennial kingdom established. Christian Reconstructionism, the movement founded by Rousas John Rushdoony (1916–2001), believes that America can hasten the advent of the millennial kingdom and Christ's Second Coming by becoming a Christian republic, governed according to biblical law. In an interview shortly before he died, Rushdoony observed that:

> Law represents the word of the God of the society. Now whose Law you have, He is your God. So if Washington makes our laws, Washington is our God. As Christians we cannot believe that. For centuries, God's law has functioned wherever God's people have been, whether in Israel or in Christendom. This is a new and modern thing that we turn to the state's law . . . Now basically you can have two kinds of law: *theonomy*—God's law, or *autonomy*—self-law. That's what it boils down to and autonomy leads to anarchy, which is what we are getting increasingly.

In another context, Rushdoony observed that democracy and Christianity must always be enemies. Critics of Rushdoony's ideas call them dominionism. "The religious utterances from political leaders such as George Bush, Tom Delay, Pat Robertson and Zell Miller are only understandable in light of Rushdoony and Dominionism," writes Chris Hedges, an ex-seminarian and Pulitzer Prize–winning journalist. "These leaders believe that God has selected them to battle the forces of evil, embodied in 'secular humanism,' to create a Christian nation."

MILLENNIALISM   *See* Millennarianism.

MILLERISM
After William Miller (1782–1849), an American farmer, Baptist layman, and millenarian visionary who in 1831 concluded, based upon his study of biblical prophecies and genealogies, that the Second Coming of Christ (the Advent) would take place in 1843. After he adjusted his calculations to conform to the Jewish calendar, he changed the date to 1844; a follower set the date more exactly, on October 22, 1844. Miller's pamphlets, books, and lectures attracted tens of thousands of followers. When 1844 passed without any signs of Christ's return (the Great Disappointment), the few remaining members of the movement, which until then had been interdenominational, reconstituted themselves as the Evangelical Adventists and the Advent Christian Church, which in turn gave birth to Seventh-Day Adventism, The Church of God, and the Jehovah's Witnesses.

MITHRAISM
The worship of Mithra, the god of the sun, contracts, justice, kings, and war in ancient Persia. Mithra had been a major Persian deity before Zoroastrianism exalted Ahura Mazdah into a position of supremacy; the sacrifice of a bull was an important ritual in the cult dedicated to him. Mithraism persisted even after Zoroastrianism became the state religion; eventually they became inextricably intertwined.

Starting in the second century CE, an altered form of Mithraism became immensely popular among the soldiers of the Roman Empire. Little is known of their beliefs, though as in ancient Persia, loyalty to the emperor played a large role. Mithraites worshipped in real or simulated caves; their ceremonies likely including a simulated death and resurrection (when Mithra sacrificed the white bull, ancient legend had it, all the good things of the earth sprung out of its flesh), and there were baptisms and sacred banquets. The parallels with Christianity have been widely noted. Some churches in Rome were erected atop Mithraic temples, which have since been excavated and can be visited today.

MONASTICISM

Withdrawal from society to live an ascetic life dedicated to religious faith. Monasticism (from the Greek *monastikos*, to dwell alone) has figured in virtually every major world religion. The Jewish Essenes lived in a self-supporting, male-only community that held its property in common; both eremitic (solitary) and cenobitic (communal) monasticism was common among the early Christians.

In the third century, Saint Anthony, an Egyptian Christian, withdrew into the desert, where legend has it he resisted every temptation the devil offered him. After twenty years of seclusion, he began to rule the colony of hermits that had grown up around him. The *boskoi,* or "grazers," spent their days outside on their hands and knees, eating grass, in an attempt to return the world to its prelapsarian innocence. The stylites lived on platforms set atop high pillars, suspended between earth and heaven. The most famous of them, Saint Simeon, a fifth-century Syrian, didn't descend for thirty-five years.

The first organized Christian monastic community was founded by Saint Pachomius in about 320 CE. Saint Basil the Great (ca. 330–379 CE) wrote the first monastic rules, which emphasize the obligations of poverty, obedience, and self-renunciation, which have remained virtually unchanged in the Eastern Church to this day. Basilian monks live in collections of cells called *lauras;* their lives revolve around devotions and manual labor. The largest Eastern monastery is at Mount Athos in Greece.

In the Roman Church, the Rule of Saint Benedict of Nursia (480–543) standardized the organization of monasteries under abbots or abbesses and mitigated many of the austerities of the monks and nuns' daily lives. Benedictine monks evangelized Germany, and their monasteries became islands of culture throughout Europe. The Cluniacs, founded in the tenth century, and the Cistercians, founded in the twelfth century, were both Bendictine reform movements. The Trappists are a Cistercian reform movement. The Dominican and the Franciscan orders, which were founded in the thirteenth century, rejected the notion of enclosure, and struck out into the surrounding communities; these uncloistered monks, or friars, were expected to either work or beg for their livings. Both orders founded universities; the Dominicans would also enforce the Inquisition. The Jesuits were founded in the sixteenth century as an intellectual order of priests (clerks regular) to serve as "soldiers of Christ" for the Counter-Reformation. Their motto is *Ad Majorem Dei Gloriam,* "for the greater glory of God." They are primarily a teaching order today; a number of major American universities are run by Jesuits, including Georgetown, Marquette, and Boston College.

Today in addition to monastic orders there are communities of priests, like the Maryknoll Order, and the Vincentians; there are also organizations of lay people who take vows, for example, the Christian Brothers (who mostly teach).

Buddhist monks (*bhikkus*) and nuns (*bhikkhunis*), with their familiar saffron robes, are celibate, vegetarian, and ascetic; they live in mendicant communities; novices can be as young as eight years old. The Hindu monks, who are called *sadhus,* dress in saffron-colored robes. Vaisnava monks (who worship Vishnu—the Hare Krishnas are Vaishnavites) shave all but a patch of the hair on the back of their heads; Saivas, who worship Siva, don't cut their hair or beards. Extremely ascetic, they are forbidden to own more than a cup and a bowl and two sets of clothes, to have any contact with women, to own or even handle money, and to have any personal relationships. Though the Koran explicitly forbids monasticism, many Sufi dervishes live in brotherhoods. In Jainism, Digambara monks go naked and are only permitted to own a feather (to brush away innocent insects) and a gourd for water. Svetambaras wear white robes and often don face masks, so as not to breathe in any insects.

MONOPHYSITISM

A variation and a continuation of the Nestorian heresy, mono-physitism held that Jesus Christ was one unitary being, entirely divine in nature. The controversy raged throughout the fifth and sixth centuries CE. One particularly vehement monophysite was Eutyches (ca. 380–ca. 456 CE), who held that Jesus' human nature was obliterated by his divinity: "like the sea receiving a drop of honey, for straightway the drop, as it mingles with the ocean's water, disappears." Eutycheanism is thus another name for monophysitism. Though condemned at the Council of Chalcedon in 476 CE and again at the Second Council of Constantinople in 553 CE, many Eastern churches stubbornly held to the doctrine. By 600 CE, the schismatic Coptic Church of Egypt, the Jacobite Church of Syria, and the Armenian Church (also called the Gregorian Church), who refused to recognize Jesus' humanity, had been established.

MONOTHEISM

A belief in one all-powerful personal God, who is intimately involved with the workings of both the spiritual and the physical worlds, and who is the source of morality and redemption. The three great Abrahamic religions, Judaism, Christianity, and Islam are all monotheistic.

MONOTHELITISM

Definitively condemned at the Third Council of Constantinople in 680 CE, monotheletism was an attempt at a compromise between orthodoxy and monophysitism. Monotheletism holds that Jesus Christ has two natures, divine and human, but only one will, which is divine. The Maronite Church of Lebanon (see Maronism) split off from the Roman Catholic Church over this issue.

MONTANISM

A Christian sect founded in Asia Minor around 170 CE that is sometimes considered a forerunner of Pentecostalism. Its founder Montanus (dates unknown) and two female prophets, Prisca and

Maximilla, declared themselves to be the Paraclete promised in the Gospel of John. In ecstatic trances they announced that Christ's Second Coming was imminent and that the town of Pepuza, in Phrygia (Turkey), would be the New Jerusalem.

The Montanists fasted frequently, encouraged sexual abstinence, and ordained women as priests and bishops. They were both admired and criticized for their zealousness. "Do not desire to depart this life in beds, in miscarriages, in soft fevers, but in martyrdoms, that He who suffered for you may be glorified," Montanus urged his followers. Though generally orthodox in their doctrines, the Montanists criticized the established church for its complacency, and challenged its belief that fallen Christians could ever be redeemed. Most damningly, they claimed to speak in the voice of God, insisting that their own prophecies superseded those recorded in the Gospels: "I am the Lord, the Omnipotent God, who has descended into a human," one of their prophecies began. Another declared, "I, the Lord, have come—not an angel, not even an ambassador." Though they were excommunicated, the sect continued for some five hundred years. Its most notable convert was the great North African theologian Tertullian (ca. 160–225 CE), which explains why he never achieved sainthood.

MORMONISM

Popular name for the beliefs and practices of the Church of Jesus Christ of Latter-day Saints (LDS). The name Mormon comes from the church's founding gospel, the Book of Mormon. The largest Latter-day Saint denomination is headquartered in Salt Lake City, Utah, and claims some eleven million members worldwide; there are many smaller denominations as well, some of which, such as the Fundamentalist Church of Jesus Christ of Latter Day Saints, still illegally practice polygamy.

Joseph Smith (1805–44) had his first vision when he was fourteen years old and living in upstate New York. In 1823, when he was seventeen, he was visited by an angel named Moroni, who told him about an ancient book inscribed on golden plates that he had buried in a nearby hill in 400 CE. Smith and a group of early disciples recovered and translated the plates, which were subsequently returned to the angel. In further visions, Smith and his disciples were ordained into the Aaronic and Melchizedek priesthoods by John the Baptist and the apostles Peter and James. The Book of Mormon, which tells the story of a group of ancient Israelites' journey to America in the seventh century BCE (the ancestors of the American Indians) and Jesus' mission to them after his Resurrection, was published in 1830, the same year that Smith founded his first church.

Smith taught that the orthodox church had been lost to apostasy since its early days. The movement of which he was the chief prophet would restore it to its original beliefs and purpose and build the New Zion in America. The LDS church continues to believe in revelation today—its followers are encouraged to listen for God's voice when they pray; its members consider the church's president to be a major prophet.

The history of Mormonism over the past century and two thirds is complex and violent, filled with schisms and succession crises. Dogged by suspicion and persecution (and accusations of unscrupulous financial practices), Smith and his followers moved from New York to Ohio to Missouri. In 1838, the governor of Missouri, responding to gunfights between new Mormon property owners and locals, issued an "extermination order," which declared that for their

> open and avowed defiance of the laws, and of having made war
> upon the people of this State . . . the Mormons must be treated
> as enemies, and must be exterminated or driven from the State
> if necessary for the public peace—their outrages are beyond all
> description.

The order wasn't officially repealed until 1976. In 1844, after the Mormons moved to Illinois, Smith was murdered by an angry mob. After a succession battle, Brigham Young (1801–77) led most of the Latter-day Saints to Salt Lake City, Utah. Smith's son Joseph III stayed in Illinois with a smaller contingent that called themselves the Reorganized Church of Jesus Christ of Latter Day

Saints. Headquartered in Independence, Missouri, they are now known as the Community of Christ Church. Though Smith and his principal followers had practiced "plural marriage," polygamy didn't become an official practice of the religion until 1852. Brigham Young married fifty-five wives (some of whom divorced him); nineteen of them bore him fifty-six children. The church banned plural marriage in 1890 as a condition for Utah's statehood; a number of breakaway groups of Mormon fundamentalists continue the practice today, in defiance of secular and church law.

Though the LDS considers itself Christian, its beliefs and ceremonies differ sharply from mainstream Christianity's in a number of particulars. The Latter-Day Saints don't believe in original sin—they teach that one atones for one's own, rather than Adam's sins. Nor do they believe in the Trinity: the Father, Son, and Holy Spirit are one in purpose but separate in being. Mormons believe, as noted above, in continual revelation and in the canonical status of the Book of Mormon and Joseph Smith's other writings. They baptize not only the living members of their churches, but also the dead, who can be retroactively converted to the church by proxy (hence the LDS's intense preoccupation with genealogy). The LDS believe in three degrees of glory for the afterlife—the telestial kingdom is for the unredeemed, who are granted the presence of neither the Father nor the Son; the terrestrial kingdom is for honorable believers—Jesus is present there, but not the Father. The celestial kingdom is reserved for scrupulously devoted Mormons (one also must be married and baptized). Children and spouses who are properly "sealed" will share eternity together. Members of the LDS tithe; abstain from alcohol, caffeine, and tobacco; and perform mandatory missionary service.

MUGGLETONIANISM

An obscure but surprisingly long-lasting English sect founded during the English civil wars by two cousins, John Reeve (1608–58) and Lodowick Muggleton (1609–98), who preached about the imminent apocalypse, declaring themselves the two witnesses in the Book of Revelation (11:3–6)—"And I will give power unto my two witnesses, and they shall prophesy a thousand two hundred and threescore days, clothed in sackcloth." Reeve wrote a book called *The Two Principles* (1656)—which Muggleton later revised—and they cowrote *Transcendent Spiritual Treatise* (1652) and *The Divine Looking-Glass or the Third and Last Testament* (1656). Both of them spent time in prison for blasphemy.

After the Restoration and the death of Reeve, Muggleton wrote two polemics against the Quakers, *A Looking-Glass for George Fox* (1667) and *An Answer to William Penn* (1668). By the 1670s Muggleton had endured several struggles over control of the sect and his message had changed radically. Now a quasi Deist, he argued that since God no longer intervened in the world, prayer was useless (his followers met in taverns for Bible readings and hymn singing). He also denied the Trinity and the immortality of the soul. He understood Hell to be the state of unredeemed man; through reason and faith, he believed, heaven could be established on earth.

The last Muggletonian, Philip Noakes, of Kent, died in 1979.

MYSTICISM

In religion, the desire (and the act) of merging with the divine. Traditional religion uses rites and symbols to represent God or the gods; in Catholicism the ceremony of the Eucharist brings the worshipper into miraculous communion with Christ. But mystics seek a more tangible experience; they ecstatically dissolve themselves into a state of "oneness" with God. This union can be described in frankly sexual terms. The Song of Solomon in the Bible and the poems of the Sufi Rumi are deeply erotic; even the autobiography of St. Teresa of Ávila contains a shockingly suggestive scene when, in a vision, a "very beautiful" angel came to her carrying a long golden spear tipped with fire.

> With this he seemed to pierce my heart several times so that it penetrated to my entrails. When he drew it out, I thought he was drawing them out with it and he left me completely afire with a great love for God. The pain was so sharp that it made

me utter several moans; and so excessive was the sweetness caused me by this intense pain that one can never wish to lose it, nor will one's soul be content with anything less than God. It is not bodily pain, but spiritual, though the body has a share in it—indeed, a great share. So sweet are the colloquies of love which pass between the soul and God that if anyone thinks I am lying I beseech God, in His goodness, to give him the same experience.

The Zohar of the Kabbalists is filled with erotic imagery—the Shekhinah, the feminized spirit of God, is the vessel into which God pours his generative energies; human couples are not only enjoined to have sex, but to enjoy it—"performing with gladness the religious duty of conjugal intercourse in the presence of the Shekhinah." The Tantrism of the Hindus employs sex as a vehicle of transcendence.

Needless to say, not all mysticism is erotic, but even in its most austere and intellectualized forms, the mystic's intensity of devotion and desire, and the disintegration of the boundaries of the self that accompany the act of union, are as suggestive of sexual as religious rapture.

NATION OF ISLAM
Also known as the Black Muslims, the World Community of Al-Islam in the West, American Muslim Mission, the Nation of Peace, the Black Muslim Movement, and NOI.

A black nationalist religious movement, founded in Detroit in 1930 by W. D. Fard (aka Wali Farad Muhammad and some fifty-plus other aliases, according to the FBI). Fard's birth date and place of origin are uncertain. His most famous follower, Elijah Muhammad, insisted that Fard was born in Mecca; the FBI stated that he was from New Zealand. Before founding the Nation of Islam, Fard belonged to a Black Nationalist religion called the Moorish Science Temple, which was established in 1913 in Newark, New Jersey, by Noble Drew Ali (born Timothy Drew in 1886, died after a police beating in Chicago in 1929). Inspired by Marcus Garvey, Freemasonry, and

Theosophy, the Moorish Science Temple taught that there are only two races: the superior Asiatic races, which include Hispanics, Native Americans, Africans, and the people of the Pacific islands, and the inferior white-skinned Europeans. Christianity is the religion of the white slave masters; Islam is the true religion of the Moors (Noble Drew Ali's preferred name for blacks).

Fard was a door-to-door clothing salesman in Detroit when he began the Nation of Islam, whose teachings differed sharply from orthodox Islam. Most striking was the origin myth he retailed, which involved space ships and eugenics. Six thousand years ago, he said, on the Island of Patmos, an evil scientist named Dr. Yakub bred a soulless, bleached race of devils: the white man. Fard's chief disciple, Elijah Poole, who would change his name to Elijah Muhammad (1897–1975), continued the story:

> Yakub promised his followers that he would graft a nation from his own people, and he would teach them how to rule his people, through a system of tricks and lies whereby they use deceit to divide and conquer, and break the unity of the darker people, put one brother against another.

When Fard vanished in 1934, shortly after he was accused of complicity in a ritual murder, Elijah Muhammad took up the reins of the movement. Muhammad declared that Fard had been the living embodiment of Allah, who had come to earth to redeem the black man from his six thousand years of oppression, and that he, Elijah Muhammad, was Allah's chosen prophet. When black men pray to Allah, he declared, when they follow the moral strictures of the Koran, when they reject their "slave names" and wholly separate themselves from their degenerate white enemies, building a separate economy and ultimately a separate nation, their mental resurrection will be complete, assuring their victory in the coming race war.

Malcolm X (born Malcolm Little in 1925) joined the Nation of Islam while incarcerated and became its leading spokesman after he was paroled in 1952. He broke with the movement in the early 1960s after Elijah Muhammad was discovered to have fathered a number of illegitimate children with his teenaged secretaries. In 1964, after his pilgrimage to Mecca, Malcolm X changed his name to El-Hajj Malik El-Shabazz, embraced orthodox Islam, and disavowed black separatism. He would be assassinated in 1965, shortly after Louis X (a former violin prodigy and Calypso singer, he was born Louis Eugene Walcott in 1933; he is better known today as Minister Louis Farrakhan), the director of the Harlem mosque that Malcolm X had formerly led, declared in the newspaper *Muhammad Speaks* that "the die is set, and Malcolm shall not escape, especially after such evil foolish talk about his benefactor, Elijah Muhammad. Such a man as Malcolm is worthy of death."

When Elijah Muhammad died in 1975, his son Warith Deen Muhammad took over the movement, radically transforming it. He changed its name several times—first to the Bilalian Community, then to the World Community of Al-Islam in the West, then to the American Muslim Mission, and finally, in the 1990s, to the Muslim Mission. He disentangled the movement's business and spiritual affairs, disavowed his father's racialism, denied the divinity of W. F. Fard, affirmed Malcolm X's legacy, conformed the movement's theology to orthodox Islam, and acknowledged the laws of the United States, allowing its members to serve in the military (the boxer Muhammad Ali was one of many Black Muslims who had been imprisoned for draft resistance).

When Muhammad invited white people to join his reformed movement, Louis Farrakhan had had enough. He and some ten thousand followers broke away and set about restoring the Nation of Islam to its original racialist vision—Dr. Yakub, flying saucers, race war, and all. More than one observer has noted that for all his radicalism, the values Farrakhan instills in his followers aren't that different from Booker T. Washington's: clean living, bootstrap entrepreneurialism, and self-sufficiency. Though his virulent homophobia and anti-Semitism have earned Farrakhan tremendous notoriety (Nation of Islam publications declare that the Jews were the dominant force in the slave trade; Farrakhan often enlivens his speeches with his impressions of mincing, effeminate homosexuals), in recent years, he has adopted a more conciliatory tone. In

1995 he reconciled with Malcolm X's widow after her daughter was arrested for plotting his murder; he has had a rapprochement with Warith Deen Muhammad as well. The Million Man Marches earned Farrakhan some positive attention from the mainstream media, but as recently as February 2006, he reverted to his familiar themes when he condemned "the wicked Jews, the false Jews" for promoting homosexuality and making "it a crime for you to preach the word of God."

NEOPLATONISM

The philosophical system developed by Plotinus (ca. 205–270 CE) and his student and biographer Porphyry (ca. 232–ca. 305 CE). Inspired by Platonic idealism, Neoplatonism provides a mechanism to account for the way that ideal forms become crude matter, and offers a contemplative path toward a mystical union with God. Though not a Christian system per se—Porphyry was a pagan; Constantine's half brother, Julian the Apostate (331–363 CE), renounced Christianity for the philosophical religion of Neoplatonism—it had an enormous influence on Christian theologians, from Saint Augustine (354–430 CE) and Boethius (ca. 475–ca. 524 CE) to Thomas Aquinas (1225–74) and Meister Eckhardt (1260–1328). The Kabbalah bears many hallmarks of Neoplatonism as well.

Neoplatonism posited a primal unity—a divine Oneness that was indivisible and transcendent, yet at the same time, the font of all existence. As the goodness of the One overflowed, it emanated the Nous, or Mind, the source of all intelligence and knowledge. Then the Nous spilled over in turn, like water in a cascading fountain, emanating a third spiritual level, the Soul. As the Soul, which contained the ideal forms of all things, overflowed in its turn, the physical universe emerged, in all its plurality. Evil comes into the world along with materiality—the greater its distance from the divine font, the more wicked a thing is. Mankind, as Plotinus wrote, "is poised midway between the gods and the beasts." As life flows down the great chain of being, love and longing flows upward. "We dare not keep ourselves set towards the images of sense, or towards the merely vegetative, intent upon the gratifications of eating and procreation," Plotinus wrote, "Our life must be pointed towards the divine Mind, toward God."

The Cappadocian fathers—Basil of Caesarea (ca. 330–379), Gregory of Nyssa (ca. 330–395), and Gregory of Nanzianzus (330–390)—were all trained in Neoplatonism. Their philosophical accounts of the Trinity and especially of the emanation of the Son and the Spirit from the Father, in which they are *homoousios*, "being of the same essence," are central to the Nicene Creed, which reads, in part, "We believe in one Lord Jesus Christ, the son of God, the only begotten of his Father, that is of the essence of the Father; God from True God, begotten, not made, being of one substance with the Father through whom all things were made, things in heaven and on the earth."

NESTORIANISM

Fifth century heresy that held that Jesus was two different people (albeit contained in one body), one divine and one mortal. Nestorianism is a variant of adoptionism, which claimed that Jesus was born human but with a divine nature—God adopted Jesus' mortal body as his son when he was baptized.

Nestorius (386–451 CE), the patriarch of Constantinople, refused to call Mary the mother of God, arguing that she had only given birth to Jesus' human body; instead he called her the mother of Christ. Like Arianism, this belief was condemned for compromising the unity of the Trinity. The Council of Ephesus was convened in 431 to settle the matter, and Nestorius was exiled to Egypt. The Assyrian Church of the East, also known as the Nestorian Church, regards Nestorius as a saint. Their liturgy refers to Mary as the mother of Christ. Though in medieval times Nestorianism reached all the way to China and India, today its members are found mostly in Iraq and Iran.

NEW THOUGHT

The philosophy behind "mind cure," New Thought is an amalgam of philosophical idealism, transcendentalism, and Eastern and Christian mysticism. Its founder is generally acknowledged to be Phineas Parkhurst Quimby (1802–66), a Maine clockmaker who discovered that he could cure sick people simply by talking to them. Quimby's son George published a biographical sketch of his father in the *New England Magazine* in 1888, which summed up the basic tenets of mental medicine: "That 'mind was spiritual matter and could be changed;' that we were made up of 'truth and error;' that 'disease was an error, or belief, and that the Truth was the cure.' "

Not only was New Thought the progenitor of a number of distinct religious denominations—Christian Science, Religious Science, Divine Science, Unity, and a Japanese offshoot called Seicho-No-Ie—its ideas have informed the sermons of popular pastors such as Norman Vincent Peale and Robert Schuller, the activities of the twelve-step movements, the prosperity programs of Napoleon Hill, Esther and Jerry Hicks, and Stephen Covey, and the teachings of a veritable pantheon of New Age writers such as Marianne Williamson and Deepak Chopra. All of these diverse movements and writers share New Thought's foundational belief that we are what we *think* we are—and that we can therefore think our way to inner peace and to the enjoyment of spiritual and physical wealth.

PAGAN RECONSTRUCTIONISM

A contemporary movement that attempts to recreate lost polytheistic and folk religions with as much historical accuracy as possible. For example, contemporary practitioners of Theodism, the pre-Christian, tribal religion of the Northern European Germanic peoples (the Saxons, Frisians, Danes, Angles, etc.), divide themselves into tribes, take oaths, and have ceremonies involving elaborate toasts and ritual boasts. Similarly, ancient Hellenistic polytheists worship the gods and goddesses of the ancient Greek pantheon. Romuva was the official religion of the Lithuanians before the country was Christianized; contemporary Romuvans kindle a fire in an *aukura* or fire altar and offer food, flowers, and grass to the flames while they sing *dainas*, or ritual hymns.

Neopaganism refers to modern, often fanciful adaptations of non-Abrahamic religions, which may or may not have much historicity. Wicca, for example, is a salad of occultism and hoary goddess lore that evokes a variety of ancient practices but in its present form dates back no further than a few decades. Some white supremacist groups espouse an Odinism that mixes myths from the Eddas with Nazi racial theories. Neo-Druids espouse a highly sentimentalized, eco-minded, politically correct iteration of a religion that in its original form most likely featured human sacrifice.

PANENTHEISM

A word coined by the German philosopher K. C. F. Krause (1781–1832) and first used in English by the English theologian William Ralph Inge in his book *Christian Mysticism* (1899), where he defined it as "the belief in the immanence of a God who is also transcendent." While pantheism (the belief that the universe *is* God) is not wholly incompatible with materialism—in fact, a movement called scientific pantheism holds that though the material world is all there is, it should be reverenced on its own terms—panentheism is theistic. When Kabbalism speaks of divine sparks that are trapped in the material world and need to be gathered up and restored to God, or when Neoplatonism describes the material world as having been emanated from a transcendent godhead (and thus containing the divine essence in a diluted form), we are in the realm of panentheism, where God is present in the world, as the soul is present in the body, but at the same time also occupies a separate and much higher level of existence.

PANTHEISM

Any religion or system of beliefs that identifies God with the universe itself. The idea is common in many ancient religions and philosophies and is central to Hinduism and Stoicism. The heretical philosophers Giordano Bruno (1548–1600) and Baruch Spinoza (1632–77) were pantheists. Romanticism and transcendentalism contain elements of pantheism (and panentheism) as well.

The word was coined by John Toland (1670–1722), an English heretic and political pamphleteer, and a dedicated student of Locke, Bruno, and Lucretius. He first used it in a letter to Gottfried Leibniz in 1710, when he referred to "the pantheistic opinion of those who believe in no other eternal being but the universe." In 1720 he published the *Pantheisticon,* in which he declared that the universe is divine: "Every material thing is in all things. All things come from all, and all is in all things."

PARSISM *See* Zoroastrianism.

PELAGIANISM
Doctrines of the heresiarch Pelagius (ca. 355–ca. 425 CE). Little is known about his life, though he was probably born in the British Isles (Saint Jerome ridiculed him as *scotorum pultibus proegravatus,* or "stuffed with Scottish porridge"). A highly educated, ascetic monk, he appeared in Rome around 380 CE and attracted a significant following. The Pelagians believed that since Adam alone was guilty of the sin of disobedience, there was no such thing as original sin. Since the human race hadn't fallen, Christ's death and Resurrection were not an atonement. To the Pelagians, Christ was a moral exemplar, not a sacrificial lamb. Finally, Pelagius taught that the Mosaic law provided as good a guide to salvation as the Gospels, and that salvation could be achieved by right-living pagans and nonbelievers as well as to Jews and Christians. After Rome was sacked in 410, Pelagius traveled to North Africa, where he fell afoul of Augustine of Hippo (354–430 CE). Eventually he withdrew to Palestine.

Though Pelagianism was roundly condemned at the Council of Carthage in 418 and then again at the Council of Ephesus in 431, a new variant of the heresy, so-called Semi-Pelagianism, soon spread throughout Gaul and especially the British Isles, which is why Pelagianism is sometimes called the English heresy. The Semi-Pelagians believed that although grace was necessary for salvation, people could desire salvation without it, and once saved, persevere in grace by their own efforts, rather than by

God's will. The Semi-Pelagians also denied the Augustinian doctrine of predestination. Semi-Pelagianism was definitively condemned at the Council of Orange in 529, but the issues it
raised—free will, predestination, and the nature of grace—would
reemerge with a vengeance during the Protestant Reformation.

PENTECOSTALISM

> And when the day of Pentecost was fully come, they were all
> with one accord in one place. And suddenly there came a sound
> from heaven as of a rushing mighty wind, and it filled all the
> house where they were sitting. And there appeared unto them
> cloven tongues like as of fire, and it sat upon each of them. And
> they were all filled with the Holy Ghost, and began to speak with
> other tongues, as the Spirit gave them utterance. —Acts 2:1–4

Pentecostalism is a Christian movement whose hallmark is the
ability of its believers to speak in tongues (a phenomenon known
as glossolalia). Pentecostals receive other charismata, or gifts of the
spirit, as well, such as faith healing, the power to exorcise demons,
to prophesy, and the ability to interpret prayer language (the gib-
berish of glossolalia). Some Pentecostals handle snakes. The name
Pentecostalism comes from the Jewish festival of Shavuot or the
Feast of Weeks, which occurs fifty days after Passover and com-
memorates the giving of the law at Mount Sinai (*pentecost* is Greek
for the "fiftieth day"). Pentecostals believe that speaking in tongues
is audible proof that one has received a Baptism of the Holy Spirit.
    Modern Pentecostalism began in Topeka, Kansas, in 1901
when a woman named Agnes Ozman (1870–1937) began to babble during a service conducted by the Holiness minister Charles
Fox Parham (1873–1929). Parham moved to Houston, where his
preaching had a similar effect on other congregants. This attracted
the attention of an African American minister named William J.
Seymour (1870–1922). Since Parham's church was segregated,
Seymour was only permitted to sit outside the door while Parham
preached inside. In 1906, Seymour launched the multiracial Azusa
Street Revival in Los Angeles, which continued for three years.

As the Pentecostal movement swiftly spread around the world, it endured a number of schisms, over race (the Pentecostal Fellowship of North America was organized in 1948 as an all-white movement) and Trinitarianism (Oneness Pentecostals baptize only in Jesus' name). The largest Pentecostal denominations today are the Assemblies of God, the United Pentecostal Church, and the International Church of the Foursquare Gospel which was founded by Aimee Semple McPherson (1890–1944). Pentecostalism has become especially popular in Latin America.

Pentecostals are not the only Christians who believe in gifts of the spirit. Since the 1970s, the charismatic movement has swept through virtually every Christian denomination. There are charismatic Catholics, Episcopalians, Presbyterians, and Lutherans; there are even Eastern Orthodox congregations that deem themselves charismatic. Not all of them speak in tongues.

PHARISAISM

The beliefs of the Pharisees, one of the two major politico-religious sects among the Jews of Palestine during the era of the Second Temple. Their name was given to them by their adversaries the Sadducees, the party of the temple priests ("Sadducee" is derived from the name Zadok, the high priest who anointed Solomon; "Pharisee" comes from *perushim,* or "separatist"). Little is known about the Sadducees, since they didn't survive the fall of the temple. They were reputed to be aristocratic, pitiless in the application of criminal law, and to believe neither in the resurrection of the dead nor the existence of spirits and angels. The anti-Talmudic Karaites sometimes referred to a Sadducean text called Sefer Zadok, which has not survived.

Following the prescriptions of Ezra, the Pharisees strictly separated themselves from non-Hebrews, observed the minutiae of Mosaic law, eschewed the temptations of secular Hellenism, and questioned the legitimacy of the non-Davidic Hasmonean dynasty that had arisen in the last centuries before Roman rule (Herod's wife Mariamne was a Hasmonean). Most important, the Pharisees believed that the priesthood was the common possession of all Jews—that Torah study and mitzvoth (observance of laws) were more legitimate forms of worship than sacrifice, and that the oral Torah (the emerging body of extrabiblical traditions, stories, and scriptural and legal interpretation) constituted a sacred text and a sacred project in its own right. After the destruction of the Second Temple, the Pharisees became the rabbis and the oral Torah the Talmud. No longer connected with a hereditary priesthood, a monarchy, a physical place, and a sacred edifice, Judaism was no longer a nation—it was a religion.

Although Jesus scorned the Pharisees' sanctimony and hypocrisy, their notion that any person could have a direct relationship with God would have a significant impact on the development of Christianity, a religion that was largely codified by Paul of Tarsus, a former Pharisee.

PIETISM   *See* Evangelicalism.

PILGRIMS   *See* Puritanism.

POLYTHEISM
The belief in many gods, who all have their own individual characteristics and functions. In the Indian Vedas, for example, Rudra is the god of storms and medicine; Soma, the god of inspiration and speech; Agni, the god of fire and sacrifice. In the Babylonian pantheon, Ishtar is the goddess of love; Shamash, the god of sun and justice; and Anu, the god of the highest heaven. The Greek Olympians include Zeus, the king of the gods, and Ares, the god of war and manliness. Not all gods were worshipped equally; in some cultures—for instance, ancient Egypt—gods were tutelaries of cities: Amon, the god of creation, was the patron of Thebes; Ra, the god of the sun, was worshipped in Annu (modern-day Cairo).

Henotheism is a word coined by the nineteenth-century German philologist and orientalist Max Müller to describe the veneration of a single god while acknowledging the existence of many. In his words, it is "monotheism in principle and polytheism in fact." In Hinduism, Rita is a supreme organizing force that the other gods are subordinate to; in some ways it resembles the Ein Sof (the infinite, indivisible, impersonal essence of God) of Kabbalism or the godhead of Neoplatonism. Some forms of Gnosticism acknowledge lesser deities; textual evidence in the Jewish Bible suggests that the earliest Jews worshipped Yahweh as the greatest and most powerful of gods rather than the only God.

POSTMILLENNIALISM *See* **Millennialism.**

PREMILLENNIAL DISPENSATIONALISM
See **Millennialism.**

PRESBYTERIANISM *See* **Protestantism.**

PRETERISM *See* **Millennialism.**

PROTESTANTISM
The form of Christianity that emerged from the Reformation in sixteenth-century Europe. Today there are more than a thousand distinct Protestant denominations in the United States, most of them rooted in the movements founded by Martin Luther (1483–1546), Huldreich Zwingli (1484–1531), and John Calvin (1509–64). There are four major "families" of Protestant churches: The Lutheran, the Anglican, the Reform (Presbyterianism in England and the United States), and the Free. The Free churches are a miscellany—they include the Congregationalists, the Baptists, the Methodists, and the Disciples of Christ. Major (and often overlapping) movements within Protestantism today include Pentecostalism, Fundamentalism, and Evangelicalism.

The five *solas*, a set of Latin slogans probably first written by Luther, provide as apt a summation of the major tenets of Reformation Protestantism as one is likely to find:

> *Sola Scriptura:* The Scripture alone is the standard of
> truth.

Soli Deo Gloria: All of life is dedicated to the Glory of
God alone.
Solo Christo: By Christ's work alone are we saved.
Sola Gratia: Salvation is by Grace alone.
Sola Fide: Justification is by Faith alone.

While Roman Catholicism and Orthodox Christianity consider
the institution of the church to be the sole legitimate medium between the people and God, and its sacraments the source of grace,
Protestantism declared that the Bible itself (not the pronouncements and dogmas of the official church) was the sole source of
truth. In addition, Protestants believe in the universal priesthood
of believers (Protestant pastors have no *charism,* or special spiritual gifts, as Catholic priests are said to) and in the doctrine of
justification by faith by grace (rather than through good works or
mere membership in a church). If Catholics accepted the notion
that the world was evenly divided into secular and religious
realms—that monks answered to the church and soldiers and
courtiers to the king—Protestants insisted that God is sovereign
over all of life.

Another major tenet of Reformation Protestantism is predestination—the idea that people are born with their fate already determined and that only an "elect" will be saved. This
was a point of contention almost from the beginning. By the
time of the evangelical revivals in the nineteenth century, most
Protestants had come to believe that the possibility of salvation
was available to all (a position known as Arminianism). There
was also disagreement over the Lord's Supper. Lutherans believed in consubstantiation (that Christ was spiritually present
in the host—a notion that is subtly different from Catholicism's
transubstantiation, or the miraculous transformation of the
bread and wine into the flesh and blood of Christ); other Protestants (mostly followers of Zwingli) believed that the Lord's
Supper was merely symbolic. Baptism (full immersion or not?
infant or adult?) and Trinitarianism are also controversial issues
within Protestantism.

American Protestantism today embraces a wide swath of beliefs and styles of worship, from the pomp and splendor of High Church Episcopalianism, with its incense, mitered bishops, and other vestiges of Roman Catholicism, to the austerities of Primitive Baptist churches, which forbid musical instruments and regard any artistic depiction of Jesus as idolatrous. Though there are any number of national church bodies, attitudes toward doctrinal and social issues can vary between church and church and region and region. Episcopalians have been sharply divided in recent years over the question of the ordination of gays; for many years Southern and Northern organizations held opposite views on the morality of racial segregation.

According to polling conducted by the sociologists Barry A. Kosmin and Seymour P. Lachman at the Graduate School of the City University of New York in 1990 and 2001, 76.5 percent of Americans regard themselves as Christians (as compared to Jews, who compose 1.3 percent of the population, and Muslims, Buddhists, and Hindus, whose combined numbers amount to less than 2 percent). While Catholicism is by far the largest single denomination, today most American Christians are Protestants. Their denominational breakdown, in terms of their percentage of the U.S. population, is as follows:

DENOMINATION	% US POPULATION
Catholic	24.5
Baptist	16.3
Methodist	6.8
Lutheran	4.6
Presbyterian	2.7
Pentecostal	2.1
Episcopal	1.7
Mormon	1.3
Churches of Christ	1.2
Congregational	0.7
Jehovah's Witnesses	0.6
Assemblies of God	0.5

These statistics are derived from respondents' self-identification, which is a very different measure of commitment from dues-paying church memberships. It would be a mistake to assume that all of these people subscribe to the specific doctrines of their chosen sects—for example, that most contemporary Presbyterians would be prepared to take up Calvin's old argument with Luther about the separation of church and state (Luther believed that the state should enforce religious orthodoxy; Calvin hoped that an independent church would Christianize the state). Church affiliation has as much to do with regional patterns of settlement (the Scandinavians who settled Minnesota brought their natal Lutheranism with them; the Pilgrims' Congregationalism is still strong in New England), family traditions, and the popularity of local ministers as it does with adherence to the specific beliefs that caused the denominations to splinter apart decades or even centuries ago. George Barna, a leading pollster of Christian trends, recently noted that nearly 75 percent of the Christians he surveyed rejected the notion of original sin and an astonishing four out of ten *Protestants* believed that their good works alone would suffice to earn them a place in heaven.

Nevertheless, it's possible to make some broad generalizations about the largest Protestant denominations (some denominations not discussed below are treated in their own entries). The so-called mainline Protestant churches in America (long established, generally recognized, and politically and doctrinally moderate) have actually fallen in membership in recent years, so they are no longer as mainstream as they once were—evangelical and fundamentalist churches are quickly overtaking them in numbers and influence. But for decades, the so-called "seven sisters" of mainline American Protestantism were understood to be the Episcopalians, Lutherans, Presbyterians, Congregationalists, Baptists, Disciples of Christ, and Methodists.

Episcopalianism is descended from the Church of England, which owes its being as much to Henry VIII's desire to divorce his wife as to the rise of Protestantism in England. Though the politics of its congregations and bishops vary widely (some

Episcopalians are as liberal on hot-button social issues like homosexuality and abortion as Unitarian-Universalists; others are as traditional as Catholics or Protestant fundamentalists), its theology, liturgy, and organization strongly resemble Catholicism's. Also very traditional liturgically and doctrinally are the Lutherans, who, as mentioned above, believe that the Lord's Supper is more than a symbolic rite.

Presbyterians are sometimes facetiously referred to as the "frozen chosen" because of the dignified austerity of their worship services and because their Confession adheres to the Calvinist notion of a predestined "elect" who are chosen for redemption—also because Presbyterians have long been noted for their willingness to "speak truth to power," to take a moral stand even if it is opposed to the government's views. Though Presbyterianism is descended from John Knox's (ca. 1514–72) Reformed Church of Scotland, and its churches are governed by regional councils of elders, there have been many schisms within the movement since its founding. In the United States alone there are nine distinct Presbyterian church bodies.

Though the Baptists are far from a monolithic group—there are tremendous differences of style, doctrine, and politics between its many organizations and self-governing congregations—Baptists sometimes use this acrostic to explain their essential tenets:

> Bible, the only rule for faith and practice
> Autonomy of the local church
> Priesthood of the believer
> Two ordinances: Baptism and the Lord's Supper
> Individual soul liberty and responsibility
> Separation
> Two officers of the local church: the pastor and
>   the deacon

Baptists do not regard the act of Baptism (always by full immersion) as a supernatural ritual—it is rather a public ceremony affirming that one has been saved and joined the church (and is thus only available to adults). The Lord's Supper is also understood to be symbolic. The most controversial of these tenets is Separation, which some Baptists interpret to necessitate a total rejection of any ecumenicism and complete withdrawal from secular society. Congregationalism is similar to Baptism in that its congregations are self-governing, and they are faithful to the Protestant *solas*. Congregationalists, however, practice infant baptism. Because most Congregational churches are in the so-called "blue" New England states, they tend to be somewhat more liberal today than their Puritan and Pilgrim heritage would suggest.

The Churches of Christ and the Disciples of Christ are creedless, Bible-based movements that dates back to the restorational activities (an attempt to return to the earliest forms of Christian organization and worship) of Alexander Campbell and Barton Stone in the early nineteenth century. Churches are autonomously governed, but there are many loosely organized movements, some deeply conservative and evangelical, some quite liberal. In recent years, a number of Disciples of Christ churches have been at the vanguard of the gay rights movement.

If Methodism began in the eighteenth century as an ardently evangelical movement, and if Methodist camp meetings and circuit riders were ubiquitous in nineteenth-century America, Methodists today tend to be less interested in aggressive proselytizing than in social justice; they are characteristically ecumenical and moderately liberal in both their theology and their politics (though Methodism, like many other denominations, is riven over the question of how to deal with homosexuality). A witticism has it that the Methodists are too Baptist for the Catholics and too Catholic for the Baptists. Most American Methodists live in the Southeast, however, and many espouse the conservative politics and evangelicalist beliefs that have come to be associated with the so-called "red states." Both President George W. Bush and Vice President Dick Cheney, for example, belong to Methodist churches.

PROVIDENTIALISM

> "There's a special providence in the fall of a
>   sparrow."
>   —Shakespeare, *Hamlet,* Act V, Scene 2

Providentialism is the belief that God's will is manifested in human affairs, and often includes the corollary assumption that power and prosperity are visible signs of divine grace. In America, this idea dates back to the Pilgrims, specifically to John Winthrop's *Arabella* sermon, "A Model of Christian Charity," in which he speaks of the special covenant between the Pilgrims and God. Should they keep their side of the compact, Winthrop promised,

> the Lord will be our God, and delight to dwell among us, as His
> own people, and will command a blessing upon us in all our
> ways, so that we shall see much more of His wisdom, power,
> goodness and truth, than formerly we have been acquainted
> with. We shall find that the God of Israel is among us, when ten
> of us shall be able to resist a thousand of our enemies; when He
> shall make us a praise and glory that men shall say of succeed
> ing plantations, "may the Lord make it like that of New En
> gland." For we must consider that we shall be as a city upon a
> hill. The eyes of all people are upon us.

George W. Bush invoked American providentialism in his speech to a joint session of Congress after the events of September 11, 2001, when he declared, "Our nation is chosen by God and commissioned by history to be a model to the world of justice." In his second inaugural in 2005, he asserted a slightly secularized variation of the same theme, in which he identified Democratic institutions rather than divine redemption with God's plan for humanity, and American foreign policy with God's will.

> We go forward with complete confidence in the eventual tri
> umph of freedom. Not because history runs on the wheels of

inevitability; it is human choices that move events. Not because
we consider ourselves a chosen nation; God moves and chooses
as He wills. We have confidence because freedom is the permanent hope of mankind, the hunger in dark places, the longing
of the soul . . .

    History has an ebb and flow of justice, but history also has
a visible direction, set by liberty and the author of liberty.

This idea, Michael Ignatieff wrote in the *New York Times Magazine* in 2004, "that when America and its soldiers promote
democracy overseas, they are doing God's work," is called Democratic providentialism.

PURITANISM

H. L. Mencken (1880–1956) defined Puritanism as "the haunting
fear that someone, somewhere, may be happy." The word *puritan*
is used today to refer to a person who is not only morally austere
and strictly orthodox in his or her religious practice, but who, in
an excess of zeal, seeks to impose religious prohibitions on others. Aggressive Sabbatarians, who not only honor the Sabbath
themselves but sponsor legislation to prevent anyone else from
violating it, are puritanical, as are the latter-day Comstockians
who turned the pop star Janet Jackson's supposed "wardrobe mal-
function" during the 2004 Superbowl half-time show, which
briefly exposed one of her breasts on national television, into a
major political and cultural event.

    Historically, the Puritans were nonconformist Protestants in
England in the sixteenth and seventeenth centuries, mostly
Calvinists, who fought to purge the Church of England of its
"popish" remnants or who illegally separated from it altogether.
England had broken with the Vatican during the reign of Henry
VIII (1509–47). During the reign of Queen Mary (1553–58) the
nation returned to Catholicism, and many Protestants were exiled
or executed (John Foxe's enormously influential *Book of Martyrs,*
written in exile and published in 1559, lovingly recounts some of
their most gruesome fates). Many Protestants returned to England

when Queen Elizabeth assumed the throne in 1558, but James I, whose reign began in 1604, strenuously resisted the Puritans' reforms, which he feared would limit his royal prerogatives. "No bishop, no king," he famously declared. Laud's persecution of the Puritans brought things to a head during the reign of Charles I. The result, by 1649, was revolution, regicide, and the establishment of a military dictatorship under Oliver Cromwell (1599–1658), who, though vehemently anti-Catholic, was surprisingly tolerant of Judaism and non-Calvinist varieties of Protestantism, such as Quakerism.

Meanwhile, starting in 1620, Puritans had begun colonizing North America. The original Pilgrims were Separatist Congregationalists who had been exiled in the Netherlands. Congregationalists believe that every church is a microcosm of Christianity, whose only true leader is Christ. Each congregation is self-governing (though they form voluntary unions with other churches—for instance, the United Church of Christ today). Their clergymen, who serve at the pleasure of their congregations and their elected officers, have no special authority.

The Pilgrims believed in predestination and the only sacraments they acknowledged were the Lord's Supper and infant Baptism. Marriage, for example, was strictly a civil matter. The Pilgrims did not celebrate Christmas or Easter, but strictly observed the Sabbath. Most of the settlers who followed the Pilgrims to New England were Puritan Anglicans. Despite their doctrinal differences—and the ostensibly egalitarian antiauthoritarianism of Congregationalism—the colonists soon established a theocracy that was more intolerant than the one they'd fled from. Their persecution of Quakers, the exile of Roger Williams and Anne Hutchinson, and the judicial horrors of the Salem witch trials are frequently adduced as cautionary tales about what can happen when governance and godliness comport too intimately with one another.

QUAKERISM

"This was Justice Bennet of Derby that first called us Quakers," George Fox (1624–91), an ex-apprentice shoemaker, traveling preacher, and the principal founder of the Society of Friends, re-called in his journals, "Because we bid them tremble at the word of God, and this was in the year 1650." Justice Bennet had sentenced Fox to six months in prison for blasphemy.

The second year of the interregnum—Charles I had been beheaded the year before—1650, was a time of unprecedented social, political, and religious strife in England. The agrarian communists known as the Diggers were agitating for the redistribution of land. Victorious Puritans were purging the Church of England of its last popish vestiges, antinomian Ranters were drinking and fornicating their way to salvation, and visionary Protestants like George Fox were beginning to question whether even Puritanism was pure enough.

"The Lord showed me, so that I did see clearly, that he did not dwell in these temples which men had commanded and set up," Fox wrote, "But in people's hearts . . . his people were his temple, and he dwelt in them." Fox—and starting in the 1650s, his fellow Children of Light in the Society of Friends that he founded—believed that every person in the world has an "Inner Light," which is literally a piece of Jesus. Worship is not a ritual obligation, but active, personal communion with the indwelling Christ; religion is not a matter of belief or knowledge, but action. As Fox exhorted,

> Be patterns, be examples in all countries, places, islands, nations wherever you come; that your carriage and life may preach among all sorts of people, and to them; then you will come to walk cheerfully over the world, answering that of God in everyone; whereby in them you may be a blessing, and make the witness of God in them to bless you.

Quakerism regards the Bible as the words of inspired but not inerrant men. Its services are conducted as open meetings in which members share their spiritual feelings rather than as a forum for a minister's sermonizing. Quakers refuse to take oaths, they are committed pacifists, and, in general, have scant regard for secular or spiritual authority that doesn't comport with their inner light.

In George Fox's words, again, "When the Lord sent me forth into the world, He forbade me to put off my hat to any, high or low." Quakers have no use for creeds, many of them eschew Baptism, Communion, and the other sacraments. Though Oliver Cromwell tolerated Quakers (unlike the American Puritans, who hounded them out of Massachusetts Bay), they were persecuted mercilessly in England between the Restoration in 1660 and the passage of the Act of Toleration in 1689. There were Quaker settlements in North Carolina, Rhode Island, and New Jersey; Pennsylvania would be founded as a Quaker colony in 1681.

The Quakers would endure several painful schisms in the 1800s. Nonetheless, they stood at the forefront of the abolition movement in both England and America, were pioneers in women's rights, and continue to be at the vanguard of many other social reform and peace movements to this day. Susan B. Anthony (1820–1906) and Jane Addams (1860–1935), for example, were both raised as Quakers. Quakers were involved in the founding of Greenpeace, Oxfam, and Amnesty International. Many major American colleges were founded by Quakers, including Bryn Mawr, Johns Hopkins, Haverford, and Swarthmore.

QUIETISM
In general usage, quietism refers to an attitude of passive withdrawal from worldly affairs. In religion, it is the notion that spiritual perfection can be attained only when the soul is purged of will, desire, and effort, so the divine can fill the vacant space. Though there are elements of quietism in most mystical systems (most notably *prajna,* in Buddhism), the term refers specifically to the teachings of the Spanish priest Miguel de Molinos (1628–97), whose *Spiritual Guide* proclaimed:

> In the throne of quiet are manifest the perfections of spiritual beauty; here the true light of the secret and divine Mysteries of our holy faith, here perfect humility, even to the Annihilation of itself, the amplest resignation, chastity, poverty of spirit, the sincerity and innocence of the Dove, external modesty, silence and

internal fortitude, liberty and purity of heart; here the forgetful-
ness of every created thing, even of it self, joyful simplicity, heavenly indifference, continual Prayer, a total nakedness, perfect dis-
interestedness, a most wise contemplation, a conversation of
Heaven; and lastly, the most perfect and serene peace within, of
which this happy Soul may say what the wise man said of Wisdom, that all other Graces came along in the company with her.

Molinos was condemned for heresy in 1687, because his teachings
had the savor of Pelagianism (in that they implied one could
achieve salvation by one's own efforts) and also because he was
said to have justified lascivious acts committed by himself and his
followers, supposedly justifying them with the argument that only
their bodies, which were under the control of Satan, had sinned.
Today many church historians believe that he was framed.

In one of the most spectacular ironies of recent years (and a
textbook instance of blowback—when a covert policy blows up
in a country's face), the state of Israel is said to have provided the
initial funding for a religious organization begun by the para-
plegic Palestinian sheik Ahmad Yassin in the 1970s because, as
the *Guardian* explained it, "of his quietism, the ideological challenge he posed to militant secular nationalism, and his opposition
to the armed struggle espoused by the Palestine Liberation Or-
ganisation." Sheik Yassin's movement is now known as Hamas,
which, though religious, is far from quietistic. The Israelis dis-
patched the sheik (and at least half a dozen bystanders) in 2004,
with a Hellfire missile launched from a helicopter. In 2006,
Hamas became the majority party in the Palestinian parliament.

RASTAFARIANISM
The word comes from Ras Tafari Makonnen, the precoronation
name of Emperor Haile Selassie I of Ethiopia (1892–1975). Rastafarianism is an outgrowth of an Afrocentric religion called the
Afro Athlican Constructive Church, whose founding document
is *The Holy Piby,* a visionary, alternative bible written by an
Anguillan-born follower of Marcus Garvey named Robert Athlyi

Rogers. Published in Newark, New Jersey, in the 1920s, *The Holy Piby*, also known as the Black Man's Bible, recounts the exile and prophesies and the redemption of the Ethiopian people:

> And it came to pass that I saw a great host of Negroes marching upon the earth and there was a light upon them, then I looked towards the heaven and behold I saw the natural man standing in the east and the star of his crown gave light to the pathway of the children of Ethiopia.

When Haile Selassie I was crowned emperor of Ethiopia in 1930, some Jamaican followers of Athlicanism believed that this prophecy had been fulfilled. Tracing his lineage back to King David (through the Queen of Sheba and King Solomon), they declared that Selassie was an incarnation of God (or Jah), the long-awaited Messiah who would lead the dispersed black nations out of Babylonia and back to Mount Zion, which is Africa. Haile Selassie is the Father and the Son and everybody is potentially the Holy Spirit. The body is a temple and, for a chosen few, immortal (many Rastas don't believe that Selassie really died). Marijuana is a sacrament; dreadlocks are worn as a celebration of Africanism and also in deference to Leviticus 21:5 ("They shall not make baldness upon their head").

ROMAN CATHOLICISM
The beliefs and practices of the Roman or the Holy Catholic and Apostolic Church. Members receive the message of the Gospels through Christ's vicar, the pope, who is infallible on matters of faith and doctrine. His authority passes down through the hierarchy of cardinals and bishops to individual priests, whose ordination gives them the power to convey the sacraments of penance and the Eucharist. Since all members of the church, living and dead, share one another's merits, members can call on the saints and the Virgin Mary in their prayers. Unlike Protestantism, which emphasizes the personal experience of grace, Catholicism conveys grace to its members through its ceremonies and rites.

The Nicene Creed summarizes the foundational beliefs of Catholicism (and many Protestant denominations as well).

> I believe in one God,
> the Father Almighty,
> maker of heaven and earth,
> and of all things visible and invisible;
>
> And in one Lord Jesus Christ,
> the only begotten Son of God,
> begotten of his Father before all worlds,
> God of God, Light of Light,
> very God of very God,
> begotten, not made,
> being of one substance with the Father;
> by whom all things were made;
> who for us men and for our salvation
> came down from heaven,
> and was incarnate by the Holy Ghost
> of the Virgin Mary,
> and was made man;
> and was crucified also for us under Pontius Pilate;
> he suffered and was buried;
> and the third day he rose again
> according to the Scriptures,
> and ascended into heaven,
> and sitteth on the right hand of the Father;
> and he shall come again, with glory,
> to judge both the quick and the dead;
> whose kingdom shall have no end.
>
> And I believe in the Holy Ghost the Lord, and Giver
>   of Life,
> who proceedeth from the Father [and the Son];
> who with the Father and the Son together
> is worshipped and glorified;

who spake by the Prophets.
And I believe one holy Catholic and Apostolic
   Church;
I acknowledge one baptism for the remission of
   sins;
and I look for the resurrection of the dead,
and the life of the world to come. Amen.

The history of the Roman Catholic Church is filled with conflicts between kings and popes who were struggling to assert their
prerogatives in one another's realms; between orthodoxy and
heresy; between the worldliness of a vast, global bureaucracy and
the personal inwardness of faith; between the Sadducean rigidity
of a priestly caste and the subversive nature of Jesus' own preaching. The forces that exploded in the Protestant Reformation in the
sixteenth century—the desire for an unmediated experience of
grace; for a personal, rather than an institutional relationship
with God; for a spirituality and morality that was as uncompro-
mising as Jesus' own—had been building up for centuries.

At the outset of the twenty-first century, Catholicism seems
to be heading toward another crisis. Pedophile scandals, rapidly
diminishing membership in the developed world, aggressive
evangelical missionizing in the third world, and a looming short-
age of priests are putting tremendous pressure on the Vatican.
Vast numbers of Catholics ignore the church's teachings on birth
control and would welcome a noncelibate priesthood; thus far
Rome's response has been to hew even harder to the right.

As Christopher Caldwell wrote in the *New York Times*:

The democratic world may offer the church a hard choice—between growing more reactionary or dying. Perhaps the church's
real arrogance was to assume at the time of Vatican II that it
had the standing to open a dialogue with modernity. The
church could never command that non-Catholics listen to it;
all it could do was expose its faithful to the siren song of
democracy, capitalism and sex.

SABBATARIANISM

The beliefs of Christians who insist upon strict observance of Sunday as the Lord's Day. Blue laws regulating certain kinds of commerce on Sundays were enacted at the behest of Sabbatarians. The word *blue*, as in *bluenose*, clearly refers to Puritanism; its etymology, however, is mysterious. Most scholars doubt Samuel Andrew Peters's claim, in his *A General History of Connecticut* (1781), that it derives from the color paper on which the laws were printed. Many states forbid the sale of hard alcohol on Sundays; it was illegal to sell housewares in Texas on Sundays until 1985.

Sabbatarian also refers to those denominations, such as Seventh-Day Baptists and Adventists, who celebrate the Sabbath on the seventh day of the week, as the Jews do. Many Christians believe that the Fourth Commandment—remember the Sabbath Day and keep it holy—was abrogated along with the rest of the ceremonial laws of the Old Testament. They regard Sunday as the Lord's Day because Jesus' Resurrection occurred on the first day of the week.

SACERDOTALISM

The notion that priests (the word *sacerdotal*, or "priestly," is derived from the Latin words *sacer*, "sacred," and *dare*, "to give"; its literal meaning is "one who makes sacred offerings") are necessary mediators between gods (or God) and human beings. While medicine men, shamans, and prophets spoke and acted independently, priests were specially trained to perform their functions. In ancient times they were often members of a hereditary caste (for example, the Cohens, or *kohanim*, of the Biblical Jews, who were direct male descendants of Moses' brother Aaron; or the Brahman caste in Hinduism).

In Eastern Orthodox and Roman Catholic churches, only priests can administer the sacraments. According to the *Catechism of the Catholic Church,*

> in the ecclesial service of the ordained minister, it is Christ himself who is present to his Church as Head of his Body, Shepherd of his flock, high priest of the redemptive sacrifice,

Teacher of Truth. This is what the Church means by saying that the priest, by virtue of the sacrament of Holy Orders, acts *in persona Christi Capitis.*

Most Protestant denominations believe in "the priesthood of believers." Their religious leaders are called ministers rather than priests because their ordination (and many Protestant clergymen aren't formally ordained) doesn't accord them any special *charism* or supernatural power.

SADDUCEEISM   *See* **Pharisaism.**

SALAFISM   *See* **Wahhabism.**

SAMARITANISM
The religious beliefs and practices of the Samaritans, descendants of the people of the ancient city of Samaria (near modern-day Nablus, in the West Bank). Readers of the New Testament know that the Samaritans, though they venerated the Torah and obeyed its laws, were regarded with contempt by the Jews of Judea. John 4:9: "Then saith the woman of Samaria unto him, How is it that thou, being a Jew, askest drink of me, which am a woman of Samaria? For the Jews have no dealings with the Samaritans."

The Samaritans claimed descent from the northern tribes of Israel, but in all likelihood their lineage was adulterated. The Assyrians, who conquered Samaria in 724 BCE, deported most of its native Israelites and replaced them with tribes from the East, as recounted in 2 Kings 17:24: "And the king of Assyria brought [men] from Babylon, and from Cutha, and from Ava, and from Hamath, and from Sepharvaim, and placed [them] in the cities of Samaria instead of the children of Israel."

According to Biblical sources and the histories of Josephus, those Easterners intermarried with the few remaining Israelites. Some of them adopted Jewish beliefs and customs while continuing to worship their own gods.

In the mid-fifth century BCE, after the Hebrews began to return from the Babylonian exile, a Judean priest named Manasseh, the son of Johanon the high priest and the brother of Jaddua, another high priest, married a Samaritan woman named Nicaso. When he was ordered to divorce her or face excommunication, Manasseh told his father-in-law, Sanballat, a man of influence (and in some accounts a notorious enemy of the Judeans), that as much as he loved his wife, he'd rather remain a priest. To entice him to stay with his daughter, Sanballat built Manasseh a temple on Mount Gerizim. This is one version of how the Samaritans came to have a Jewish temple (there are others). Needless to say, the Judeans regarded the Samaritans as heretics, an attitude that hadn't changed by the time of Jesus.

A small number of Samaritans still live in Israel and Nablus. Some of their Hebrew and Aramaic texts, though not terribly ancient, include interesting variants on the canonical Hebrew Torah.

SANTERIA   *See* Syncretism.

SCIENTOLOGY

Founded in 1953 by the science fiction writer and pop psychologist. L. Ron Hubbard (1911–86), Scientology, an outgrowth of Hubbard's best-selling self-help book *Dianetics* (1950), is a vexing amalgam of Gnosticism, pseudoscience, space opera, psychotherapy, and organized religion. Its members (Scientology claims there are millions of them worldwide; skeptics estimate their numbers in the tens of thousands) are inculcated (skeptics would say indoctrinated) into a radical regime of therapy rather than ritual and prayer. Though Scientology, after years of litigation, has achieved tax exempt status as a charity in the United States, Germany regards it as a criminal cult. The United Kingdom and many other countries tax it as a business.

The word *scientology* is derived from the Latin *scio,* "to know," and the Greek ending *ology,* "the study of." As in Gnosticism, Scientology introduces its adepts to a higher dimension of knowledge in gradual stages, reserving its most esoteric teachings for a special elect. Also like Gnosticism, it teaches that what we think of as the real world is not only illusory, but is deliberately and maliciously misleading. In Gnostic mythology, the world is the creation of a lesser God, or even Satan. Scientology's creation story features a wicked alien being named Xenu, who ruled over a vastly overpopulated galactic federation some seventy-five million years ago. In a fiendish subterfuge, Xenu ordered billions of his subjects to report to his government's offices so their income tax returns could be audited. When they arrived, they were paralyzed, injected with alcohol, loaded onto "space planes" (which looked exactly like DC-8s), and transported to earth, where their bodies were piled up near volcanoes. Than hydrogen bombs were detonated, causing the volcanoes to erupt. Though the captives' bodies were vaporized, their souls, known as Thetans, were sucked into "vacuum zones" and then transported to a movie theater, where they were compelled to watch a 3-D movie for thirty-six days. This movie indoctrinated them into the tenets of traditional religion and other falsehoods, while depriving them of their sense of identity. These Thetans are our souls. Because of the trauma and the brainwashing they endured seventy-five million years ago, we suffer from fear, violence, addiction, and many other symptoms of "the reactive mind" today. Scientology gradually restores its members to health by "auditing" them—asking them leading questions, then tracking the electrical currents that pass through their skin while they answer with a patented device known as an E-meter.

Scientology has long cultivated celebrities; some of its most prominent members are the movie stars Tom Cruise and John Travolta, the jazz musician Chick Corea, and Elvis Presley's daughter, Lisa Marie.

SECULAR HUMANISM   *See* Humanism.

SEMIPELAGIANISM   *See* Pelagianism.

SEPARATISM   *See* Evangelicalism.

SETHIANISM *See* Gnosticism.

SEVENTH-DAY ADVENTISM

Formally organized in 1863 in Battle Creek, Michigan, by three former Millerites—Ellen White (1827–1915), James White (1821–81), and Joseph Bates (1792–1872)—the Seventh-Day Adventist Church, drawing its authority from Mrs. White's prophetic visions, believes that Miller had predicted the right date but the wrong event: rather than the Second Coming of Christ, what began in 1844 was a period of Investigative Judgment, in which Jesus entered the presence of God to pass judgment on the living and the dead. The Advent would occur as soon as this essential preliminary work was completed.

The Seventh-Day Adventists believe that it is essential to keep the Jewish Sabbath, as the first Christians did, beginning at sundown on Friday. They also follow a healthful lifestyle, avoiding pork and shellfish and red meat, as well as alcohol and tobacco. (Ellen White financed the medical education of Dr. John Harvey Kellogg, of Corn Flakes fame, though he was later excommunicated from the church.) According to Seventh-Day Adventist teachings, there will be two resurrections. The first, of the righteous, will occur at the instant of the Second Coming. The second will occur one thousand years later when the unsaved are all revived, only to be destroyed along with Satan and his angels.

Victor Houteff, a self-styled prophet, broke away from the Seventh-Day Adventists in the 1940s to start the Branch Davidian movement. On April 19, 1993, after a fifty-one-day siege by federal agents, the church's compound near Waco, Texas, burned to the ground, killing some eighty men, women, and children, including the church's leader, David Koresh.

SHAKERISM

Originating in a Quaker revival in England in 1747, the sect began to grow when Ann Lee (1736–84) joined them. Ridiculed as the Shaking Quakers because of the convulsive movements they made while praying, their official name was the United Society of Believers in Christ's Second Appearing. They were also known as the Millennial Church and the Alethians.

Lee, an illiterate textile worker from Manchester, an unhappy wife, and the mother of four dead children, spoke in tongues and had visions, in one of which she learned that marriage and the Holy Spirit are incompatible. In another she became the vessel of the feminine part of Christ's spirit. In 1774, after she was briefly imprisoned for blasphemy, she immigrated to America with her brother, six other followers, and her husband (who deserted her soon after) and established a community near Albany, New York.

By 1826 there were eighteen Shaker communities in eight states. The Shakers lived in sexually segregated dormitories, practiced celibacy, and held their possessions in common. New members were added through conversion or the adoption of children. They supported themselves by farming and by selling crafts, especially wooden furniture, which is widely admired and highly sought after by collectors to this day.

The Shakers were pacifists and believed in the equality of sexes and the sanctity of labor. Rather than the Trinity, they worshipped God the Father-Mother; they denied the divinity of Jesus and did not believe in resurrection. Salvation was achieved through atonement. According to the official creed of the church, "The true cross is not of wood but a life of self-denial, a crucifixion of the lower nature. Every soul must work out its own salvation by practicing the self-denials of Jesus, aided by baptisms of the Holy Spirit of Christ, an influx of the saving power of the Divine Creator; salvation is not otherwise found."

SHAMANISM *See* **Animism.**

SHIISM *See* **Islam.**

SHINTOISM
Ancient animistic religion of Japan. The word Shinto comes from the Chinese Shin Tao, "the way of the Gods"; the Japanese equivalent is *kami-no-michi*. Shinto shrines are dedicated to rivers, rocks, trees, mountains, and other natural objects; they house a large pantheon of generally benign, but not particularly individ-

uated, gods. Although no god is supreme, some are more powerful than others. Amaterasu-o-mi-kami, the sun goddess, is one of
the more important deities. Shintoists believe that she gave birth
to the first Japanese emperor, Jimmu, in 660 BCE.

Starting in the eighth century, Shinto and Buddhist beliefs
were amalgamated and some of Shintoism's ancient practices were
lost. Strong efforts were made to revive traditional Shintoism
starting as early as the seventeenth century. After the Meiji
Restoration between 1866 and 1869, Shinto mythology was used
to glorify the emperor and promote imperial aggression. In 1946,
Emperor Hirohito formally disavowed his divinity, and the American occupation forbade the use of public funds to support Shinto.

Many Japanese houses have an altar (a *kami-dana,* or "shelf of
gods"); public shrines are sometimes decorated with origami. The
four affirmations of Shinto are the importance of family, love of
nature, physical cleanliness, and Matsuri, the honor due to gods
and ancestors.

SIKHISM

Religion established in the Indian state of Punjab in 1499 CE,
which amalgamates elements of Hinduism and Sufism. Its
founder and first guru, Nanak Dev Ji (1469–1539), was raised as
a Hindu. When he was about thirty years old, he disappeared for
three days; his first words upon his return were "There is no
Hindu, there is no Muslim." Nanak argued that organized religions were corrupt and that rituals and pilgrimages were a waste
of time. He opposed the caste system, believed in the equality of
men and women, and advocated living a life of pure love—both
for one's fellow man and God. After enough lifetimes of meditation and virtuous activities, he taught, one can escape the cycle of
birth and death and permanently enter the realm of God.

Under succeeding gurus, the Sikhs founded a sacred city, Amritsar, compiled devotional poetry into a scripture (the *Guru Granth
Sahib*), and formed an army. Govind Singh (1666–1708), the tenth
and final guru, created the military fraternity called the Khalsa, or

the pure. After they are initiated into it, Sikh men wear a turban, carry a ceremonial dagger, and cease cutting their hair and beards.

The Sikh wars with the British in the 1840s cost the Sikhs their autonomy; in 1947, when India was partitioned, millions of Sikhs were displaced or killed. After Indira Gandhi was assassinated by her Sikh bodyguards in 1984 (in retaliation for the destruction of the Golden Temple at Amritsar by Indian troops), thousands of Sikhs were massacred throughout India.

SOCINIANISM

A religious movement of the sixteenth and seventeenth centuries (an important influence on Unitarianism) inspired by the ideas of the expatriate Italian theologians Laelius Socinus (1525–62) and his nephew Faustus Socinus (1539–1604). Neither of the Socinuses believed in the Trinity: they both taught that Christ was the mortal son of God. Salvation, in their view, was achieved through fidelity to the teachings of Christ and obedience to God's will. To the Socinians, the Crucifixion was not a sacrifice. Christ did not "ransom" sinners; rather, he showed them the way to achieve their own salvation. While the faithful could hope to attain immortality, nonbelievers didn't face an eternity of punishment; they simply ceased to exist. Socinians considered the Eucharist to be an important but symbolic rite—they did not believe in transubstantiation. They also advocated the separation of church and state, and opposed capital punishment.

Faustus Socinus became a leader of the Minor Reformed Church of Poland (or the Polish Brethren), whose Racovian Catechism (1605) was largely based on his teachings. Under pressure from the Counter Reformation, the Polish Diet banned Socinianism in 1658; many Socinians emigrated to Germany, Transylvania, the Netherlands, and England.

SUFISM   *See* Islam.

SUNNISM   *See* Islam.

SUPERSESSIONISM

Also called replacement theology. The belief that since Christianity is the fulfillment of the Old Testament, the Jewish people have not only forfeited their "chosenness" but their very existence as a nation—the *true* Israel is now Christianity.

In Martin Luther's words:

> Listen, Jew, are you aware that Jerusalem and your sovereignty, together with your temple and priesthood, have been destroyed for over 1,460 years? . . . This work of wrath is proof that the Jews, surely rejected by God, are no longer his people, and neither is he any longer their God.

Though supersessionism is as much a symptom as a cause of anti-Semitism, there can be no denying that the doctrine has made it easier for even the most fair-minded of Christians to tolerate hostility to Jews. Passages can be found in the Gospels that either support or undermine the notion; much of the Christian faith remains ambivalent on the subject today. Some liberal Protestant denominations and Pope John Paul II have formally renounced supersessionism. Dispensationalist evangelicals, who believe that the End Times will bring about mass conversions of Jews, reject the idea as well.

SWEDENBORGIANISM

The religious teachings of the Swedish scientist and mystic Emanuel Swedenborg (1688–1772) and the tenets of the Church of the New Jerusalem, which is based on his visionary writings. Ardently anti-Trinitarian, Swedenborg preached that heaven and hell are invisible presences. After our deaths, he said, we will choose which one we will live in. Grace through faith alone is insufficient for redemption—love is the guiding principle of Christianity and the key to salvation. From *The New Jerusalem and Its Heavenly Doctrine*:

> The church is in the internal spiritual man, because that is in heaven, and not in the external without it . . . The merely natural man is in hell, unless he be made spiritual by regenera-

tion . . . All who are in the external without the internal, or with whom the spiritual internal is shut, are in hell . . . The interiors of man are actually turned according to his loves.

The son of a Pietist bishop, Swedenborg was a prominent mining engineer and wrote prolifically on philosophy, religion, science (especially anatomy), and psychology. After he was ennobled, he was active in the House of Knights, where he pursued a liberal, reformist agenda. But then, in 1745, "heaven was opened to him" and he began to receive visitations from angels; in 1747 he retired from his occupations so he could concentrate on spiritual matters full time. He wrote some fourteen more books before he died, and continued to visit not just with angels, but with Jesus, Paul, Abraham, Moses, Plato, Cicero, and Saint Augustine. He also traveled to other planets.

In 1787, The New Church, based on Swedenborg's teachings, was founded in England; it was planted in the United States a few years later. There was a schism in 1897, when members who regarded Swedenborg's writings as the revealed word of God withdrew to establish the General Church of the New Jerusalem. Swedenborgians reject the doctrine of substitutionary atonement; they believe that all religions can provide salvation as long as they acknowledge God and the moral law. Like Mormons, they believe in eternal marriage.

John Chapman (1774–1847), better known as Johnny Appleseed, was a Swedenborgian missionary; William Blake (1757–1827), Ralph Waldo Emerson (1803–82), Samuel Taylor Coleridge (1772–1834), Henry James, Sr. (1811–82), Carl Jung (1875–1961), Joseph Smith (1805–44), Helen Keller (1880–1968), and Jorge Luis Borges (1899–1986) are only a few of the writers, thinkers, and public figures who were influenced by Swedenborg's writings.

SYNCRETISM
In religion, belief systems that fuse the rituals, practices, and doctrines of more than one preexisting faith. For instance, Gnosticism fuses elements of Hermeticism, Christianity, Judaism, and

Zoroastrianism; Manichaeanism combines elements of Buddhism, Zorastrianism, and Christianity. Though perhaps it doesn't qualify as a religious movement in itself, enough contemporary Jews combine Buddhist meditation and beliefs with traditional Judaism in their spiritual practice that the name Jubu has caught on. The Jewish poet Rodger Kamenetz described his explorations of Tibetan Buddhism in his best-selling book *The Jew in the Lotus.*

In 1844, Ali Muhammad of Shiraz, Persia (1819–50), proclaimed himself the Báb (Arabic for "the gate") to the knowledge of God, abrogated Islam, and established a new mystical system based on the number nineteen, which foretold the imminent arrival of the Promised One, who would complete his revelation. He was executed in 1850 after his followers revolted against the shah. In 1863, one of Babism's earliest and most ardent followers, Mirza Husayn Ali Nuri (1817–92), who called himself Bahá'u'lláh (Arabic for "glory of God"), declared himself the Promised One, a prophet in the line of Abraham, Zoroaster, Moses, Krishna, Buddha, Jesus, and Muhammad. After he died, his son Abdul Bahá (1844–1921), having battled with his brother for the succession, promulgated the religion of Bahaism. Baha'is believe that God created life through the process of evolution and sent his prophets to all nations as parts of an unfolding revelation. The central tenets of their faith are the oneness of humanity (they advocate equality of the sexes, world government, and the adoption of a universal language) and the unity of all religions. For the Baha'is, spiritual transformation is not an end in itself: Once enlightened, Baha'is work to eliminate racial prejudice, sexism, and ignorance, and to bring about world peace.

The Theosophical Society, founded in 1875 by the Russian-born clairvoyant and spiritualist Helena Petrovna Blavatsky (1831–91), and the lawyer, journalist, Civil War veteran, descendent of Puritans, and convert to Buddhism Colonel Henry Steel Olcott (1832–1907), presents a dauntingly esoteric stew of Buddhism, Neoplatonism, Hinduism, Zorastrianism, Hermeticism, Kabbalah, and Christianity. Theosophists believe that peoples' higher selves are immortal and are slowly, through history, culture, religion, and the divinely ordered processes of the universe, evolving toward a higher consciousness. Theosophy's purpose, in Madame Blavatsky's words, is to "reconcile all religions, sects and nations under a common system of ethics, based on eternal verities."

The Austrian architect, educator, literary scholar, philosopher, playwright, and social thinker Rudolf Steiner (1861–1925) began the Anthroposophy movement after parting ways with Theosophy. He described his philosophy as "a path of knowledge, to guide the Spiritual in the human being to the Spiritual in the universe." Through Anthroposophy people would become more human by becoming more conscious. Steiner pioneered biodynamic farming, alternative medicine, and eurhythmic dance. His Waldorf Schools offer a revolutionary approach to early childhood education.

The Unity Church, founded in 1889 in Kansas City, Missouri, by Charles and Myrtle Fillmore, draws from New Thought, Hinduism, Buddhism, Theosophy, and Rosicrucianism. "We have borrowed the best from all religions," Charles Fillmore declared. "Unity is the Truth that is taught in all religions, simplified . . . so that anyone can understand and apply it." Today Unity and New Thought have blurred into the New Age, which adds a "spiritualized" version of quantum physics and a psychological therapeutic aspect to the doctrinal mix. Marianne Williamson (who is a Unity pastor), Gary Zukav, and Wayne Dyer are only a few best-selling writers who proclaim that spiritual growth (and worldly success and happiness) follows from a transformation of our ways of thinking. "Personal transformation," writes Marianne Williamson, "can and does have global effects. As we go, so goes the world, for the world is us. The revolution that will save the world is ultimately a personal one."

Santería (also known as Lukumi or Regla de Ocha), which combines features of Catholicism with West African Yoruban animism and the religions of the indigenous people of the West Indies, began as early as the sixteenth century, when African slaves in Cuba, who were forbidden to practice their own religion, pretended to venerate saints (who actually stood in for the Orishas, or spirit emissaries). What began as camouflage continues today as fusion. Olodumare, the supreme spirit, is identified with

Christ; Elegba, the spirit who stands at the crossroads between the spirit and human worlds, is identified with Saint Anthony; Obatala, the father of the Orishas and the accidental creator of humanity (he drank too much palm wine while he was fashioning the Orishas; the imperfect figures he created while he was tipsy are humanity) is sometimes identified with the Virgin Mary. Babalu Aye is the god of epidemics and healing (Desi Arnaz's 1946 hit "Babalu," which became his signature song, invokes him); he is associated with Saint Lazarus. There are many others.

Voodoo (from the Fon, the language of Benin, word for spirit, *vodún*), which arose in Haiti, shares some aspects of Santería, particularly its magical practices and ritual animal sacrifices. Though Hollywood has seen to it that Voodoo dolls (the miniature likenesses of enemies that Voodoo practitioners stab with pins) are its best-known feature, Voodoo is much more than sorcery. Both a system of healing and a complex polytheistic faith, in April of 2003 the government of Haiti accorded Voodoo official status as a religion, giving its priests and priestesses full legal authority to conduct weddings and baptisms. Interestingly, the so-called 'Voodoo doll,' a staple of sympathetic magic, is unique neither to Haiti or Voodooism. A ninth-century Jewish treatise on magic offered the following instructions to its readers who "wish to kill a man."

> Take mud from the two sides of the river and form it into the shape of a figure, and write upon it the name of the person, and take seven branches from seven strong palm-trees and make a bow from reed with the string of horse-sinew, and place the image in a hollow, and stretch the bow and shoot with it.

Perhaps we could call this sinister practice Jewdoo.

TANTRISM
Esoteric sexual/religious practices rooted in Hinduism but present in Buddhism (especially Tibetan Buddhism), Jainism, and even some South Asian versions of Islam.

Though the contemporary New Age movement tends to identify Tantra exclusively with "sacred sex" (Kundalini yoga awakens the chakras or energy centers in the body, particularly those at the base of the spine; unorthodox sexual techniques and positions can extend intercourse and intensify orgasm), most Tantric practices are not actually erotic. Some of the ones that seem to be sexual—the so-called right-handed Tantras—are actually meant to be meditated upon rather than enacted. The transgressive left-handed Tantras, however, not only include sexual acts, but drunkenness and the eating of forbidden meat. Many traditional Hindi regard Tantra much as Christians regard black magic—as blasphemous and dangerous.

Tantrism is so ancient and so various that it's difficult to generalize about it without distorting it beyond recognition. (It has been vulgarized in popular Western culture, which as often as not transforms its sacred texts into high-toned sex manuals. It's worth noting in this context that the *Kama Sutra* is not actually Tantric.) The following definition by the scholar David Gordon White is both accurate and succinct.

> Tantra is that Asian body of beliefs and practices which, working from the principle that the universe we experience is nothing other than the concrete manifestation of the divine energy of the godhead that creates and maintains that universe, seeks to ritually appropriate and channel that energy, within the human microcosm, in creative and emancipatory ways.

The operative words are *channel* and *appropriate*. Through direct and personal instruction from a guru, by meditation on gods and mandalas and the body, by the use of mantras and physical exercises and, in some cases, by deliberately challenging and breaking taboos, the devotee literally becomes divine.

As in many Western mystical traditions, part of this process involves the transformation of sexual energy into spirituality. As Sir John Woodroffe (1865–1936), a prominent British jurist and Orientalist, wrote,

> It is a fundamental error to regard the Vedanta as simply a speculative metaphysic in the modern Western sense . . . It claims

that its supersensual teachings can be established with certainty by the *practice* of its methods. Theorizing alone is insufficient. The Shakta, above all, is a practical and active man, worshipping the Divine Activity; his watchword is Kriya or Action. Taught that he is Power, he desires fully to realize himself in fact as such.

TAOISM

Reversing the evolutionary path of many other religions, Taoism came into the world as an abstract philosophy and later turned into a full-fledged religion, with a large pantheon of gods, occult practices, monasteries, and an ecclesiastical hierarchy. The philosophical system begins with the *Tao Te Ching,* a book supposedly written by Lao Tzu in the sixth century BCE, but which some scholars believe was written as late as 300 BCE by several different writers who adopted Lao Tzu (its literal meaning is Old Sage) as their pen name.

Tao Te Ching, or *The Book of the Way and Its Virtue,* teaches the way of effortless action, of freeing oneself from desire and striving, and simply surrendering oneself to the eternal flow.

> Stand before it—there is no beginning.
> Follow it and there is no end.
> Stay with the Tao, Move with the present.
> Knowing the ancient beginning is the essence of Tao.

One should endeavor to do nothing (*wu wei*), the Old Sage counseled, and then you'll be able to do what you should.

Chuang Tzu (399–295 BCE) deepened Lao Tzu's paradoxes and added a touch of wit:

> Once I, Chuang Tzu, dreamed I was a butterfly and was happy as a butterfly. I was conscious that I was quite pleased with myself, but I did not know that I was Tzu. Suddenly I awoke, and there was I, visibly Tzu. I do not know whether it was Tzu dreaming that he was a butterfly or the butterfly dreaming that he was Tzu. Between Tzu and the butterfly there must be some

distinction. [But one may be the other.] This is called the transformation of things.

Other Taoist philosophers were Yang Hsiung (53 BCE–18 CE),
and Wang Ch'ung (27–100 CE).

Religious Taoism, which developed alongside philosophical
Taoism, was much less austere. Alchemy and Tantrism enter into
it, as do astrology and other forms of divination. There was a
large pantheon of gods, probably adapted from local religions, including Lao Tzu, Yu-Huang, the Jade Emperor, and the Three Officials: Tien-kuan, the Ruler of Heaven; Ti-kuan, Ruler of Earth,
and Shui-kuan, Ruler of Water. Taoism also contained a strong
element of Buddhism.

The Taoist ideal of least resistance would have a strong influence on the martial art Tai Chi.

THEISM
The belief that at the ultimate level of reality there is one all-
powerful God who involves himself in human affairs and who,
though incommensurable and eternal and infinitely powerful, occasionally reveals himself to selected people. Judaism, Christianity, and Islam are all theistic religions.

THEOSOPHY   *See* Syncretism.

TIBETAN BUDDHISM
The forms of Buddhism practiced in the Himalayan region (Tibet,
Nepal, Bhutan, Sikkim), Mongolia, and parts of China and Russia, all of which incorporate significant elements of Hindi yoga
and Tantrism.

Tibetans believe that some high lamas (the word has a similar meaning to the Sanskrit *guru*) are reincarnated, especially the
Dalai Lamas, the leaders of the Gelug, or Yellow Hat school,
founded by Tsongkhapa (1357–1419). Upon the death of a Dalai
Lama, his monks begin a search for his new carnation among
newborn babies; when a child exhibits familiarity with the previ-

ous Dalai Lama's personal possessions, he is declared his rightful successor. Beginning in the 1600s, the Dalai Lama was the political leader of Tibet as well as the bodhisattva (an enlightened being who helps mortals achieve Buddhahood) of compassion. The current Dalai Lama, Tenzin Gyatso, is fourteenth in the succession; he has lived in exile since 1959, when Communist China annexed Tibet. Tibetan Buddhists venerate a pantheon of Buddhas, bodhisattvas, and Dharmapalas (fierce deities who protect believers). The *Bardo Thodol,* or the Tibetan Book of the Dead, dates back to about the eighth century CE in its written form, but is almost certainly much older; A guide for newly departed spirits that instructs them how to achieve enlightenment, it is traditionally read out loud to the dying.

TOTEMISM   *See* Animism.

TRACTARIANISM
Also called the Oxford movement, Tractarianism began in 1833, in opposition to the proposed disestablishment of the Irish Anglican Church. John Henry Newman (1801–90), a fellow of Oriel College and vicar of St. Mary's, would write the majority of the ninety tracts that appeared over the next eight years, arguing that secular powers had no right to interfere in churchly matters; more so, that High Church Anglicanism was directly in the line of the church founded by Christ's apostles. Not surprisingly, he converted to Roman Catholicism in 1845. Newman was elevated to cardinal in 1879; in the speech he gave upon the occasion he declared himself an enemy of liberalism, "the doctrine that there is no truth in religion, but that one creed is as good as another."

ULTRAMONTANISM
Ultramontanism has nothing to do with Montanism—its literal meaning in medieval Latin is "beyond the mountains," referring to the Alps and the Vatican. Ultramontanism is the belief that the pope has absolute authority in religious matters. Gallicanism, the opposing belief that temporal states can lawfully exercise power

over the church, takes its name from Gaul, or France, whose Philip IV moved the papacy to Avignon and destroyed the Templars in the fourteenth century. Gallicanism intensified and spread throughout Europe during the upheavals of the Reformation. In the nineteenth century, liberal Catholicism was seen to pose as potent a threat to papal authority as Europe's restive monarchs had in previous centuries. The doctrine of papal infallibility, decreed at the First Vatican Council (1870) reaffirmed the principle of ultramontanism in no uncertain terms.

UNIFICATION CHURCH

Religious movement founded in Korea in 1954 by the Reverend Sun Myung Moon. In 1971, Moon moved to America, where the Unification Church's headquarters are now located (its official name is the Holy Spirit Association for the Unification of World Christianity). Though Moon served time in prison for tax evasion in the 1980s, he continues to be active in conservative causes (one of the church's many investment properties—which include hotels, resorts, restaurants, and publishing houses—is the right-leaning *Washington Times*).

The fall of man occurred because Eve was seduced by the serpent and then seduced Adam in turn. The Unification Church thus demands strict celibacy before marriage. Couples are sometimes matched up by Moon himself and other church elders and are then wed in mass ceremonies—twenty thousand couples made their vows in Seoul Stadium on February 13, 2000. Ethnically and nationally mixed marriages are favored as a way of bringing the world together. The teachings of the Unification Church are summarized in Moon's book *Exposition of the Divine Principle*. In a nutshell, it declares that Moon himself has been chosen by God to finish what Jesus left undone.

According to a document titled "A Cloud of Witnesses" (which can be found on the Unification Church's official Web site), at 12:00 noon on Christmas Day in the year 2001, a seminar was held in heaven. Attendees included Jesus, Confucius, Muhammad, and Buddha, all of whom were accompanied by their entourages as well as a host of lesser luminaries, including Karl Barth, Martin Luther, Saint Peter, Saint Augustine, and Jonathan Edwards. All of them signed a resolution affirming that, among other things, "Reverend Sun Myung Moon is the Savior, Messiah, Second Coming and True Parent of all humanity." Four surprise guests (Marx, Lenin, Stalin, and Deng Xiaoping) were also present. Each of them addressed messages to the Communist world. Deng's was that "there is no way for Communists to live, but by following Reverend Moon's guidance." Even God offered a brief testimonial.

Moon believes that democracies are a temporary stage in human development that pave the way for the establishment of the worldwide theocracy that will succeed them. According to him,

> America's intellectual establishment is liberal, godless, secular, humanistic, and anti-religious. We are declaring war against three main enemies: godless communism, Christ-less American liberalism, and secular-humanistic morality. They are the enemies of God, the True Parents, the Unification Church, all of Christianity, and all religions. We are working to mobilize a united front against them.

UNITARIAN UNIVERSALISM

Universalism began in the eighteenth century in the United States as a dissident Protestant movement that rejected the notion of predestination and hell. Unitarianism arose in Central Europe in the sixteenth century as an outgrowth of the anti-Trinitarian heresy of Socinianism. In the nineteenth century United States, Unitarianism would be closely associated with the Harvard Divinity School and the transcendentalists. Its hallmarks were unconditional religious toleration, a belief in human decency, and the possibility of universal salvation. William Ellery Channing (1780–1842) summarized Unitarian beliefs in a sermon in 1819:

> We are said to exalt reason above revelation, to prefer our own wisdom to God's . . . Our leading principle in interpreting Scripture is this, that the Bible is a book written for men, in the

language of men, and that its meaning is to be sought in the same manner as that of other books . . . all books, and all conversation, require in the reader or hearer the constant exercise of reason; or their true import is only to be obtained by continual comparison and inference . . .

We believe that God is infinitely good, kind, benevolent, in the proper sense of these words; good in disposition, as well as in act; good, not to a few, but to all; good to every individual, as well as to the general system.

Unitarianism and Universalism formally merged in 1961. Today Unitarian Universalism is a creedless faith whose members believe "that personal experience, conscience and reason should be the final authorities in religion." Unitarian Universalists accord the same respect to Moses, Buddha, and other spiritual leaders from different belief systems as they do to Jesus. Some of them reject the idea of a supernatural God altogether. To the Unitarian Universalist, salvation is defined broadly as "spiritual health," which is to be achieved from the pursuit of social justice, the practice of art, and the study of science and philosophy rather than from any profession of faith.

UNITY CHURCH   *See* Syncretism.

VALENTINIANISM   *See* Gnosticism.

VOODOOISM   *See* Syncretism.

WAHHABISM
Reactionary Islamic movement whose history is inextricably intertwined with Saudi Arabia's. Its founder was Muhammad Ibn Abd al Wahhab (1703–92), a Sunni cleric who was deeply inspired by the writings of Ibn Taymiya (1263–1328). Ibn Taymiya read the Koran literally and held that only the teachings of the first, second, and third generations of Islam had any validity—all subsequent innovations, especially Sufism, were to be rejected (this belief is

called Salafism, which literally means "the teachings of the early generations"). Taymiya also preached that faithful Muslims were required to engage in jihad against the impure Mongols, despite the fact that they had declared themselves to be fellow Muslims.

Expelled from his tribe (his own brother wrote a treatise denouncing him), Wahhab formed an alliance with a tribal chieftan named Muhammad Ibn Saud, who launched jihads against his own impure Muslim neighbors, extending his sway far into the Arabian peninsula. Though the Saudis, as Saud's tribe was known, were beaten back twice in the next century, by 1924 they had seized the sacred cities of Mecca and Medina. The modern state of Saudi Arabia was officially founded in 1932, with Wahhabism as its official religion, though nowadays its adherents prefer to call themselves al-Muwahhidun, "the monotheists," or Ikhwan, "the Brotherhood." Wahhabism has exerted a major influence on such modern militant Islamist movements as the Muslim Brotherhood of Egypt, Palestine's Hamas, and Osama bin Laden's Al Qaeda.

ZOROASTRIANISM

Religion founded by Zoroaster (the name is a Hellenized version of Zarathustra), who lived from approximately 628 to 551 BCE (though this date is hotly contested—some maintain that he lived as early as six thousand years before the birth of Christ).

The Zoroastrian scriptures—a collection of prayers, hymns, commentary, and laws—are written in Old Iranian, a language that is closely related to Sanskrit. Some of these texts are ancient, fragmentary and much corrupted. Zoroastrianism is henotheistic in that while it features many gods from the Persian pantheon, Ahura Mazdah ("Sovereign Knowledge"), is the only one who is actually worshipped. Ahura and the lesser gods who serve him (originally they were personifications of his attributes; over time they developed personalities of their own) are at war with the army of evil spirits led by Angra Mainyu. Humans participate in this battle as well; the side they fight on depends upon whether they are good or bad, as do the rewards or punishments they receive after they die. Since Ahura's ultimate triumph over Angra Mainyu is foreordained (at the end of time, a savior—conceived by a virgin from Zoroaster's preserved seed—will appear, after which the righteous will be resurrected and all evil destroyed), Zoroastrianism isn't exactly dualistic, though it almost certainly influenced Gnosticism and Manichaeanism, which are. Its messianic eschatology clearly had an influence on both Judaism and Christianity.

Zoroastrianism went underground after Alexander invaded Persia in 334 BCE; it reemerged in the second century CE as the state religion of Persia and thrived until the advent of Islam some five hundred years later. The Indian Parsis are descendants of Zoroastrians who emigrated from Persia in the eighth century to escape religious persecution. Small Zoroastrian communities still exist in Iran and Pakistan, though their numbers are dwindling. Magianism refers to the practices of the Magi, the Zoroastrian priestly caste; in general usage a Magus is a sorcerer or a magician.

Sexual Perversions

EXHIBITIONISM

The clinical name for flashing, mooning, or otherwise exposing one's private parts while in public. Alcohol, peer pressure, and/or fraternity high jinks can be responsible for such behavior, but when an individual achieves sexual arousal by exposing his or her genitals to an unsuspecting stranger (sometimes while masturbating), it rises to the level of a perversion. Almost all exhibitionists are men; the stereotype of the dirty old man notwithstanding, they tend to be well below the age of forty. Although the compulsive exhibitionist may appear to be aggressive, he rarely poses a physical threat.

Not all exhibitionists, of course, are mentally ill—some are simply narcissistic or attention starved. Web cams and blogs can provide an innocuous and, in some cases, a remunerative outlet for these individuals.

FETISHISM

People with this paraphilia (the preferred clinical term for *perversion*) can only achieve sexual arousal with the aid of a particular type of inanimate object, such as lingerie, gloves, shoes, and balloons (balloon fetishists call themselves "looners"—there are a number of Web sites on the Internet that cater to their special interests). Object fetishes are further broken down into two subcategories: form fetishes and media fetishes. With form fetishes, what matters is the type of object—black, stiletto-heeled shoes, say, or lace stockings. With media fetishes, what matters is what material the object is made of: leather, rubber, latex, or silk, for example. Though fetishists usually use the objects when masturbating in private, some incorporate them into sex acts with partners. Even so, the sex they engage in tends to be depersonalized and ritualistic. Some common fetish objects include boots, corsets, diapers, gloves, pantyhose, school uniforms, and spandex.

Partialism is a variety of fetishism that's focused not on objects but on specific body parts, such as feet, breasts, or buttocks. Races, pregnancy, obesity, or hair color can all be the objects of obsessive attraction as well. *Abasiophilia* is the technical name for an attraction to disabled people with leg braces or crutches, or who are confined to wheelchairs; *acrotomophilia* is a compulsive attraction to amputees. Activities can be fetishized as well, such as spanking or tickling, having enemas administered (the clinical name for this is *klismaphilia*), or being urinated on (*urolagnia*).

FROTTEURISM

From the French verb *frotter,* "to rub." In clinical terms, a compulsive desire to rub one's genitals against a nonconsenting partner in order to achieve sexual arousal, usually in a public place, like a crowded subway or elevator, preferably without being discovered. When obsessive fantasies about this activity interfere with the normal conduct of life, or when they are put into practice (which is considered a form of criminal sexual assault), Frotteurism rises to the level of a mental illness.

MASOCHISM

The psychologist Dr. Richard von Krafft-Ebing succinctly defined masochism in his *Psychopathia Sexualis* (1886) as "the opposite of sadism. While the latter is the desire to cause pain and use force, the former is the wish to suffer pain and be subjected to force." Krafft-Ebing named the condition after Leopold von Sacher-Masoch (1836–95), a distinguished author of Galician birth who wrote in German; his best-remembered book is the semipornographic (and, according to the sexologist Havelock Ellis [1859–1939], unabashedly autobiographical) "bondage" novel *Venus in Furs*.

"Yes I am cruel," the beautiful dominatrix of the title tells her wretched lover before inflicting a bout of punishment on him. "Through his passion nature has given man into woman's hands, and the woman who does not know how to make him her subject, her slave, her toy, and how to betray him with a smile in the end is not wise."

Venus in Furs captivates James Joyce's Leopold Bloom when he finds it in a bookstall during his wanderings around Dublin; it is broadly parodied in the "Circes," or "Nighttown," chapter of *Ulysses* as well.

PARAPHILIA

From the Greek *para* "beside" and *philia* "loving." Coined by the Viennese psychologist Wilhelm Stekel in 1925 to describe out-of-the-mainstream sex practices, it has become the preferred clinical term for perversions, because it is less implicitly pejorative. It acknowledges that many alternative forms of sexual expression (cross-dressing, for example) can only be considered pathological when they cause profound distress to the individual who engages in them (or to the individual's partner or partners). (See Relativism.)

A very partial and highly selective list of paraphilias follows: *agalmatophilia*, attraction to statues, mannequins, or extremely still partners; *amaurophilia*, desire for sex while blindfolded or in total darkness; *coprophilia*, sexual attraction to feces; *eproctophilia*, sexual excitement from flatulence; *galactophilia*, attraction to lactating women; *gerontophilia*, sexual attraction to the elderly; *hematolagnia*, sexual attraction to blood; *macrophilia*, sexual attraction to large people and/or oversized genitalia; *necrophilia*, attraction to corpses; *plushophilia*, sexual attraction to people in animal costumes, such as sports team mascots or theme park characters, or to stuffed animal toys; *telephone scatologia*, arousal from talking dirty on the telephone; *zoophilia*, sexual attraction to animals.

PEDOPHILIA

Pedophiles both fantasize about having sexual relations with prepubescent boys and girls and act them out. Most pedophiles are heterosexual males; contrary to myth only a distinct minority of them were sexually abused as children themselves. Though the causes of pedophilia are mysterious, many pedophiles suffer from narcissistic disorders. Totally lacking in empathy for the objects of their infatuation, they tend to either blame their victims for enticing them or idealize them as objectifications of their own lost childhoods. Although pedophiles frequently fantasize that their passion is fully reciprocated—indeed, that they are the children's benefactors—more often than not the children they abuse are so objectified that sex with them amounts to a form of masturbation.

Ephebophilia, an adult's sexual attraction to postpubescent boys or girls, is a more complicated issue. While many see the power imbalances implicit in such relationships as problematic enough to qualify as a milder form of pedophilia, evolutionary psychology, an approach to behavior which hearkens back to the adaptive strategies that helped early primates evolve into human beings, suggests that they are endemic to our species—primate males generally prefer younger, and hence more fertile, sex partners. In some countries, the age of consent for girls is as low as thirteen or fourteen years old. The advertising industry frequently utilizes suggestive pictures of adolescents of both genders to sell products to adults.

SADISM

After Donatien Alphonse François, comte de Sade (1740–1814), better known as the Marquis de Sade, prolific writer of pornography, philosophy, plays, and fiction. Sade's most famous works include *Justine* (1791), *Juliette* (1798), and *Crimes of Love* (1800). Many of his books were written in prison, where he spent twenty-nine years of his life.

Because of the contents of his novels and plays, which include many scenes of degradation and erotic violence, and the notoriety of his own escapades (he blasphemed, engaged in orgies and flagellation, sodomized and otherwise abused prostitutes and his servants), his name is inextricably associated with the paraphilia that finds erotic satisfaction in giving pain. Sadism is a long continuum, however, with spanking and scolding on one end and mutilation, necrophilia, and cannibalism on the other. Though Sade was the personification of aristocratic decadence, and his sexual debaucheries were undoubtedly disturbing and extreme, they didn't necessarily rise to the level of psychosis—or of the extreme ritualized violence associated with notorious torturer-rapist-murderers like the cannibal Jeffrey Dahmer, Wichita, Kansas's BTK killer, or the ghoulish necrophile Ed Gein, who terrorized Wisconsin in the 1940s and 1950s, and whose ghastly predilections provided inspiration for the novels and movies *Psycho* and *The Silence of the Lambs,* among many others.

Modern psychologists would probably describe Sade's obsessions as fetishistic. Simone de Beauvoir saw him as a protoexistentialist moralist who ceaselessly tested the boundaries of behavior in a world that had lost its religious underpinnings. "Yes, I am a libertine, I admit it freely. I have dreamed of doing everything that it is possible to dream of in that line," Sade wrote of himself. "But I have certainly not done all the things I have dreamt of and never shall. Libertine I may be, but I am not a criminal, I am not a murderer."

TRANSVESTITISM

Cross-dressing, or wearing clothing associated with one's opposite gender, only rises to the level of a paraphilia when it's engaged in compulsively by heterosexual males, and when it is the only way that they can achieve sexual arousal. Typically the transvestite fantasizes that he is having sex with his "female" counterpart. For some individuals, one item of female clothing (such as lingerie) suffices to stimulate them; others require a feminine coiffure, cosmetics, and a complete wardrobe.

VOYEURISM

A compulsive voyeur (literally "one who sees" in French) attains arousal by secretly watching people undress or engage in sex. An enormous amount of economic activity—peep shows, pornographic magazines and Web sites, topless bars, the adult film industry, even downloadable pornographic content for cell phones—is seemingly dedicated to satisfying people's "normal" voyeuristic predilections. As with the other paraphilias, voyeurism only rises to the level of a mental illness when it becomes the sole means of attaining sexual arousal (or when it impinges on other people's privacy).

Eponyms, Laws,
Foreign Words

◦⟨∞⟩◦

ANGST

A German word meaning "dread"—most often used in the sense that Søren Kierkegaard (1813–55) did: as a global, nonspecific feeling endemic to the human condition, particularly when it's unanchored by the certainties of religious faith. "Dread is the dizziness of freedom which occurs when . . . freedom . . . gazes down into its own possibility, grasping at finiteness to sustain itself," he wrote. "In dread there is the egoistic infinity of possibility, which does not tempt like a definite choice, but alarms and fascinates with its sweet anxiety." Another term for this emotion is "existential anxiety."

BABBITRY

After George F. Babbit, the title character in Sinclair Lewis's (1885–1951) novel *Babbit* (1922). Prosperous, middle-aged, vaguely dissatisfied but congenitally unimaginative, Babbit "made nothing in particular, neither butter nor shoes nor poetry, but he was nimble in the calling of selling houses for more than people could afford to pay." Babbit briefly dabbles in bohemianism, only to return to the safe harbor of complacent conformity. His name became synonymous with the vulgar philistinism of the American social class that Lewis's contemporary H. L. Mencken memorably called the "booboisie."

BOWDLERIZE

After Dr. Thomas Bowdler (1754–1825), an English physician, philanthropist, and editor, whose *Family Shakespeare* (1818) omitted "those words and expressions . . . which cannot with propriety be read aloud in a family." Bowdler also published expurgated (or bowdlerized) versions of Gibbon's *Decline and Fall of the Roman Empire* and *The Old Testament*.

BROBDINGNAGIAN

An adjective meaning "enormous," from Brobdingnag, a country of giants, which the hero of Jonathan Swift's (1667–1745) *Gulliver's Travels* (1726) visits. After Gulliver proudly discoursed on England's history and institutions, Brobdingnag's monarch was "perfectly astonished," protesting that "it was only a Heap of Conspiracies, Rebellions, Murders, Massacres, Revolutions, Banishments, the very worst Effects that Avarice, Faction, Hypocrisy, Perfidiousness, Cruelty, Rage, Madness, Hatred, Envy, Lust, Malice, or Ambition could produce . . . I cannot but conclude," added the King, "[that] the Bulk of your Natives [are] the most pernicious Race of little odious Vermin that Nature ever suffered to crawl upon the Surface of the Earth."

BUSHISMS

"The accidental wit and wisdom of George W. Bush," collected in a recurring feature in *Slate,* the online magazine, by its editor Jacob Weisberg, and in a burgeoning series of books and calendars. Never noted for his eloquence, the forty-third president of the United States proves himself a surreal, if inadvertent, comedian in these notably silly snippets from his public utterances: "I know how hard it is for you to put food on your family," he once declared at a campaign event. "It's in our country's interests to find those who would do harm to us," he affirmed in a speech on the war on terror. And then he added, "And get them out of harm's way."

CASANOVA

In familiar usage, a Casanova is a skilled and tireless seducer, an attractive but faintly disreputable figure. Pop psychology's Casanova complex is another name for sex addiction.

In real life, Giacomo Girolamo Casanova (1725–98) was a

Venetian adventurer, ecclesiastical lawyer, soldier, gambler, diplomat, Mason, occultist, violinist, playwright, translator, librarian, duelist, and unapologetic sensualist—the seducer, by his own account, of more than one thousand women (and a handful of men as well). He lived in almost every major European capital and was expelled from many of them; he was acquainted with such illustrious figures as Benjamin Franklin, Voltaire, and Frederick the Great, and he charmed as many people as he scandalized.

"There are three real wants which nature has implanted in all human creatures," he wrote in his memoirs.

> They must feed themselves, and to prevent that task from being insipid and tedious they have the agreeable sensation of appetite, which they feel pleasure in satisfying. They must propagate their respective species; an absolute necessity which proves the wisdom of the Creator, since without reproduction all would be annihilated—by the constant law of degradation, decay and death. And, whatever St. Augustine may say, human creatures would not perform the work of generation if they did not find pleasure in it, and if there was not in that great work an irresistible attraction for them. In the third place, all creatures have a determined and invincible propensity to destroy their enemies; and it is certainly a very wise ordination, for that feeling of self-preservation makes it a duty for them to do their best for the destruction of whatever can injure them.

CATCH-22

From Joseph Heller's (1923–99) satirical novel of the same name (published in 1961) about the travails of Captain John Yossarian, a bombardier in the 256th Squadron of the Army Air Force during World War II. Though written in the 1950s, *Catch-22* would become one of the signature novels of the Vietnam era.

Catch-22 is the ultimate bureaucratic absurdity: a rule that is so circularly illogical but at the same time so irrefutable that it justifies any injustice. For instance, army regulations stipulated that an airman who was crazed with fear could be legitimately excused from flying any more missions. To receive his exemption, all he had to do was formally request it. But there was one catch . . .

> and that was Catch-22, which specified that a concern for one's safety in the face of dangers that were real and immediate was the process of a rational mind. Orr was crazy and could be grounded. All he had to do was ask; and as soon as he did, he would no longer be crazy and would have to fly more missions. Orr would be crazy to fly more missions and sane if he didn't, but if he was sane he had to fly them. If he flew them he was crazy and didn't have to; but if he didn't want to he was sane and had to. Yossarian was moved very deeply by the absolute simplicity of this clause of Catch-22 and let out a respectful whistle. "That's some catch, that Catch-22," he observed. "It's the best there is," Doc Daneeka agreed.

Another clause of Catch-22 required military men to obey their commanding officers at all times, even when their orders were blatantly illegal.

Though its ostensible subject was the excruciating inanity of life in the military—what Paul Fussell, in his book *Wartime* (1989), memorably dubbed as the "chickenshit" that was mercilessly inflicted on servicemen in the name of "necessary discipline"—*Catch-22* casts its net much wider. In fact, it is a thoroughgoing critique of the cynical amorality of capitalism and especially of corporatism. One of its characters, an entrepreneurial-minded American quartermaster named Milo Minderbinder, signs a contract with the Nazis to bomb and strafe his own base. Despite widespread calls for his prosecution and punishment, all charges against him are dropped when he opens his books and reveals the tremendous profit he's made.

CHAUVINISM

Blind patriotism; excessive partiality to one's own race, gender, region, or country. The term is taken from the name Nicolas Chauvin, a character in Théodore and Hippolyte Cogniard's play *La*

Cocarde Tricolore (1831) who was an ardent (to the point of silliness) admirer of Napoléon. People who remember the sixties-vintage epithet "male chauvinist pig" but don't know its meaning frequently misuse *chauvinist* as a synonym for *sexist* (see Sexism).

COLLYER BROTHERS SYNDROME

A mania for collecting and hoarding worthless items; a pathological disinclination to throw anything away (sometimes called disposaphobia).

Homer and Langley Collyer, an admiralty lawyer and an inventor, lived together in a luxurious mansion at Fifth Avenue and 128th Street in Manhattan. It was a fashionable address when they moved there in 1909, but by the 1930s, the neighborhood was run down and crime ridden and the reclusive brothers had virtually boarded themselves into their house. In 1942, the Bowery Savings Bank initiated eviction proceedings, but the brothers paid off their mortgage with a single check. Five years later, police broke into the mansion when they received an anonymous call about a dead body. After fighting their way through mountains of junk, they found Homer's body. Blind and paralyzed since the 1930s, he had apparently died of a heart attack. Three weeks later, after removing 136 tons of refuse—stacks of newspapers dating back decades, guns, bowling balls, ten grand pianos, a car chassis, an x-ray machine, thousands of medical and engineering texts, jars containing preserved human medical specimens—they discovered Langley's badly decomposed body, just ten feet away from his brother's. He had been crushed under a pile of debris.

COMSTOCKERY

After Anthony Comstock (1844–1915), a tireless-to-the-point-of-monomaniacal crusader against obscenity. In 1873 he founded the New York Society for the Suppression of Vice. Later he successfully lobbied Congress to pass what became known as the Comstock Law, which forbid the transporation of "obscene literature" through the U.S. mail. "Obscenity" was interpreted so broadly that it included family-planning literature and anatomy textbooks. "I have convicted persons enough to fill a passenger train of 61 coaches, 60 coaches containing 60 passengers and the 61st almost full," Comstock bragged to the *New York Evening World* in 1913. "I have destroyed 160 tons of obscene literature."

DON JUANISM

Don Juan is a legendary Spanish libertine, who remains defiantly immoral and impenitent, even while burning in hell. A figure of folk culture, his first appearance in literature was in 1630 in Tirso de Molina's play *El Burlador de Sevilla* ("The Seducer of Seville"), in which he seduces the daughter of the commander of Seville and then kills her father in a duel. When he sees the father's effigy on his tomb, he jeeringly invites it to dine with him—and it does.

Molière used Don Juan as a character in a play in 1665. He also appears in George Bernard Shaw's *Man and Superman* (1903) and is the antihero of Mozart's opera *Don Giovanni* (1787) and Byron's scandalous and never completed poem *Don Juan*.

Much of Don Juan's appeal lies in his wit and charm; if he is damned, he is fiendishly entertaining—and he speaks uncomfortable truths. Molière's Don Juan sounds disturbingly contemporary in Richard Wilbur's translation:

> It's no longer shameful to be a dissembler; hypocrisy is now a fashionable vice, and all fashionable vices pass for virtues. The part of God-fearing man is the best possible role to play nowadays, and in our present society the hypocrite's profession has extraordinary advantages.

DOPPELGÄNGER

Literally "double walker" in German, a doppelgänger is a ghostly apparition of a still-living person, the sight of which, in German folklore, usually foretokened one's death. The minister and Gaelic scholar Robert Kirk (ca. 1641–92) gathered Scottish lore about fairies in his posthumously published *The Secret Commonwealth*.

In the following passage (modernized, annotated, and edited by R. J. Stewart), he describes a similar phenomenon:

> They call this Reflex-man a *coimimeadh* or Co-walker, every way like the man, as a Twin-brother and Companion, haunting him as his shadow and is oft seen and known among men, resembling the Original both before and after the Original is dead. And [this Co-walker] was also often seen, of old, to enter a house; by which the people knew that the person of that likeness was to visit them within a few days.

The doppelgänger is a common trope in literature, from Jean Paul Richter's (1763–1825) novel *Siebenkäs* to Joseph Conrad's (1857–1924) short story "The Secret Sharer," from Henry James's (1843–1916) novella *The Jolly Corner* to the rival pederasts Humbert Humbert and Clare Quilty in Vladimir Nabokov's (1899–1977) *Lolita*.

FLOCCINAUCINIHILIPILIFICATION
See Antidisestablishmentarianism.

GEMÜTLICH
German word meaning "warm and friendly," "cozy," "comfortable," generally in an agreeably middle class sort of way. "Germany's geeks love Munich's Gemütlich feel," wrote *Global Finance*. "This may be the world's neatest, coziest city—and Germany's new generation of techies love to call it home."

GERRYMANDER
To gerrymander is to redraw the map of a voting district (the prerogative of the ruling political party) to capture as many members of its own party as possible or to exclude as many members of the opposition party. If, for example, a congressional district has reliably elected Democrats in the past, but most of its registered Democrats reside in one populous city, a newly elected Republican majority might move the borders of the district so that that

city is no longer a part of it, virtually guaranteeing the election of a Republican in subsequent elections.

The word *gerrymander* is a portmanteau of *salamander* and the surname of Elbridge Gerry (1744–1814), a signer of the Declaration of Independence, governor of Massachusetts, and a vice president of the United States. It dates back to 1812, when a political cartoonist reproduced a map of Massachusetts's congressional districts. To one serpentine-shaped district whose members were overwhelmingly Democratic-Republicans, Governor Gerry's party, the cartoonist had added a salamander's head, wings, and claws, and labeled it a "Gerrymander." Ironically, Gerry had not approved of the legislation that created the monstrosity that now bears his name. By all accounts he had signed it reluctantly.

GESTALT

In general use, the *gestalt* of something is its total, holistic quality—tangible and intangible, qualitative and quantitative, subjective and objective. A gestalt is more than the simple sum of its parts. A jury is composed of twelve separate individuals, but when they are in the jury room, slowly coming to a consensus on a verdict, they form a unique gestalt.

A back-formation from the Old High German word *ungestalten,* which means "misshapen," the word was coined by the philosopher Christian von Ehrenfels in 1890 to describe perceptions that require more than the basic physical senses to comprehend. A musical melody is more than just a sequence of notes and we "hear" it with more than our ears. A listener will recognize "The Star-Spangled Banner" whether it's played on a clarinet in the key of C or on a piano in the key of D—despite the fact that the notes and their timbres are different. We recognize that a table is a table, even if we are looking down on it and can't see its legs, even if it is covered with books and papers.

Max Wertheimer (1880–1943), Wolfgang Köhler (1887–1967), and Kurt Koffka (1886–1941) founded the school of Gestalt psychology, which studied the ways that the mind shapes raw sensory data into perceptions. Fritz Perls (1893–1970), with his wife Laura (1905–90), were the founders of the Gestalt school of psychotherapy. Drawing on insights from phenomenology and existentialism, Gestalt therapy encourages the patient to attend to the ways they experience the world and their bodies in the present so that they can become aware of negative feelings and behaviors engendered in the past and begin to change them, ultimately reintegrating the mind/body/spirit into a balanced whole.

GOLDWYNISM

From the movie mogul Samuel Goldwyn (ca. 1879–1974), whose unintentionally revealing slips of the tongue were widely quoted. "Anybody who goes to a psychiatrist ought to have his head examined," is one Goldwynism; "When I want your opinion, I'll give it to you," is another.

GRADGRINDISM

From the character Thomas Gradgrind, a wealthy, retired hardware merchant and educator, in Charles Dickens's (1812–70) *Hard Times* (1854). A callous exponent of a utilitarianism that is so unsentimental that it would bring a blush to the cheeks of Jeremy Bentham himself, Gradgrind prides himself on being

> A man of realities. A man of facts and calculations. A man who proceeds upon the principle that two and two are four, and nothing over, and who is not to be talked into allowing for anything over . . . With a rule and a pair of scales, and the multiplication table always in his pocket, sir, ready to weigh and measure any parcel of human nature, and tell you exactly what it comes to.

HOBSON'S CHOICE

A choice that is no choice at all. The English essayist Joseph Addison (1672–1719) introduced Hobson to the world in his magazine the *Spectator*:

Mr. Hobson always kept a stable of 40 good cattle, always ready and fit for travelling: but when a man came for a horse, he was led into the stable, where there was great choice, but he obliged him to take the horse which stood next to the stable door: so that every customer was alike well served according to his chance, and every horse ridden with the same justice: from whence it became a proverb, when what ought to be your election was forced upon you to say "Hobson's Choice."

When someone tells you to "take my way or the highway," they're offering you a Hobson's Choice.

KITSCH

The etymology of this word is uncertain, though most dictionaries agree that it was first used by art dealers in Munich in the 1860s and 1870s to describe cheap paintings. Some suggest that it is a mispronunciation of the English word *sketch*; others that it is German slang for "to slap together," and "to smear"; still others that it is derived from the German dialect verb *kitschen,* which means "to scrape mud off the street." The French poststructuralist Jean Baudrillard defines kitsch as

> one of that great army of "trashy" objects, made of plaster of Paris . . . or some such imitation material: that gallery of cheap junk—accessories, folksy knickknacks, "souvenirs," lampshades or fake African masks—which proliferate everywhere, with a preference for holiday resorts and places of leisure . . . To the aesthetics of beauty and originality, kitsch opposes its *aesthetics of simulation.*

If that were all there was to kitsch—Eiffel Tower pencil sharpeners, Empire State Building paperweights, brass-plated reproductions of Rodin's *The Thinker*—then it wouldn't agitate cultural critics half as much as it does. Some tchotchkes may not be pretty to look at, but they needn't offend. A better example of kitsch might be a photograph, suitable for framing, of the World Trade Center, sold in the months after September 11, 2001.

Kitsch doesn't just imitate art—it counterfeits an aesthetic experience by offering a ready-made, mass-produced emotional experience in its stead. In his novel *The Unbearable Lightness of Being* (1984), Milan Kundera wrote that

> Kitsch causes two tears to flow in quick succession. The first tear says: How nice to see children running on the grass! The second tear says: How nice to be moved, together with all mankind, by children running on the grass! It is the second tear that makes kitsch kitsch.

It is not just its shoddiness per se that makes kitsch so infuriating—it is its sentimentality, what James Joyce (1882–1941) so aptly defined as "unearned emotion." Even more, it is the smug sense of self-satisfaction that follows from what Theodor Adorno (1903–69) called kitsch's "parody of catharsis."

A crudely rendered velvet painting of, say, Elvis Presley and Princess Diana sharing a cloud in heaven, hanging on a cheaply paneled wall in a mobile home, would undoubtedly qualify as kitsch, but as vulgar as it is, it's relatively harmless in and of itself. A certain sensibility—albeit an ironic one—might enjoy it as an instance of camp, in Susan Sontag's (1933–2004) sense of the word. That same painting hanging on the wall of a museum, credited to a trendy conceptual artist as a "found object," could induce yawns or grins depending upon one's mood. Hanging on the wall of a chic Soho gallery with a multimillion-dollar price tag on it, it might provoke a certain sense of outrage. But if you talked to the owners of the mobile home, and they told you how beautiful the painting was to them and how moved they are every time they look at it, that a dealer had charged them much more for the painting than they could afford, but that they hoped to pass it on to their children as a repository of their deepest values, then you might begin to think about kitsch in a less easygoing way. As Hermann Broch (1886–1951) wrote, "Kitsch is the element of evil in the value system of art."

LILLIPUTIAN

An adjective meaning "miniature"; also, by implication, "small-minded" or "petty." In Jonathan Swift's *Gulliver's Travels* (1726), Lilliput is an island nation inhabited by six-inch-tall people who, though they are less technologically advanced than Europeans, in all other respects—especially their propensity for slaughtering one another over meaningless abstract principles—bear a startling likeness to them.

MACHIAVELLIANISM

> I can add colors to the chameleon
> Change shapes with Proteus for advantages
> And set the murderous Machiavel to school.
> —Shakespeare, *Henry VI, Part 3*

Niccolò Machiavelli (1469–1527) was a Florentine diplomat and scholar whose name would become synonymous with political ruthlessness and opportunism. His short treatise *The Prince* (1513) is a primer for princes who want to gain and hold on to power. In it, he espoused a hardheaded, brutally realistic notion of statecraft—instead of urging leaders to live up to the highest standards of philosophical or religious virtue, he wrote frankly about the necessity "for a prince wishing to hold his own to know how to do wrong, and to make use of it or not according to necessity." While it is not necessary for a ruler to have good qualities, he wrote:

> It is very necessary to appear to have them. And I shall dare to say this also, that to have them and always to observe them is injurious, and that to appear to have them is useful; to appear merciful, faithful, humane, religious, upright, and to be so, but with a mind so framed that should you require not to be so, you may be able and know how to change to the opposite.

Because his political thinking is based on how people in power really behave, he is considered the father of modern political science.

Machiavelli's plays, his *Discourses on Livy,* and his vast history of Florence reveal a much more humane sensibility than he displayed in *The Prince,* which was written while he was in disgrace and exiled from Florence. Machiavelli dedicated *The Prince* to Lorenzo di Piero de'Medici in the hope that it would facilitate his return to the political sphere. Unfortunately for his reputation, it is the book that he is most remembered for.

MALAPROPISM

The unintentional misuse of a word with comic effect, from Mrs. Malaprop, a character in Richard Sheridan's (1751–1816) play *The Rivals* (1775), who is given to using impressive-sounding words that she doesn't understand. "He is the very pineapple of politeness," Mrs. Malaprop gushes about a gentleman. In speaking of her efforts to quash her niece's unsuitable romance she exclaims, "Oh! it gives me the hydrostatics to such a degree. I thought she had persisted from corresponding with him; but, behold, this very day, I have interceded another letter from the fellow; I believe I have it in my pocket."

MICAWBERISM

Irrepressible optimism coupled with chronic destitution, after Wilkins Micawber, a character in Charles Dickens's *David Copperfield* (1850), whose grandiose schemes only land him deeper and deeper in debt.

> [Mr. Micawber] solemnly conjured me, I remember, to take warning by his fate; and to observe that if a man had twenty pounds a year for his income, and spent nineteen pounds nineteen shillings and sixpence, he would be happy, but that if he spent twenty pounds one he would be miserable. After which he borrowed a shilling of me for porter, gave me a written order on Mrs. Micawber for the amount, and put away his pocket-handkerchief, and cheered up.

Ironically, Mr. Micawber does eventually make his fortune, in Australia.

MRS. GRUNDY

A prig or prude, whose judgment is widely feared, from an off-stage character in Thomas Morton's (1764–1838) play *Speed the Plow* (1798). Throughout the nineteenth and early twentieth centuries "What will Mrs. Grundy say?" was shorthand for the fear of social censure. "No unprotected woman can do the least thing that is unconventional," Emily Post's *Etiquette* (1922) noted regretfully, "without having Mrs. Grundy shouting to everyone the worst possible things about her."

MURPHY'S LAW

"If anything can go wrong, it will." Attributed to Captain Edward A. Murphy, an engineer at Edwards Air Force Base in 1949, who was a member of a team studying the physiological effects of rapid deceleration. When he noticed that a technician had wired a transducer incorrectly, he snapped, "If there is any way to do it wrong, he'll find it." The project manager, George E. Nichols, who was collecting humorous adages and laws, added it to his list as "Murphy's Law." In a press conference shortly afterward, Dr. John Paul Stapp attributed the project's safety record to their cognizance of Murphy's law and the necessity to try to circumvent it. He was widely quoted in the media and eventually the phrase found its way into advertisements for aerospace firms.

In England, the same adage is called Sod's law. The science fiction writer and editor John W. Campbell popularized the axiom as Finagle's law of dynamic negatives. A corollary to Finagle's law (of uncertain origins) that is often quoted by hackers is Hanlon's razor, which states: "Never attribute to malice that which can be adequately explained by stupidity."

Project manager George E. Nichols gave his own name to a catchphrase: Nichols's fourth law, which states, "Avoid any action with an unacceptable outcome." And from Dr. Stapp there is Stapp's ironical paradox: "The universal aptitude for ineptitude makes any human accomplishment an incredible miracle."

PANGLOSSIAN

An absurd and baseless optimism, based on principle rather than facts. The word comes from Master Pangloss, a character in Voltaire's (1694–1778) satirical novel *Candide* (1759). Master Pangloss "taught the metaphysico-theologo-cosmolonigology," which proved "that things cannot be otherwise than as they are; for as all things have been created for some end, they must necessarily be created for the best end." When Pangloss catches syphilis from a serving wench, he faces the consequences with serene equanimity, knowing that

> it was a thing unavoidable, a necessary ingredient in the best of worlds; for if Columbus had not caught in an island in America this disease, which contaminates the source of generation, and frequently impedes propagation itself, and is evidently opposed to the great end of nature, we should have had neither chocolate nor cochineal.

Pangloss is a broad caricature of the philosopher and mathematician Gottfried Wilhelm Leibniz (1646–1716), whose *Theodicy* (1710) argued that God permits evil to enter the world only in order to avoid a greater evil—"an imperfection in the part may be required for a greater perfection in the whole." To refute the arguments of atheists, who assert that the existence of an all-powerful and perfectly good God is incompatible with the suffering and injustice that mars his creation, Leibniz argued that it would be "sufficient to show that a world with evil might be better than a world without evil; but I have gone even farther . . . and have even proved that this universe must be in reality better than every other possible universe."

The biologist Richard Lewontin (b. 1929) and the paleontologist Stephen Jay Gould (1941–2002) coined the term *Panglossian fallacy* to describe teleological views of evolution, which spuriously assume that any and all evolved attributes of a creature must by definition be ideally suited to its needs.

PARKINSON'S LAW

"Work expands so as to fill the time available for its completion." From *Parkinson's Law: The Pursuit of Progress* (1957), by the British historian, novelist, and veteran bureaucrat C. Northcote Parkinson (1909–93). An important corollary of Parkinson's law is that if work expands, so does the bureaucracy that's paid to do it. Thus, as the number of ships in the Royal Navy diminished by 67.4 percent between 1914 and 1928, the staff of officials at the admiralty grew by 78.45 percent.

> An elderly lady of leisure can spend the entire day in writing and dispatching a postcard to her niece at Bognor Regis. An hour will be spent finding the postcard, another in hunting for spectacles, half an hour in a search for the address, an hour and a quarter in composition, and twenty minutes in deciding whether or not to take an umbrella when going to the pillar box in the next street. The total effort that would occupy a busy man for three minutes all told may in this fashion leave another person prostrate after a day of doubt, anxiety, and toil.
>
> Granted that work (and especially paperwork) is thus elastic in its demands on time, it is manifest that there need be little or no relationship between the work to be done and the size of the staff to which it may be assigned.

PECKSNIFFIAN

Hypocritically sanctimonious. From the character Seth Pecksniff in Charles Dickens's *Martin Chuzzlewit* (1844).

> It has been remarked that Mr. Pecksniff was a moral man. So he was. Perhaps there never was a more moral man than Mr. Pecksniff: especially in his conversation and correspondence . . . He was a most exemplary man: fuller of virtuous precept than a copy-book . . . his manner, which was soft and oily in a word, even his plain black suit . . . all tended to the same purpose, and cried aloud, "Behold the moral Pecksniff!"

PETER PRINCIPLE

"In a hierarchy every employee tends to rise to his level of incompetence," from *The Peter Principle* (1969), a humorous look at the foibles of organizations by the educator Laurence J. Peter (1919–90). An example of the Peter Principle: a mechanic does outstanding work because he's so meticulous and patient. When his performance is acknowledged with a promotion to manager, those same virtues become liabilities. He doesn't know how to delegate, his perfectionism makes him oblivious to deadlines, and he constantly meddles with his subordinates' work. His promotion has elevated him to his "level of incompetence."

Another one of Peter's many memorable aphorisms: "The incompetent with nothing to do can still make a mess of it."

POLLYANNA

A naively optimistic person, almost always used pejoratively. From the title character of *Pollyanna* (1913), a popular children's novel by Eleanor Porter, which spawned a number of sequels, a silent movie starring Mary Pickford, a Disney film starring Hayley Mills, and many other adaptations. *Pollyanna* tells the story of an orphaned eleven-year-old girl whose infectious sunniness lightens the hearts of every dour soul she meets up with.

> "Well, goodness me! I can't see anythin' ter be glad about—gettin' a pair of crutches when you wanted a doll!"
>
> Pollyanna clapped her hands.
>
> "There is—there is," she crowed. "But *I* couldn't see it, either, Nancy, at first," she added, with quick honesty. "Father had to tell it to me."
>
> "Well, then suppose YOU tell ME," almost snapped Nancy.
>
> "Goosey! Why, just be glad because you don't—NEED—'EM!" exulted Pollyanna, triumphantly.

QUIXOTISM

Impractical, delusory idealism, from the eponymous hero of Miguel de Cervantes' (1547–1616) classic novel *Don Quixote* (1605). Don

Quixote de la Mancha was a Spanish gentleman of about fifty who
became so obsessed with reading chivalric romances that

> his wits being quite gone, he hit upon the strangest notion that
> ever madman in this world hit upon, and that was that he fancied
> it was right and requisite, as well for the support of his own hon-
> our as for the service of his country, that he should make a
> knight-errant of himself, roaming the world over in full armour
> and on horseback in quest of adventures, and putting in practice
> himself all that he had read of as being the usual practices of
> knights-errant; righting every kind of wrong, and exposing him-
> self to peril and danger from which, in the issue, he was to reap
> eternal renown and fame.

RABELAISIAN

Extravagantly gross, earthy humor. When little boys entertain
each other by imitating farts, they are being Rabelaisian.

François Rabelais (ca. 1484–ca. 1553) was a monk, an inno-
vative physician, a humanistic scholar of Greek and Latin, and
the irrepressible author of farcial, verbally profligate, bibulous,
earthy-to-the-point-of-obscenity novels about the giant Gargan-
tua and his son Pantagruel, which were promptly banned by the
church. The *Catholic Encyclopedia,* while noting Rabelais' genius,
observes that his vocabulary, while "rich and picturesque," is "licentious and filthy." All in all, it concludes, his work "exercises a
baneful influence."

Perhaps the most infamous passage from Rabelais is Gargan-
tua's discourse on his quest for the perfect toilet tissue, a small
portion of which is quoted below.

> I wiped my bum, said Gargantua, with a kerchief, with a pillow,
> with a pantoufle, with a pouch, with a pannier, but that was a
> wicked and unpleasant torchecul; then with a hat. Of hats, note
> that some are shorn, and others shaggy, some velveted, others
> covered with taffeties, and others with satin. The best of all

these is the shaggy hat, for it makes a very neat absterion of the fecal matter.

Shakespeare's Falstaff evokes the spirit of Rabelais, as does James Joyce's Leopold Bloom, whom we accompany to the bathroom early on in *Ulysses*. To the Russian critic Mikhail Bakhtin (1895–1975), Rabelais' spirit is triumphantly subversive and anarchistic; his "carnivalesque" exuberance representing "a victory not only over supernatural awe, over the sacred, over death; it also means the defeat of power, of earthly kings, of the earthly upper classes, of all that oppresses and restricts."

SAPPHISM

A synonym for lesbianism, or female homosexuality, taken from the name of the poet Sappho (ca. 610–ca. 570 BCE). An aristocratic woman from the Isle of Lesbos (hence the word *lesbian*), who spent some years in exile in Sicily, Sappho was considered the greatest of the Greek lyric poets. Plato called her the tenth muse. Only one of her poems ("Hymn to Aphrodite") survives intact today; there are also several hundred fragments. Deeply personal and frequently dedicated to the subject of "limb-loosening Eros," almost all of her verses allude to intimate relationships with women.

SCHADENFREUDE

German compound from *schaden* (harm) and *freude* (joy), it translates loosely as "pleasure in someone else's misfortune." Thus Jeffrey Toobin, writing in the *New Yorker* about the courtroom ordeal that led to the billionaire Martha Stewart's prison sentence, noted that hers was "a distinctly American story of self-creation—of a dramatic rise and sudden fall—which invested an essentially banal trial with the weight of meaning and the potential for a schadenfreude festival."

SPOONERISM

Errors of speech in which syllables of neighboring words are accidentally interchanged, after the Reverend William Archibald

Spooner (1844–1930), dean and warden of New College, Oxford, whose mind was notoriously nimbler than his tongue. "You have deliberately tasted two worms," he chastised a lazy student, "and you can leave Oxford by the town drain." The student had wasted two terms; the "down train" was a train out of London. "The weight of rages will press hard upon the employer," was one of his oft-quoted economic maxims.

URIAH HEEP
Another character from Charles Dickens, Uriah Heep is David Copperfield's nemesis. Servile and fawning, Heep's ostentatious humility masks a "base, unrelenting, and revengeful spirit," full of "meanness . . . craft and malice."

> "When I was quite a young boy," said Uriah, "I got to know what umbleness did, and I took to it. I ate umble pie with an appetite. I stopped at the umble point of my learning, and says I, 'Hold hard!' . . . I am very umble to the present moment, Master Copperfield, but I've got a little power!"

VOLSTEADISM
After Andrew J. Volstead (1860–1947), a ten-term congressman from Illinois who sponsored the legislation that gave the federal government the power to enforce the notorious Eighteenth Amendment to the Constitution, which prohibited the "manufacture, sale, or distribution of intoxicating liquors." The Volstead Act, wrote Clarence Darrow, "has brought a reign of terror and oppression, outrage and assassination, to all classes of people; and this will not end until Volsteadism and all its kind are dead and done with." Prohibition was officially repealed with the passage of the Twenty-first Amendment in 1933.

WELTANSCHAUUNG
German compound word that literally means "worldview"—a philosophy, an ideology, a comprehensive and consistent set of ideas. " '*Weltanschauung*' is, I am afraid, a specifically German no-

tion, which it would be difficult to translate into a foreign language," wrote Sigmund Freud. "If I attempt to give you a definition of the word, it can hardly fail to strike you as inept. By *Weltanschauung*, then, I mean an intellectual construction which gives a unified solution of all the problems of our existence in virtue of a comprehensive hypothesis, a construction, therefore, in which no question is left open and in which everything in which we are interested finds a place."

"A pundit," wrote William Safire, in the *New York Times,* "carries an ax not to murder but to grind; he (the pronoun embraces 'she') develops a mindset, elevated to a Weltanschauung, that enables him to glance at an encyclical and meet a deadline to pontificate."

WELTSCHMERZ
German compound that literally means "world pain," coined in 1810 by the German writer Jean Paul Richter (1763–1825). The word is usually used to describe the pervading sense of sadness that an idealist feels when he or she compares the way the world should be to the way that it is. "To really enjoy drugs you've got to want to get out of where you are," wrote P. J. O'Rourke in *Republican Party Reptile* (1987), "but there are some wheres that are harder to get out of than others. This is the drug-taking problem for adults. Teenage weltschmerz is easy to escape. But what drug will get a grown-up out of, for instance, debt?"

YAHOO
From Jonathan Swift's *Gulliver's Travels.* The noble talking horses called the Houyhnhnms used Yahoos ("the most filthy, noisome, and deformed animals which nature ever produced") as beasts of burden. "Upon the whole," Gulliver confesses, "I never beheld, in all my travels, so disagreeable an animal, or one against which I naturally conceived so strong an antipathy." The Yahoos, alas, were human beings.

The word is used today to mean any ignorant, coarse, ill-mannered person. Writing of the 2004 Republican convention,

Tom Shales, of the *Washington Post* acidly noted that the delegates "behaved like a bunch of yahoos who'd been bused in expecting *The Jerry Springer Show*. Nothing makes a worse case for the Republican Party than seeing a mob of them congregating."

ZEITGEIST

German word, coined by G.W. F. Hegel (1770–1831), that literally means "spirit of the age"—the general moral, ideological, aesthetic, and political tastes and trends that characterize an era.

"Oppressed people cannot remain oppressed forever," Martin Luther King (1929–68) wrote from his cell in the Birmingham Jail in 1963.

> The urge for freedom will eventually come. This is what happened to the American Negro. Something within has reminded him of his birthright of freedom; something without has reminded him that he can gain it. Consciously and unconsciously, he has been swept in by what the Germans call the Zeitgeist, and with his black brothers of Africa, and his brown and yellow brothers of Asia, South America and the Caribbean, he is moving with a sense of cosmic urgency toward the promised land of racial justice.

INDEX